The Sugar's at the Bottom of the Cup

ELDA DEL BINO WILLITTS
PATRICIA LYNN HENLEY

Zucchero Press • Sonoma, CA

THE SUGAR'S AT THE BOTTOM OF THE CUP

published by Zucchero Press

International Standard Book Number: 0-9708-257-2-2

Cover design by Gary Tompkins
Interior design and typeset by Katherine Lloyd, The DESK

Printed in the United States of America

For information:
Zucchero Press
P.O. Box 529 • Sonoma, CA 95476

04 05 06 07 08 09 10—10 9 8 7 6 5 4 3 2 1 0

This book is dedicated to

Sabina and Domenico Del Bino

and to all determined immigrants—

past, present, and future.

ACKNOWLEDGMENTS

*A*s is undoubtedly common, many, many people helped us shape this book. We appreciate the ongoing support of both of our families. Special thanks go to Elda's son and daughter-in-law, Bill and Patti, for their unwavering enthusiasm and invaluable help; and to Elda's nephew Fred Abballo, for his assistance with dates and his corrections of Elda's rusty Italian spelling. We are indebted to Eric Weber for his professional guidance; Jennifer Gott for her dedicated copy-editing eye; and Paul Sigrist and the staff at Ellis Island for aid in verifying the facts. Our appreciation also goes to Flora Durfee for use of her Golden Gate Bridge slide; Jim and Jeannette Turrini; Elvira Pueblo; Shannon and Michael Falk; Sally Lycke; Phyllis H. Henley; Kathey Hale; Lilla Weinberger of Readers' Books; Kathleen Caldwell; Robbi Pengelly; Elda's lifelong friend Etta Soldavini; Candi Smucker; Tina Luster; Linda Kalber; Shirley Wishingrad; and the numerous others who graciously read the manuscript at one stage or another and gave us valuable feedback.

FOREWORDS

From Patricia

As a reporter for a small-town newspaper, my first interview with Elda was a routine assignment. My reaction was anything but routine. Usually I meet someone, take notes, write an article, and move on to the next story. But that hour or so with Elda touched me deeply. I marveled at everything she had experienced, and I was intrigued by the deep love, faith, and optimism that had carried her through it all. Faced with the increasing indignities of old age, Elda was cheerful, loving, serene, and at peace with herself and with the prospect of her eventual death.

I wanted to know how she did it. As time went on, I felt a deep need to share Elda with as many people as possible. This book is the result of more than six years of conversations, many of them over delicious Italian dinners prepared by Elda. I tape-recorded our sessions, transcribed the tapes, and—paragraph by paragraph—organized those notes into topics. Elda and I worked out a rough timeline of her life, figuring out exactly what happened and when. Then I began shaping her memories into book form.

After I finished the rough draft of a chapter, Elda would read it aloud to me. That was her first glimpse of each portion of this book. I paid close attention if she stumbled over a phrase or replaced it with other, more comfortable words. I took out anything that didn't sound like Elda. Then we would talk about the chapter and any new memories it evoked. Those details would be added to the story, increasing its richness and flavor.

The events, phrases, and ideas in this book are all Elda's. The structure and organization of the story are mine. It is my fondest hope that I have captured enough of what she has taught me these past six and a half years to convey at least a hint of how delightful it is to have a conversation with Elda, enjoying her warmth, wit, and wisdom.

—*Patricia Lynn Henley*
July 2004

From Elda

I get a real sense of fulfillment from this book, as if I had accomplished something. And yet I feel like Patricia did all the work while I just enjoyed the process. She's the one who slaved over it while I had fun cooking meals and visiting with her.

When we started, I don't know if I was as interested in the book as I was in Patricia and having her in my life. It seemed like we had something in common from the first time we met. As we worked together, that connection developed into a wonderful friendship.

This book wouldn't have been possible without Patricia. Her many questions brought the little details of my life back into my mind. She even took me on a trip to San Francisco and Marin County to visit all the places I had lived over the years.

I give thanks to Patricia for making the book what it is. As I read it, my life seems kind of glamorous—and I certainly didn't think it was glamorous at the time I was living it.

—*Elda Del Bino Willitts*
July 2004

9

THE SUGAR'S AT
THE BOTTOM OF THE CUP

CHAPTER 1

*T*he first time my mother cooked a turkey for Thanksgiving, she wasn't quite sure how to do it. We had all heard the bird should be stuffed, so Mamma whipped up a batch of ravioli filling and used it in the turkey. That was pretty unusual back in the 1920s, but even our American-born dinner guests told us they loved it. No one in my family knew anything about the Mayflower or the Pilgrims. We had no idea why we were fixing turkey on Thanksgiving, but that's what we ate, just like everyone else in our San Francisco neighborhood. My family dined on ravioli-stuffed turkey for quite a few Thanksgivings before we finally cooked it more American-style.

Although she lived almost half her life in the United States, Mamma never did learn English. So I always spoke Italian at home and English at school and, later on, at work. Even after I grew up, married, and had a family of my own, I still spoke only Italian with Mamma and translated for her whenever she needed help. Sometimes I've felt like that turkey: American on the outside and Italian on the inside.

I was born Teresa Elda Del Bino on April 29, 1909, in Lucca, Italy. I came to the United States in 1916, when I was seven years old. Now here it is, the twenty-first century. Because of when I was born and how long I've lived, I feel I'm getting to see most of one century and a good bit of the next. It's not a bad deal at all. I started life among the rolling foothills and rich farmlands of the Tuscany region of Italy. I'm choosing to spend what are undoubtedly my last years in the small Northern California town of Sonoma, in an area surrounded by golden hills and covered with rows of lush vineyards. In between my first days and what will eventually be my final ones...well, in between there's been a whole lot going on. Hopes, secrets, betrayals, triumphs, failures, poverty, luxury—they have shaped me into who and what I am today.

It hasn't always been easy but I have no regrets. It's not that I think I'm all that different from anybody else. We all have stories to tell. We've all had secrets. We've all been betrayed in one way or another. We've all had sorrows, and we all get a chance or two at happiness. But after years of stress and worry, I have finally learned to savor the small daily miracles of love, joy, forgiveness, appreciation, and gratitude. I'd like to share my story—all of it, not just the parts I'm proud of—while I still have the time and the energy.

It's important to understand that I'm a ninety-five-year-old woman looking back. I can only give you my memories, such as they are. I'm a widow with a son, a daughter-in-law, five grandchildren, and seven great-grandchildren. Thinking back to when I was a little girl—first in Italy and then growing up in San Francisco—well, some things stand out and other details are pretty fuzzy.

I don't know if I actually recall our life in Italy and our trip to

America or if I've just imagined some of the events based on the family stories I heard over and over as I grew up. A few of my memories are quite real, I'm sure, like the sheer terror I felt on Ellis Island. Others you'll have to take for what they are—the dim pieces that come up as I look back and marvel at how lucky I've been. Even with all the ups and downs in my life, I've always felt blessed by God. Did I create my good luck by believing in it and always expecting it? I don't know. But even with my body starting to wear out on me, my everyday reality is full of beauty, and I give thanks for that.

I was born in an ancient, dusty farm town in northwestern Italy, about ten miles inland from the Mediterranean Sea. If you picture the classic boot shape of Italy, Lucca is on the far left side, just a little bit down from where the boot flares out to hang onto the rest of Europe. Lucca is a walled city, and our family lived on the wrong side of the ancient wall—the poor side. My father was a gardener and took care of rich people's estates.

When I visited my hometown as an adult tourist, it was an easy drive to the nearest beach along the coast. But during my childhood in Lucca, we walked everywhere we went. Occasionally a peddler would wander down the gravel and dirt road in front of our house, hauling his wares in a mule-drawn wagon. At times the mule would get stubborn, Mamma said, and wouldn't want to move. Then the peddler would have to curse or coax or do whatever it took to get the animal back to work pulling the load.

But mostly our street was filled with people on foot—my family and our neighbors, out on one errand or another. Once or twice my family took a short trip on the steam train that huffed and puffed its way through our town. This was a rare luxury, reserved for important occasions like weddings or funerals in other cities. Otherwise we walked anywhere we needed to go. In all those years, we never went to the beach or saw the bright water of the Mediterranean, even though it was only ten miles away.

We lived in a tiny brick and stone house built in the sort of straight-up-and-down, two-story construction that's common in Northern Italy. Our home had one main room downstairs, with a fireplace where all the cooking was done. There was no kitchen to speak of, just the open fireplace and a table that served as a work surface as well as a place to eat. Upstairs were a few small bedrooms. That was all the space we had for our family of ten.

I remember that as a little girl I used to eat my breakfast sitting on a wide windowsill instead of at the table. The window looked out on an area paved with crushed rock, a common backyard for all the neighborhood houses. There were no fences, and I could usually see other children playing or their mothers coming to talk with them. Someone was almost always out there, and I liked to watch them while I sipped my milk laced with coffee and ate my bread, which I loved to dunk in the warm drink.

Beyond the gravel area behind our home lay acres of flat, open fields full of weeds and wildflowers. I was told in no uncertain terms never to go out there by myself. Heading in the other direction—toward the wall and the center of town—I was only allowed as far as the railroad tracks, no more than a block away. Two blocks from our home was the Catholic church. That was my world, or as much of it as I can recall.

I was the youngest of eight children. Our parents were Domenico Del Bino and Maria Sabina Fedi Del Bino. My sister Beppa was the oldest, followed by Jenny, Algisa, and Paolina. There was great joy when the fifth child was a boy, Rico. Next was my brother Joe; then came my sister Eda; and six years later there was me, Elda.

As the eldest daughter, Beppa was the most serious of my six sisters, but I always knew that her stern exterior hid a soft heart. Jenny was the family comic, able to find humor in almost anything. Algisa was much quieter than Jenny, but the two were always the best of friends. I think Jenny's constant jokes helped Algisa feel a part of everything. As the fourth girl in a family that had been waiting for a boy, Paolina was a bit of a loner and kept her thoughts to herself. Of our two brothers, Rico was temperamental and moody while Joe was the family peacemaker, always trying to avoid conflict. Eda was good-looking and enjoyed the attention it brought her. I was simply everyone's baby.

All of us, even our mother, called our father Babbo—that's Italian for Poppa. Not quite six feet tall, Babbo had olive skin, a prominent nose, piercing brown eyes, and a beautiful handlebar mustache, which he kept carefully trimmed. He always took pains to make sure his clothes were immaculate, and he wore them well. A lifetime of manual labor had left him trim and muscular.

Mamma also had olive skin, a fairly long nose, and brown eyes. However, at barely five feet tall, she was much shorter than Babbo. Mamma was pretty but with a narrower face than Babbo's round one. She wasn't fat exactly, but Mamma's waist had been permanently expanded by eight pregnancies. I can still remember following her solid figure down the street. Like all the adult women in our neighborhood, she kept her hair pulled back in a tight bun and always wore floor-length, high-necked dresses. All eight of us inherited our parents' dark hair, brown eyes, and distinctly Italian complexions. I favor Mamma somewhat in looks; I have her narrow face. So did my brother Joe. My five sisters all had softer, rounder faces, like our father. Only our brother Rico was the maverick in appearance—he didn't resemble Mamma, he didn't favor Babbo…he just looked like Rico.

Eight children is a lot, and Mamma really did work from morning until night taking care of us all. She was always in motion. If Mamma sat down, it was because she was chopping vegetables, mending clothes, or working at some other job that could be done while sitting. As soon as they were big enough to be any help at all, my older sisters were just as busy as Mamma, keeping up with all the household chores.

Our home had no indoor plumbing. We fetched what water we needed from a nearby pump. We'd push the handle of the pump up and down to make the water gush into our bucket; then we'd haul the heavy container back to our home. There was an outhouse in our backyard, and we kept our "pee pots"—also known as chamber pots— under the beds at night. They had to be carried out and dumped into the outhouse every morning. We were used to it back then, but that's one household chore I can gladly do without. I wonder how many people today truly appreciate flush toilets.

We washed our dirty clothes and linens in *il fosso,* the series of ancient ditches that once formed the moat around the walled city of Lucca. The man-made stream had a wide spot where some large, flat rocks had been placed in the water. Mamma and my older sisters would get down on their knees to swish our clothes through the rushing water. They would rub them with soap and pound each item on the rocks to get out the dirt and stains. Then we'd carry everything to the fields behind our house, where we draped our wet laundry on tall bushes, letting everything dance in the breeze to dry.

Mamma came from a wealthy family, but they would have nothing to do with her once she married Babbo, who had worked as their gardener. After she left home, Mamma never saw her parents or her two sisters again. Of her two brothers, only the one who was a priest kept in touch with her. He visited with her while we were still in Italy and wrote letters to her after we moved to California.

Once I was old enough, I became his chief correspondent since Mamma never learned to read or write in any language. In Italy in her day education cost money and was a luxury not to be "wasted" on girls. So even though her family was well-off by local standards, Mamma never got to go to school, as I did in America. I think that's why Mamma and Babbo took the risk of coming to America—to give us eight children a better chance in life than they ever had. For them the United States really was the land of opportunity and their only hope for us.

They certainly had a hard life in Italy. When my oldest sisters were babies, Mamma added to Babbo's meager earnings by wet-nursing other newborns in the neighborhood. Between babies, if things got bad, she sometimes went out and picked crops in the fields. By the time I was born, my oldest sister, Beppa, was twenty-one. In their early teens, Beppa, Jenny, Algisa, and Paolina all got jobs at the J. P. Coats factory, which manufactured sewing thread. They walked five miles along a country road to the factory each workday and five miles home. At lunchtime our brother Joe walked to the factory and back to deliver the hot meal Mamma made daily.

My family had originally lived in a small town called Monsummano about twelve miles west of Lucca. They moved to Lucca shortly after Eda was born—probably just to be near the sewing thread factory. My older sisters gave every cent they earned to our parents. That may be why Eda, as the second to the youngest, got to go to school even though she was just a girl. I guess times had changed from my mother's day, because Eda went to the local grammar school and then learned dressmaking from a neighbor in the afternoons. I was too young to start school until after we moved to America.

Of course the boys got as much education as possible. Joe even graduated from high school before leaving Italy. His classes cost money, but Joe paid for them by working at a rock quarry after school and on weekends. He couldn't add anything to the family's finances, but he did earn enough to be able to go to high school. My four older sisters weren't as lucky. Algisa was the smartest and the most determined. She managed to learn to read and write in Italian as part of going to catechism classes at the Catholic church. Beppa, Jenny, and Paolina didn't have much energy for lessons after all the household chores—especially once they started working their ten- to twelve-hour-a-day jobs at the thread factory. Just like Mamma, those three never learned to read or write.

For several years, Mamma ran our household in Italy by herself. That's because when I was three years old, Babbo and Rico went off to San Francisco to try to earn enough money to bring the whole family to America. Babbo had been working as a gardener for an Italian doctor who spent several months each year in San Francisco. The doctor told our father all about the advantages of life in the United States, and Babbo told Mamma. Together they decided that, even with all the upheaval involved, moving to America was the best thing they could do for their eight children. Babbo was forty-seven years old at the time, and Mamma was forty-three.

There was no way all ten of us could afford to go to America at once. So on March 26, 1912, Babbo and fifteen-year-old Rico went to San Francisco by themselves. Looking back now, it must have been so hard for my parents to say good-bye. I'm sure they had absolutely no idea how long it might be before we could all be together again.

After arriving in California, Babbo found a job growing produce at the Italian Swiss Colony in Asti, about ninety miles north of San

Francisco. He earned room, board, and a small stipend. Set up by immigrants to employ immigrants, this somewhat remote farm grew all kinds of crops, but eventually became famous for its wine. Rico went to work as a busboy in a San Francisco restaurant, which left him living on his own in the city. I doubt he and Babbo saw each other much because transportation was so difficult. Even in a big city like San Francisco, only a few people had cars. Everyone else got around by horse and wagon or had to pay to ride the train. Babbo and Rico were both working long hours, trying to save every penny. They couldn't have made the ninety-mile trip between Asti and San Francisco very often—if at all.

The rest of us stayed in Italy, living on my sisters' wages while also saving as much money as possible. Mamma was frugal. We ate a lot of greens—she would go out into the fields around our house picking mustard plants for salads and turnip greens for boiling. Sometimes she'd fix dried fish, cooking it in a broth so we could dip our bread in it. She really knew how to stretch things as far as possible and still make delicious food. We might not have had much, but we always had something tasty to eat.

Our routine changed after World War I broke out in 1914 because my four sisters were transferred to the night shift. They had to start work at 2 A.M. Joe walked them to the factory every night and then turned around and walked the five miles back home.

Finally, four years after Babbo and Rico went to California, we had enough money for the rest of us to join them. Mamma made arrangements for us to sail out of the northern Italian seaport of Genoa on April 1, 1916. But the world was at war, and at sixteen years old, Joe couldn't leave Italy without an official form saying he didn't have to serve in the Italian army. The paperwork didn't come on time, so we missed our ship, which was a big disappointment.

One week later we were told that that particular ship had been torpedoed by the Germans. We heard that it sank with no survivors. Our sadness at the delay turned into shocked relief—and fear at what might happen when we finally did sail. All eight of us had avoided death because of a missing piece of paper. Although we now had the proper signed form that would let Joe leave the country, traveling to America meant we had to risk drowning like the people on that first ship.

"In ogni modo andiamo lo stesso. Se siamo destinati d'arrivare in America, allora ci si arriva"— "We're going anyway. If we're meant to make it to America, we will," Mamma said.

I don't know how she did it. I watched the movie *Titanic* a few years back, and when I saw all those people in the icy water, I kept thinking about how that might have been me and my family. I was struck by what a horrible death it would have been. But Mamma was a strong-willed woman, and she wanted her children to have better opportunities in life. My father and brother had left for California when I was three years old. I was now six and didn't even remember what Babbo and Rico looked like. I'm sure Mamma knew that we had to take a chance if we were going to get the whole family together again.

So about a week after we heard that the first ship had sunk without a trace, the eight of us boarded the local steam train heading north to Genoa. We carried all our belongings in a battered suitcase and a couple of bundles tied with rope. We didn't own any toys and I don't remember Mamma packing any pans or other kitchen stuff. I think the few things we had in our kitchen in Italy were too worn out to be worth carrying with us. Mostly we took clothes and blankets—stuff to keep warm. Tucked carefully into the middle of our bundles were our spotlessly clean pee pots. Unaware of the wonders of flush toilets, Mamma just assumed we would need the chamber pots in our new home.

On April 15, 1916, the eight of us carried our precious possessions up the gangplank of the SS *Caserta*, which was bound first for Napoli in southern Italy and then for New York.

CHAPTER 2

The *Caserta* was considered a medium-sized steamship—420 feet long and 51 feet wide. It had two masts and one steam funnel pointing toward the sky. It seemed huge to me and a bit overwhelming.

My family told me the *Caserta* had carried horses and cattle on its trip from America to Italy. Then the cargo area was cleaned and whitewashed to get it ready to carry poor people from Italy to America. Although a few people traveled graciously in first-class accommodations and others fairly comfortably in second-class cabins, we were among the hundreds sailing the cheapest possible way in what was known as steerage. It left a lot to be desired.

We were assigned beds in the huge cargo hold, where narrow wooden bunks were stacked three high with just enough room to walk in between. Conditions weren't too bad at first because only a handful of people got on with us at Genoa. But when our ship arrived in Napoli, hundreds of people were waiting on the dock. I couldn't believe my eyes as I watched them coming up the gangplank, carrying all their belongings just as we had done earlier. The line seemed endless, and I didn't think there would be enough room. In a way there wasn't. Just as we had done, all those people climbed down the white wooden stairs that led to the steerage area. The huge room was packed to overflowing with bodies and noise. Each person had been assigned a bunk bed, but nothing more.

I know that sailors refer to "above deck" and "below deck," but to me it was just upstairs and downstairs—and downstairs it was dark, crowded, and stinky. When we hit the open ocean, the waves really affected the boat, swinging it from side to side. People were sick all the time. There was vomit all over the floor, and no one cleaned it up. What I remember most is the awful smell and the dirt—real filth. Going downstairs felt like stepping into a nightmare.

At first my family slept in our assigned bunks. But after a few nights we couldn't bear going down below. For the rest of our sixteen-day journey, we wrapped ourselves in every sweater, jacket, and blanket we owned and stretched out on the open wooden deck. The freezing nighttime ocean air was better than the stench downstairs. It's impossible for me to describe that odor. Think of the worst thing you've ever smelled and then triple it. That should be about right.

Since everyone went downstairs as little as possible, a huge crowd was on the open deck most of the time. People just plopped down anywhere they could find room. Mamma or someone would take me for a walk at least once a day, to stretch my legs. We had to pick our way through the crowd, being careful not to step on anyone. Everybody was nice about it, but it felt odd that there were people everywhere we went. It was a real change from our quiet little street in Lucca.

Everyone on board spoke Italian but with slightly different dialects. We understood each other, but the differences stood out. My family was soon labeled *i Toscanini* because we were from the Tuscany region. I especially remember when the new people came on board in Napoli because Mamma didn't approve of them. Like a lot of northern Italians, Mamma always thought people from southern Italy could stand to learn a lot about cleanliness.

"Come sono sudici," she would say. "How dirty they are."

She took special pains to see to it that we were always neat, with our faces washed and our hair combed. Her opinions about the southern Italians made a real impression on me. I thought about it in later years, when I met up with hurtful anti-Italian prejudice that left me ashamed of both myself and my family. It took a while for me to learn that we are all the same, no matter what our surface differences, and that we all have value.

Even though conditions in steerage were horrible, my family was lucky. One of the ship's officers had a soft spot in his heart for my fourteen-year-old sister, Eda, because she reminded him of his own daughter. He arranged for our family to work for the first-class galley. This was a real advantage since we were allowed to eat some of the food we helped prepare. It was wonderful. We worked on deck and ate there after we were done. We ate well, especially compared to everyone else traveling steerage. To earn that privilege, our whole family spent hours cleaning and cutting up vegetables, including peeling bushels of garlic and potatoes. The garlic was Eda's job; years later she claimed she peeled five to six pounds of the stuff every day. None of us really minded, though, because it was such a bonus to have decent, tasty food.

But even with the good meals, it was a difficult trip. I was so young that I didn't really understand everything that was going on. I don't think Mamma and the others ever completely forgot that the first ship had sunk. I'm sure they couldn't help but worry about the Germans lurking out there somewhere, searching for targets to torpedo. There were lots of safety drills to make sure the passengers would know what to do if there was an attack. We were each given a lifeboat number and told to go to a certain spot anytime we heard a siren.

"Per carita"—"Have mercy," Mamma would mutter every time there was a drill. *"Speriamo che Dio ci aiuta. Speriamo che non ci sara bisogno"*—"I hope God is good to us," she'd say as our family gathered next to our assigned lifeboat. "I hope we never have to use this."

I don't know if Mamma's prayers helped, but we did have a safe journey, reaching New York on May 2, 1916, just three days after my seventh birthday. There had been no party, of course—traveling steerage on a steamship didn't lend itself to celebrations, and my family never did pay any attention to birthdays. It had been just another day at sea, like all the others. So I was seven years old when I first saw New York and the Statue of Liberty. As we sailed into the harbor, customs inspectors came on board the *Caserta* to help the first- and second-class passengers. Those of us in steerage boarded smaller boats heading to Ellis Island for immigration processing. The place was known as *Isola di Lachrime*—the island of tears. Immigrants who didn't pass the medical exams were kept back for more examinations or were deported. Some families split up, the one person who didn't pass the physical making the lonely journey home while everyone else went on to new lives in America.

"Se uno non passa, si ritorneia indietro insieme"—"If one of us doesn't pass, we'll all go back together," Mamma said firmly. At the same time, she was silently praying we would all make it through the inspections because she didn't want to go back to Italy.

With great determination Mamma got us off the small boat and through the huge, imposing doors of the main building on Ellis Island. Even more people were there than had been on our ship. We stood for hours in long lines that snaked back and forth across the immense, cavernous building. The immigration processing area was basically a massive, high-ceilinged warehouse decorated in an imposing nineteenth-century public-institution style. Most of the floor space was filled with tall dividers made of metal pipe. Designed to keep people in orderly rows, they stretched from one side of the huge room to the other and back again, over and over. It looked like something you'd use to control cattle.

The wait seemed endless. We shuffled ourselves and our belongings back and forth across the huge floor, carefully following the people in line in front of us. *"Dove sono i bagagli? Non perdete i bagagli"*—"Where are the bundles? Don't lose the baggage," my mother kept saying to us. She feared that everything we owned might be lost.

I was even more afraid than she was, but for a different reason. An older man had befriended our family on the boat. Mamma paid attention to his advice because he had been through the Ellis Island immigration process many times. He worked and earned money in Chicago but had made a number of trips back and forth, visiting his family in Italy. Mamma listened intently to anything this man said, so of course I did too. One day he took me for a walk around the crowded boat deck. I think he decided to tease me, all in fun, but I took him seriously.

"When we get to Ellis Island, they're going to be examining your eyes with a big hook. Don't let them do it," he told me, shaking his finger at me. "Don't let them get near you with that hook because you know what happened when they did it to me?"

I stood still and faced him, wide-eyed, waiting for him to go on.

"Why, one of my eyes fell right out and rolled into my vest pocket," he said, sliding two of his fingers into his pocket for emphasis.

My mouth dropped open in shock. I'm sure he must have been joking and meant me no harm, but I took every word to heart. I had been taught to respect all adults and saw no reason to disbelieve a man my mother listened to so carefully. No one else in my family had heard what he told me, and I kept my fears to myself. But my silent panic grew during the hours we spent inching our way slowly through the long lines on Ellis Island.

Finally it was our turn. The doctor looked over everyone else in my family and then turned toward me. They really did use a small hooked instrument to turn down immigrants' eyelids, checking for disease. My examination never got that far because I wouldn't let the doctor—or any other immigration official—get near me. I simply fell to the floor and started screeching in total, complete terror. I couldn't help myself and I certainly couldn't explain why I was so afraid. My family didn't know what was wrong, but they were panicked by the thought that I might be rejected. Mamma started shouting loudly at me, trying to get me to stop screaming. In the middle of that immense room, surrounded by hundreds of other immigrant families, I howled and Mamma yelled back at me. The officials just stood there in shock. But instead of rejecting me or my family, they passed us all.

"Go on, go on," the doctor said, gesturing to Mamma to move along and take us all with her. Maybe he figured that seven of us had been found to be healthy so I probably was too. At the very least, he knew I had good lungs. Whatever the doctor's reason for waving us forward, suddenly we were standing outside in the sunshine. We had made it through the immigration inspections.

My whole family cried in relief. I was glad the ordeal was over and my eyes were safe. Mamma and the others were thankful their dream had finally come true: We were in America. We stood there on Ellis Island, within sight of the Statue of Liberty, with tears running down our faces. But our journey wasn't over, not by a long shot. Many of the people on our boat reached their destination when we docked in New York, while others had just short trips to get to where they were going. We still had a cross-country train trek in front of us. It probably helped that none of us had any idea how far it was from New York City to San Francisco.

Mamma carried a total of eighty dollars for the eight of us. She had the cash and our train tickets in a sort of purse on a chain around her neck so they were always nestled safely inside her bosom. I think that's where she tucked every important document we had.

A barge took us off Ellis Island and dropped us at a pier in Jersey City, New Jersey, right next to the train station. No one in our family spoke English, and the people around us all looked and acted differently than the folks back home in Italy. Everything was so big and strange to us. Mamma made sure somebody was always holding my hand. When it got really crowded, she insisted we all hold hands so we wouldn't get separated. The eight of us must have been quite a sight, weaving our way through the busy train station in a long line, our dilapidated suitcase and bundles bobbing along with us. Once we found the right platform, we quickly boarded the train and settled into our seats. That's where we sat, day and night, for the next five days.

We had been given box lunches at Ellis Island, and Mamma thought those would be enough for us to eat on our trip to San Francisco. The boxes held sandwiches, cookies, and bananas. We'd never even seen a sandwich before, much less a banana. At first we tried to eat the long yellow fruit peel and all, but we soon figured out that couldn't be right. Our box lunches lasted a couple of days, but eventually they were gone. We didn't have a lot of money to spend on food, so for the rest of the five-day trip we lived mainly on candy bars and cold drinks sold in paper cups—not a bad diet from a child's point of view, but I'm sure it bothered Mamma.

We could only sleep sitting upright on those hard benches, so we never really slept at all. We couldn't change our clothes, either, or take a bath. It wasn't as bad as steerage on the boat, but it was still a pretty uncomfortable way to travel. So when the train stopped for a long break in Chicago, we all hopped off, glad for the chance to stretch our legs by walking up and down the platform. I was a little wobbly from the constant motion of the train. Mamma decided I looked much too pale. She considered me a sickly child because I was naturally thin, and she was always giving me something to make me healthier.

Mamma spotted a food stand and hurried to it. She was pleased when she found a small baked dish topped by cooked egg yolks, which she considered especially nourishing. I bit into it reluctantly—and broke into a grin of absolute delight. It turned out to be a delicious open-faced pie. What Mamma thought were egg yolks were actually apricots. I gobbled it down happily, but it sure wasn't the nutritious meal Mamma had meant to feed me.

The rest of the trip was uneventful—or at least my memories start to get fairly sketchy at this point. I think I just couldn't take in any more new sights and experiences. It was quite a journey for a seven-year-old girl, and I was worn out. Mamma, my five sisters, and my brother must have been exhausted as well. In the following years they told all kinds of stories about most of our trip, but they just glossed over the last few days—as if the open spaces of the Midwest, the sharp peaks of the Sierra Nevada mountains, and the fertile fields of the Sacramento Valley flashed past the train windows in a blur.

We arrived in San Francisco on May 6, 1916, exactly three weeks after we left our home in Lucca. We headed straight to the restaurant where Rico was working as a busboy. I was so tired I really don't remember much, but it had to have been an emotional reunion, with lots of hugging. I do know the restaurant fed us a nice Italian dinner. That detail was always mentioned in the family tales because it was our first familiar-looking meal since arriving in America. I think my family was grateful to be given something to eat that didn't need to be explained, served by people who spoke Italian.

A man at the restaurant telephoned up to Asti and talked to Babbo, who came to San Francisco the next day. I was so exhausted from the trip that I must have slept through his arrival. I know there was a lot of joy when Babbo and Mamma finally saw each other again after being apart for more than four years, but I didn't see it myself. I was just glad to be somewhere in a bed that didn't move and sway like a train or boat.

All the planning, working, and saving had finally paid off. We had a new home: San Francisco, California, in the United States of America.

CHAPTER 3

At some point while I was growing up in San Francisco, someone told me that all the sugar was at the bottom of the cup. I have no idea who said that to me. Maybe it was a common phrase at the time and I heard it from several different people. Or perhaps only one person said it to me, just once, and I've forgotten who it was. I really don't know. I doubt that anyone in my family said it because their outlook tended to be more fearful than that. After all the hardships in her life, Mamma didn't expect the best from the world. I'm sure it must be an English saying; it's not something I tend to say in Italian.

I'll never know who spoke that phrase to me, but I'm grateful I heard it. Young as I was, I believed it with total certainty. I looked around at my life, at how little our family had compared to other people, and told myself "all the sugar's at the bottom of the cup." Things might be hard now, but the sweetness will come.

And it's true. My life today is sweet in spite of the fact that at age ninety-five my body is like an old car with one part after another starting to wear out. I don't let the bitterness of my various physical problems distract me from the daily joys that surround me. One of the many lessons I've learned in my long life is that the only real disability is a bad attitude. Watching and waiting for the sugar at the bottom of my cup has given me a positive outlook, which lets me be happy even while my body puts more and more limits on what I'm able to do.

It's astonishing to sit here as an old woman and reflect on all that has happened during my lifetime—the Great Depression, two World Wars, Korea, Vietnam, and men walking on the moon, plus the introduction of everything from electric lights to microwave ovens, computers, and cell phones. Sometimes I can't believe everything I've seen and done. Of course, most of the time I was so busy living that I didn't think about the significance of any of it. I just got on with my life.

I loved growing up in San Francisco. I tend to remember the city as it was rather than as it is, but it's still a beautiful place. If you look at it on a map, San Francisco is basically a square surrounded on three sides by water. To the west lies the Pacific Ocean and Ocean Beach, which is the long stretch of sand that makes up the city's western coastline. North of the city is the opening to San Francisco Bay. The wide channel is named the Golden Gate, but the impressive bridge that stands there now didn't exist when I was a little girl. North of the Golden Gate are the green, rolling hills of Marin County. Today they are covered with high-priced homes and all types of businesses, but those gorgeous hills used to hold only a few sleepy little towns. The Bay itself is to the east, with the cities of Berkeley and Oakland across the water. Until I grew up I had only a hazy impression of the East Bay communities that were somehow "over there." They weren't San Francisco, so in my mind they barely existed. South of San Francisco is the peninsula, which nowadays has houses and buildings everywhere you look. Back then there were just a handful of towns surrounded by acres of orchards. I remember lots of apple and cherry trees. They were so beautiful, especially when they were full of blossoms.

The San Francisco you see now is nothing at all like the one I knew as a child. Except for a few public parks, today almost every square inch of the city is covered with houses, high-rise buildings, and parking lots. When I was young, there were still lots of open spaces. Just inland from Ocean Beach are the heavily populated Richmond and Sunset districts, where rows of houses stretch in tight lines along every street without a single empty lot. In my childhood those areas were nothing but open sand dunes. Sandwiched between those dunes were the thousands of acres of greenery that are Golden Gate Park, which was created long before my family arrived in 1916. Once isolated from most of the rest of the city, today the park is hemmed in by buildings on three sides, with Ocean Beach as its western border.

The Marina district along the northern edge of San Francisco was also mainly sand dunes in 1916. I remember when I came home and told Mamma that people were building homes out there. She threw her hands up at such foolishness. Who would buy a house built on sand? Today almost every square inch of the Marina has something built on it.

When I was young, there were several distinct districts in San Francisco, each identified mainly by the nationality of the people living there. It was a city of neighborhoods; you could almost tell where you were just by listening to the residents' accents and checking what kind of things were for sale in the stores. The Italians generally settled in North Beach, which occupied most of the northeastern corner of the city. You could buy any type of Italian food and goods, like cold meats and pasta, and the storekeepers all spoke Italian in addition to English. That's where my family felt most comfortable, of course. Except for the tremendous number of people living there, North Beach wasn't much different from our hometown in Italy.

On the southern edge of North Beach is Broadway, a wide main street running on an angle from east to west. Broadway was (and still is) the dividing line between North Beach and the next area to the south, exotic Chinatown. In those days we still saw Chinese women hobbling around. Their feet had been bound tightly when they were young girls because tiny feet were a mark of beauty. Most of the men we saw in Chinatown wore long robes and pigtails. The grocery stores had rows of dead ducks hanging by their necks in the front window and bins full of strange-looking vegetables. There was often an odd smell in the air, which I realize now might have been opium. It was all much too foreign for Mamma, who believed the Chinese couldn't be trusted. Anytime we walked through Chinatown, Mamma would caution me not to step on the metal sidewalk grates that led down to the buildings' basements.

"Non caminare vicino al'inferiata. Ti prendano e ti portano abbasso e non ti vedo piu"—"Don't go near there. They'll take you down there and I'll never see you again," Mamma told me. She put such a fear into me—it took me years to get over it.

South of Chinatown were all the offices and fancy stores of the downtown area. It had what I considered to be huge buildings—four stories high and about twice as wide as the average house. Downtown San Francisco was filled with them, each with its own distinctive style and architectural decor. Forget today's massive skyscrapers that take up a whole block and soar overhead. Back then there were only a handful of buildings taller than four or five stories. South of downtown was the

Mission district, where mainly Irish people lived. My family said disapprovingly that the Irish always got drunk on hard liquor. I got the impression that there was nothing wrong with good, healthy Italian wine, but hard liquor was a terrible thing to drink.

Of course, other people had similar stereotypes about the Italians, but I wasn't really aware of that until I was older. It wasn't just my family or the people around me; back then it was generally acceptable to be suspicious of anyone who was different or foreign. Slang words like *wop* or *dago* for an Italian or *mick* for an Irishman were often used as descriptions in conversation. It took me years to slowly unlearn the fears and false images that were pretty commonly accepted when I grew up.

Our first San Francisco home was a downstairs flat in a building on Lombard Street near Octavia—that's in the northern part of the city, just south of the Marina district. The area is known as Cow Hollow, which was an appropriate name back then because there were still cattle pastures on the north side of the street. The south side held a short stretch of buildings; we lived in one of them. Today that part of Lombard Street is also Highway 101, and it's packed solid on both sides with motels and restaurants. The building where my family once stayed is gone now, replaced by a tiny parking lot.

Although we finally had the whole family in America, Babbo still couldn't live with us. We desperately needed the money he earned at Asti, where he slept in a dormitory with a bunch of other men. There was no way the family could move in with him or get jobs up there. So Babbo stayed in Asti while Mamma settled in San Francisco with the rest of us. This was hard on Rico, who was nineteen years old and had been living on his own for four years. He couldn't stand to have anyone give him orders, and he would never do anything Mamma asked him to do. My two brothers were like night and day. Rico was highly argumentative, while soft-spoken Joe would do anything to avoid even a minor disagreement.

Despite Rico's rebellious attitude, we settled down fairly comfortably once Joe and my sisters found work and we had enough money to move into a larger apartment. With only four rooms including the kitchen, our first flat on Lombard Street was way too small for nine people. We only stayed there a few months, and I don't remember much about the place. Although there wasn't any hot water, it did have a bathtub, a toilet, and a sink with easy-turn faucets instead of a hand-operated pump. It was our first indoor plumbing. My family didn't have any trouble getting used to these improvements, but we were so accustomed to having our pee pots under our beds that we kept them there for a couple of weeks. Finally Mamma realized we didn't need them anymore and got rid of them.

Beppa, Jenny, Algisa, and Paolina were soon busy working at a cannery, the California Packing Company. Since it was run by Italians with Italian-speaking supervisors, it didn't matter that my sisters didn't know any English. The only important thing was that they quickly earned reputations for being reliable and hardworking on their twelve-hour shifts. That was crucial in seasonal cannery work, because it meant they were hired anytime jobs were available, which was practically year-round.

Even fourteen-year-old Eda was employed. Back then there weren't child labor laws like there are now. She was hired as a factory worker at the Ghirardelli Chocolate Company. Rico still had his job at the restaurant, and Joe went to work at a men's clothing store. Nobody in the family earned much money, but together it was enough to let us move a bit east, to a larger place—a cold-water flat near the cannery and chocolate factory.

Our new home was on North Point Street, between Hyde and Larkin streets. The Ghirardelli Chocolate factory was also on North Point, one block west of our flat. The California Packing Company cannery was a block behind us to the north, down a short hill, and there was a stretch of open land to the east of us. The city's Fisherman's Wharf, with its docks full of small ships, was a bit to the northeast, within easy walking distance. Although this area wasn't officially part of the North Beach district, almost everyone living there was Italian-American, so we fit right in.

That was a magical time to be a child in San Francisco. Few people had cars, and most deliveries were made by horse and wagon. Many of the streets were still paved with cobblestones to give better footing for the horses. Even now, when I close my eyes and concentrate, I swear I can hear the *clop-clop-clop* of the animals working their way up and down the city's steep hills.

The streets were lit by gas, not electricity. Every night the lamp-lighter would come by, lighting all the streetlamps. Each morning he came back and turned them off. For many years we had gas jets in our home instead of electric lights. I thought the gas lights were pretty, but they provided a rather faint glow. We could see enough to walk around the room, but we had to light candles to be able to read.

Our block of North Point Street was fairly level and had a row of two-story wooden buildings on its north side, which is where we lived. There were only two houses on the south side of the street, plus a vacant lot that ran all the way to the corner. Today the whole area is a solid mass of side-by-side buildings, with no empty lots. The chocolate factory and the cannery have been converted into tourist attractions filled with boutique stores. Back then they were just good sources of factory jobs.

Our new home was in a two-story, light-colored building, which was fairly old and somewhat plain. It had a set of wide outside steps that led to a smoothly polished entrance area where my friends and I loved to play marbles. My family's front door opened onto a flight of stairs leading up to our second-story apartment. There were two rooms in front, one room on the side and then the large kitchen in back, all connected by a long hallway. One of those front rooms was supposed to be a living room, but we used it as a bedroom, with the kitchen as our main gathering place. It wasn't until years later, when I was in my twenties, that we had a real living room complete with living room furniture.

When we first came to this country from Italy, we had only the bare essentials: beds, a kitchen table, and chairs. That was all we could afford. And we didn't have decorations on the walls either. The only exception was Mamma's crucifix hanging in her bedroom so she could burn a candle to the Sacred Heart of Jesus. To this day, I have a crucifix on the wall in my bedroom too. I guess it reminds me of how safe I felt as a child when I watched Mamma light her candle and kneel to pray. The candle and crucifix were comforting symbols in my family, telling us we were not alone. Praying for us each day seemed a natural thing for Mamma to do. It was one of the ways she showed how much she loved and cared for us.

We six girls shared a room. That meant we slept in two double beds, three to a bed. As the littlest I was always in the middle, squashed between two older—and much larger—sisters. One night I crawled down to the foot of the bed and stretched out across it. Although I didn't like having my sisters' feet in my face, it was better than being jostled awake all night long. I slept at the end of the bed from then on.

There was another disadvantage to being the youngest: going last at bath time. Like I said, we had a cold-water flat. Although there was running water, we had to heat it ourselves on our wood-burning kitchen stove. Then we carried the pan of hot water down the hall to the bathroom, poured it into the built-in tub, and mixed it with the cold water that came out of the bathtub faucet. Taking a real, sit-down bath was quite a production.

We'd scrub ourselves over the wash basin every day, but we only took baths on Saturday night. Mamma and my sisters would heat the water and then fill the tub. The oldest got the first bath, followed by the next oldest and the next oldest, and so on. Even though we added a little more hot water as each person took his or her turn in the tub, basically we all shared the same bathwater—so you can see why I thought being the youngest was a drawback. Mamma was sad when my sisters started getting married and moving into their own homes, but I was delighted. It meant more bed space and fewer people using the bathwater before I got my turn.

I spent that first summer playing with the children in the neighborhood, and in the fall I trooped off to Sherman Grammar School with all the other kids. The campus was about a mile west of our home. Today there's an impressive-looking school on that site, with massive buildings that take up the whole block. When I went there it was a simple, two-story wooden building of eight classrooms, with wooden stairs running up and down the outside. The whole block was fenced off, with the school building on one side of the lot. The rest of the property held a big paved area where we would play jump rope and tag during recess and lunchtime. There were no plants or trees, but it still looked a lot more like a rural schoolhouse than a city campus.

Even though I was seven years old, I was put in the first grade because I had never been to school before. The funny thing is, I don't remember learning English. Somehow I must have picked it up over the summer, at least enough to get by in school. My teachers insisted on calling me by my first name, Teresa, since they couldn't come up with an English equivalent for Elda. It was the first of many divisions in my life: As Teresa at school I spoke only English, and then at home I was Elda, speaking Italian. They were two separate worlds and I had to live in both of them.

About half a dozen of us kids walked together to school. The mile-long trek wasn't too bad by San Francisco standards—we only had to climb one short hill and the rest was flat. We would kick pebbles along the way to see who could knock one the farthest. Some mornings would be so foggy that we couldn't see where we were going. We'd bump into things, and by the time we got to school our hair would be soaking wet from the misty fog. Mine always frizzed and curled something awful when it got damp. I hated that.

If it was pouring down rain, my girlfriend's father would take us to school in his Model-T Ford. We had to leave early because the car needed to be cranked to get it started. He'd crank, and then he'd cuss, and then he'd jiggle something, and then he'd crank, and then he'd cuss, and then he'd crank again. It was a riot from our point of view, but I don't think he saw the humor. Finally the Model-T would roar to life and off we'd go.

I enjoyed school and did well there. The teachers were kind and looked out for me. One sent a note home to a neighbor who could read English to let Mamma know I needed warmer clothes. We still had only the few things we'd brought with us from Italy in the spring, and I guess in the cool San Francisco weather I was turning kind of purple on the playground.

"Gli farò una maglia"— "Oh, I'll knit her a sweater," Mamma said, once the problem was explained to her. She could knit anything. Trouble was, she didn't want to go to all the work of making some-

thing and then have me grow out of it right away. She wanted the sweater to last me two or three years, so she made it big. Really big. The arms came way down over my hands, and the bottom hem was around my knees. I got to school and all the kids started laughing, but I laughed too because it was funny. My sweater was also very soft and warm, so I didn't really mind.

I got along well with my classmates, but I did feel kind of different at lunchtime. Someone told Mamma I should take sandwiches to school, so that's what she made me—slicing big hunks of Italian bread and filling them with any leftovers she had. I was the only one with pasta sandwiches. Having them in my lunch bag made me feel funny—sort of embarrassed because they were so different from what everyone else brought. However, the other kids were happy to trade with me. To them my pasta sandwiches were great.

Like I said, I enjoyed going to school. Maybe that was because I always got top grades. I worked hard at it—I had to because there was no one at home who could give me any guidance with my homework, which was all in English. After working all day in the chocolate factory, Eda went to night school, so she wasn't available. Rico worked at the restaurant most nights. By the time Joe learned enough English to be of any use to me, he had started his own grocery store. He left early each morning and came home late, exhausted.

Mamma and my four older sisters were generally more available, but only Algisa could read in Italian and none of them wrote or spoke English. I was pretty much on my own as far as school was concerned. I must have done all right, though. They let me skip second and fourth grades so that I was no longer the oldest one in my class. I still felt different from my classmates, in part because of Mamma's endless rules, which were strictly enforced.

43

We knew Mamma loved us, but she was very much in charge and no one except Rico dared disobey her. For the rest of us, whatever Mamma said, that's what we did. She never slapped or spanked us; we just knew she was the boss. She didn't let me go out and play after dinner like the other children did. I wasn't allowed to go anywhere with my friends, not even to a birthday party. Sometimes the excuse was money. Mamma wouldn't let me have roller skates because she said the family couldn't afford it if I fell down and broke my leg. Mostly, though, Mamma just liked to know where we were and what we were doing. She didn't want anyone to ever find us doing something improper, and she made it very clear that we should never, ever disgrace the family.

"Guai! Se qual cuno dovessa svergognare la famiglia sarebba la mia morte"—"If that happened, it would kill me," Mamma told us. She saw to it that we didn't have any opportunity to get into trouble.

After school I always had to head straight home to help Mamma with the household chores and so she could keep me under her watchful eye. At night our family would gather around our well-worn kitchen table for dinner. Space was so tight that we would open the door to our hallway and put chairs there too. Mamma sat at the head of the table with Rico and Joe at the other end, in the doorway. Each of us girls had our "usual" spot along the sides—Eda and I always sat next to each other, every night. Most nights Joe sat alone at the foot of the table, facing Mamma, since Rico's restaurant job meant he worked during the dinner hour. We never really knew when Rico would be around. He pretty much came and went as he pleased. Everyone else was always home for dinner or they told Mamma exactly where they would be and for how long. It was, "I'm going to be late, Mamma," or, "I have to stop and see so-and-so, Mamma."

That was what Mamma expected of us. Rico was a different story. Mamma never knew if he was working that night or not. If he showed up at dinnertime, she fed him and was happy. If not, we went ahead and ate without Rico.

My four oldest sisters worked long hours, so they were usually the last to get home. Mamma always managed to have dinner hot and ready to go on the table when they came in the door. There was lots of laughter as we ate Mamma's delicious food and talked about what had happened to each of us that day. Jenny always had the funniest tales. She could see the humor in almost any event, and she'd soon have the rest of us laughing with her. Of course we all had something to say, usually with everyone trying to talk at the same time. Even today I tend to speak loudly because when I was a kid it was the only way to be heard.

Two of our friends were musicians and would often come over to play for us after dinner. The guitarist was a short man, not much more than five feet tall. He would stand with one foot on his chair, resting his guitar on his knee. The other man was quite tall and always sat down to play his mandolin. They played lots of instrumental Italian music for us, but I liked it best when Rico or Algisa would sing. Although my brother and sister knew all the standard Italian folk songs, my favorites were the arias from the Italian operas. The musicians would play softly and either Rico's tenor or Algisa's soprano voice would just soar on those lovely solo pieces. They both had wonderful voices. I often wonder what might have happened if there had been enough time and money for them to take lessons.

The only word I can think of to describe Algisa as she performed for our family is *humble*—she'd just sit there and sing, not for praise but because she enjoyed it so much. Rico was much more of a show-off;

you could tell he really craved the attention. Of course, Rico also loved music with a passion. Maybe it was his only escape from having to work long hours and live with so many family members. He'd sing to himself in the morning while he was shaving. Rico's wonderful voice would come floating out through the closed door.

Other families also lived squeezed into small apartments. This, combined with the fact that there were few cars in the city, meant that much of our daily neighborhood life spilled out onto the street. An organ grinder passed by our house every week, playing lovely songs. I was so enchanted with his music that I'd follow him all the way down the block. I never had any money to give him, but I was definitely one of his admirers. The ice man also came regularly to refill everyone's ice-box. He wore a thick leather vest to keep his clothes dry if the blocks of ice started to melt as he carried them around. He'd also put a soft pad on his shoulder where he balanced the large piece of ice, which was about a foot or so square—it was cut to fit inside the standard ice-box. He'd grab the ice with a pick, sling it up on his shoulder, and then carry it into the kitchen—or at least he did that for folks who could afford an icebox. We didn't own one. We just had a screened container in the window to keep things cool and away from the flies. So we never got ice delivered to our flat.

The white ice wagon was enclosed, looking a bit like a modern pickup truck with a camper shell on the back. We children kept a sharp watch for this wagon, which had a step on the back. We'd sneak behind the wagon when the ice man drove by and jump onto the step. We'd get a free ride until he spotted us and yelled at us to get off. In the summer-time we'd scoop up the little ice shavings that littered the wagon's floor and let the small bits of ice melt in our mouths.

Another familiar sight was the milkman's horse-drawn wagon,

bringing glass bottles of milk to our house every day. We'd leave the empty bottles outside our front door, and early each morning the milkman would replace them with full ones. Milk wasn't homogenized the way it is now, so there was always thick cream at the top of the bottle with a kind of watery milk underneath it. I loved to drink that rich, delicious cream before Mamma had a chance to shake the bottle to mix it all together.

"Non lo sai che lo lasci annaquato per l'altri?"—"Don't you know you're leaving it diluted for everybody else?" Mamma would ask me crossly. But it was so good that I just couldn't stop.

Occasionally we bought fruits and vegetables from a peddler who wandered through our neighborhood with his produce arranged color-fully in the back of his horse-drawn wagon. And every day the bread wagon delivered five loaves to our house—we ate a lot of bread. Mamma always told us to fill up on bread first and then eat the rest of the meal. Once a month or so, Mamma would take me with her and we'd go to the bakery in North Beach to pay for our bread deliveries. She usually couldn't pay all the money we owed, but she'd give the man what she had. He wouldn't argue with Mamma but just cheerfully take what she offered. I figured that was how everybody did it. I guess he must have known we were honest and would pay the whole amount when we could.

My family found many different ways to get the things we needed. Mamma even sewed our underpants out of flour sacks. Back then flour came in big cloth bags made of strong but soft cotton. The name of the flour company and other information was stamped on the bag, so Mamma would bleach the material to get all the writing off. Sometimes it wouldn't all come out and some lettering could still be seen.

"Questo si mette di dietro"—"We'll put that part in the back of the pants," Mamma would say.

When our finances got a little better, Mamma switched to buying inexpensive underpants and making dish towels out of the flour sacks—but she still turned every one of them into something useful.

As I said, I was expected to pitch in and help as much as possible. Trouble was, I hated housework; I just hated it. Mamma and my older sisters all appeared to accept the endless chores as their role in life and even seemed to enjoy cooking meal after meal. Not me. I always wanted to be doing something else with my time—anything else.

The only task I didn't mind was going shopping. In those days, every street had its own little neighborhood shops, like a small grocery, a butcher shop, a bakery, and almost anything else you needed. Since the local storekeepers spoke Italian as well as English, Mamma got along as if she were still in Northern Italy. She bought groceries practically every day since we didn't have an icebox to keep our food cold.

I always went with her to help. Because she couldn't read or write, Mamma kept a mental list in her head. She bought all the items she needed for huge meals with soup, pasta, salad, two kinds of meat, and dessert—and she never forgot anything. Me, if I leave my list at home, I'm sunk and I buy only half the things I need. Mamma always remembered everything. As she gathered what she wanted, I'd add the prices in my head and then at the end I'd tell her how much it was going to cost.

"Sei ingegnosa," Mamma would tell me. "You're so smart."

It made me feel so proud of myself. I liked being able to help Mamma and, despite my family's continued poverty, I liked our new life in San Francisco.

CHAPTER 4

When Mamma needed to buy things we couldn't get in our little neighborhood shops, she would head to the big stores in the downtown area. She always took me along so I could interpret for her with the English-speaking clerks.

I think Mamma enjoyed our downtown shopping trips because it gave her something different to do other than cooking or cleaning. And if we went, it was because she had a little extra money put aside, which always made her happy. It was a treat for both of us since Mamma often spent a nickel on some little thing for me too. She'd say, *"Andiamo, Elda, poi parlare per me"*—"Let's go, Elda, so you can talk for me," and we'd head off to the downtown stores.

Mamma always wore a hat when we left home because in those days every respectable woman did anytime she went downtown. Mamma didn't even look in a mirror, but just stuck a hat on her head as we went out the door. I don't think she ever spent much time in front of a mirror or on her appearance at all. I suppose nowadays she would be considered a prim little figure with her high-necked, floor-length dresses and her hair carefully pulled back into a severe bun.

Mamma never cut her hair. It was quite long and beautifully wavy, but no one outside the immediate family ever saw it. Mamma's wonderful hair was always captured in that tight little bun, with hairpins all over her head to keep every lock strictly in its proper place. When we were ready to head downtown, she'd just jam her hat on her head and off we'd go, hurrying to catch the streetcar. It would take us across Chinatown, through what is known as the Stockton Street tunnel. We'd get off on Market Street, the main downtown road. That meant we went right past Union Square, a fancy shopping area at the south end of Chinatown. Until I was older, I didn't even know the high-priced Union Square stores existed. All the places Mamma shopped at were along Market Street and had much more reasonable prices.

Translating for Mamma made me feel important. I guess I did all right in English because the sales clerks all seemed to understand me. One time a clerk asked me what my father did for a living. Mamma had just told me that Babbo had helped kill some pigs up on the farm, I guess to use the meat for sausage, bacon, and pork. Anyway, I smiled sweetly at the clerk and said, "My father kills pigs." She laughed. She had a friendly laugh, so I didn't mind.

Mamma loved Woolworth's, which was what used to be known as a five-and-dime store. It had big, wide aisles, and you could find almost anything there—socks, underwear, thread, pots and pans, silverware, hair clips, inexpensive jewelry, and so on. Nothing cost more than ten cents. Mamma had a field day buying something for a nickel here and a nickel there. She felt like she was a big spender and really doing a lot. We'd walk from aisle to aisle, checking to make sure we hadn't missed any bargains.

Then we'd go next door to the Emporium basement to buy clothes, shoes, linens, and things like that. The Emporium was a big, fancy department store, with several floors. On the main level and upstairs, everything was really nice. There were all kinds of salespeople to help you find what you needed. It was great. Downstairs in the bargain basement you were on your own. I understood clearly that the basement was where the poor people shopped. It was where Mamma and I always went.

Our shoes never lasted long, maybe because we bought the cheapest ones we could find. First the sole would wear out, so we'd fold a piece of cardboard in half and stuff that in. The cardboard had to be changed every day because it would wear out too. We couldn't afford to buy shoes very often, so we'd keep using cardboard until the whole shoe fell to pieces.

One thing I longed for as a child was a doll of my very own. When I was about eight years old, I saw the dolly of my dreams while I was translating for Mamma in the Emporium. The doll was standing on a glass counter in the middle of the store, where I couldn't help but see her. She took my breath away—she was exactly the doll I had always dreamed of. I'm not sure how tall she was—maybe a foot and a half to two feet, with a beautiful white porcelain face. Her hair was dark and curly, just like mine. Her eyes would open and close, and they were dark brown—just like my eyes. She even had adorable dark brown lashes. I thought she was the most beautiful thing I had ever seen. More than anything in the world, I wanted her for my very own.

The price tag said $1.25, and I begged Mamma to buy her for me. We didn't have enough money at the time, but for several months Mamma saved up her pennies and nickels until she had an extra $1.25. I was so excited the day we went to buy her. I remember taking the streetcar down to Market Street and the Emporium. I rushed Mamma inside, leading her directly to the counter where "my" doll was standing.

"We want to buy that dolly—the one that costs $1.25," I told the salesclerk.

She explained that the $1.25 price tag was only for the doll's dress. We would have to go upstairs to buy the doll. I translated for Mamma. She took me by the hand and we headed upstairs. But the doll I wanted was too expensive. In fact, all the dolls cost at least four or five dollars. It had taken Mamma months to save the $1.25. Spending more than that was simply out of the question. We went home, both of us disappointed. I'm sure Mamma wanted to be able to buy the doll for me almost as much as I wanted to own her.

But I did get an unexpected treat. A neighbor, Mrs. Casassa, noticed that I didn't own a single book. Since most of my family didn't understand English, I don't think it ever occurred to them to buy me something to read. Dear Mrs. Casassa gave me a brand-new copy of *The Three Little Pigs,* and I read it cover to cover, over and over.

When Mamma and I were out walking or shopping, often she would say, *"Si va a cende un paio di candele"*—"Let's go light a couple of candles," and we'd head for the nearest Catholic church. When she prayed, Mamma was—well, I'd look at her, and it was like she was in another world. She was so focused; her face was transformed. If I close my eyes today, more than eighty-five years later, I can still see her peacefulness and serenity. It's an image that continues to comfort me.

My mother's relationship with God and the Catholic church was interesting. I think Mamma felt she had special dispensation to skip Mass because of her brother Luigi, the priest. One time, when we still lived in Italy, she took all of us on the train to visit Father Luigi in

Pescia, which is about fifteen miles west of Lucca. When Father Luigi started his evening prayers, Mamma told him she was exhausted and needed to go to sleep.

"Avete fatto il tuo dovere verso il Signore d'aver avuto tutti questi figli, state tranquilla con le mie grazie"—"You've done your duty to God by having all these children, so go to bed with my blessings," he told her.

Mamma did as he said and then apparently decided that her brother's words applied not just to that one night but to all of her life—and not just in Italy but after we came to the United States as well. She prayed regularly, but she wasn't much of an official church-goer. Remembering what Father Luigi had said, Mamma figured her real duty to God was to care for her children. Rather than attending Mass, she liked to drop in when she had the time and talk with God on her own.

Of course, Mamma saw to it that faith in God was a big part of our lives. Our family attended Sts. Peter and Paul Church, in the heart of North Beach. The church has been rebuilt since then, but at the time it was a small wooden building with a sanctuary that held maybe a hundred people. In a way it was a lot like many small-town Catholic churches. There were a couple of stained glass windows and the usual statues of saints. The basement held a sort of meeting room that also served as a classroom. It was there that I attended catechism classes just before I turned nine years old. The classes were required so that I could take my First Communion. Catechism was really something then, all about hell, purgatory, and heaven. God help you if you went to hell—and I figured purgatory was even worse.

I believed every word the nuns told us. I could see it all vividly in my mind, and I figured, *Oh my God, you have to be really good or forget it.* But Mamma kept such close tabs on me that I never had much chance to get into trouble. I felt sorry for the kids who would end up in hell because they didn't have someone like Mamma to look after them.

With catechism completed, it was time for my First Communion. I don't know how my parents managed to afford it, but I got a fancy white dress and veil for this special day. My outfit was so beautiful. I just couldn't believe it. We went to church in the morning, then home for a big family meal where I was the center of attention. After that I was given enough money to go off with my friends to see a movie. I could do anything I wanted that day. At nine years old, it gave me a rare feeling of freedom. Usually Mamma had her watchful eye on me and seemed to know exactly where I was and what I was doing every minute. For that one day, I got to feel grown-up and special, able to move freely into the world beyond my family.

And there were more special events soon after—family weddings that were held, of course, in the Catholic church.

I don't know why my four eldest sisters didn't marry in Italy. They were certainly old enough. Beppa turned twenty-eight about a month after we came to the United States. The day we landed at Ellis Island, Jenny was twenty-six, Algisa was twenty-two, and Paolina was twenty. Maybe our family was so poor in Italy that their prospects weren't good. Or maybe since a group effort was needed to make it to America, Mamma and Babbo told them they'd have to wait. I really don't know.

Anyway, Paolina and Beppa both married in 1919, and both married Italian immigrants. Paolina wed Luigi Abballo, who was originally from a village south of Rome. He worked with her at the canning company, and that's where they met. The two of them started talking, perhaps at lunchtime or after work; then they started keeping company for a while—strictly chaperoned of course—and then they got married.

Originally from Tuscany just like our family, Giuseppe Vinci worked in a San Francisco restaurant near the cannery where my older sisters were employed. Every morning and every evening he would watch them walk by. Finally he got up the nerve to stop Beppa and say a few words to her. Once again a little conversation led to a carefully chaperoned courtship and then to marriage.

I loved my sisters' weddings. In addition to the fact that I gained more bed space and cleaner bathwater, the celebrations were great fun. They all pretty much followed a traditional Italian format. The bride wore a simple long, white dress, not formal, with a short veil decorated with orange blossoms. The couple getting married and several witnesses went to church for the ceremony, then came back home for a big family meal. There was good Italian food everywhere, music, a nice long party, and then the newlyweds went home and started their life together.

None of my oldest sisters ever dated before marriage or "broke up" with a boyfriend. They went along with their lives, working hard every day until they met a guy they were interested in. They spent some time with him—carefully chaperoned by the family—then got married and spent the rest of their lives working hard every day. Even when they were single and at an age to be considered old maids, my four oldest sisters never said anything about wishing that they had a date or that they might somehow meet an interesting man. I think they simply accepted whatever happened in their lives and never questioned anything.

I don't mean to make it sound as if the four of them were boring or somehow identical. Each one had her own likes and dislikes and a distinct personality. As the oldest, Beppa never lost her somewhat gruff exterior. She and her husband, Giuseppe, were always so kind to me. I think Beppa put up a stoic facade to the outside world to cover her embarrassment at not being able to speak much English and not knowing how to read or write in any language.

Jenny, the second oldest, didn't care what anyone thought; she knew she belonged here. Who cared if her English wasn't that great and she was illiterate? She was a natural born storyteller and would have made a great stand-up comedian. Jenny had an infectious laugh and would begin chuckling anytime she started telling a good joke. I'd end up giggling long before the punch line because Jenny was laughing so hard at her own humor.

Algisa was quieter than Jenny and an extremely private person. Whatever was going on inside her and whatever secrets she might have, she kept to herself. However she and Jenny were great friends and spent a lot of time together.

Our fourth-born sister, Paolina, was more serious than the others and also fairly shy. She cried easily, sometimes for no reason that I understood, and was softhearted, sensitive, and fairly stubborn. She knew her own mind. After they had been married a few years, she and her husband bought a house on the far side of the city, so Paolina didn't share her day-to-day life with the family the way my other sisters did. I don't think that bothered her at all. I suspect she liked time to herself and being able to run her household without help or comment.

Beppa's husband, Giuseppe, quickly became a favorite of Eda's and mine. He had a good, steady job and was really a generous guy. At the end of the week he'd come by our house and give Eda and me each a quarter. Every Saturday the two of us would watch from our second-story front window, keeping an eagle eye on every streetcar to see if Giuseppe was on it. Finally we'd see him hop off the streetcar and head to our house. Eda and I would act nonchalant when Giuseppe walked in the door, but we were on pins and needles until he gave us each our quarter. Eda and I first had to ask Mamma's permission, and then we would race off to see a movie at the Palace Theater in North Beach.

We'd buy candy with whatever money we had left after buying our tickets. Back then you could really pick and choose which sweets you wanted for just a penny.

The movies were silent—and exciting. There were a lot of cowboy pictures, but mostly I loved the cliff-hanging serials that always ended with the heroes in some awful spot. They'd be falling off a mountain, and when you came back the next week you'd find out there was a tree or something that saved them. Sometimes my older sisters would come with us, and they had a great time because they didn't need to know English to enjoy silent movies.

My sisters' marriages brought other excitement to our family: babies. On March 14, 1920, my sister Paolina gave birth to her son, Fred. Just like Mamma, Paolina had her baby at home with the help of a midwife. At that time Paolina and her husband, Luigi, lived in a downstairs flat in the building right next door to ours. I knew Paolina was pregnant because I saw her most every day, and then suddenly I found out I had a nephew. I guess Mamma and the family didn't think I needed to know any more than that.

A short while later, Beppa's husband, Giuseppe, introduced one of his friends to our sister Algisa. Lorenzo Parenti was originally from a small town near my native Lucca in Tuscany, but at that time he was working on a ranch in Rio Vista, in California's huge Central Valley. Lorenzo came to visit Giuseppe and to enjoy a bit of the big-city excitement in San Francisco. After a brief—and of course carefully monitored—courtship, Lorenzo moved to the city, found a better job, and married Algisa in June 1921.

Along with this third family wedding, there was another exciting change: Babbo was finally able to live with us again. After Joe opened his own grocery store in North Beach, our father quit Italian Swiss

Colony, moved to our home in San Francisco, and started helping Joe at the store. Mamma was delighted. Besides the fact that she loved him, in her eyes Babbo always was the real head of our family. I think she felt she had played that role on her own for long enough and was glad to have him take charge. Now when we sat down for dinner, Mamma and Babbo sat side by side at the head of the table. Joe and Rico still had the place of honor at the other end—if Rico was around that night. Even with Babbo home, Rico still kept his own schedule. And, as always, we girls sat along the sides of the table.

In a lot of ways we were living just as we had in Italy. We always spoke Italian at home; our food was Italian; even our family friends were all of Italian descent. Eda, Joe, Rico, and I were meeting non-Italians outside the family circle, but that didn't have much effect on what happened at home. Which wasn't unusual. Most of the immigrants we knew lived pretty much as they had in the old country. Those who came here later in life—like Babbo, Mamma, and my older sisters—were much too busy earning money or keeping house to learn a new language or new customs. They lived in a neighborhood where they could work in Italian, shop in Italian, go to church in Italian. I had to speak English at school, and Eda, Joe, and Rico all spoke English on their jobs because they worked with non-Italians. But otherwise our family life continued as it always had.

Babbo bought a horse and wagon and kept it in a stable near our home. The wagon let him pick up produce and other items to take them to Joe's store. Sometimes Babbo let me ride with him on the wagon, which was always exciting. I loved going anywhere with my handsome father. For the first time I could remember, I had both my father and mother around on a daily basis. It was wonderful. Babbo and Mamma would be there when I got home from school. They'd sit at the kitchen table and talk with me while I drank some milk and ate the long, crunchy Italian cookies known as biscotti.

Then Babbo would help me with my math homework. He'd never been to school, but he had taught himself to read and write and could do all kinds of math in his head without any trouble. I'd read a problem aloud and start working it out on paper, but before I was done Babbo would have figured out the right answer without writing anything down. I thought he was a genius. He was also definitely in charge. If he thought I was talking too much or getting out of line at the dinner table, he had a way of looking at me that just made me freeze and clam up. Even so, I was never afraid of him. I was the baby of the family and he was so good to me. I loved spending time with him.

One thing hadn't changed: Rico was still the family maverick and a source of growing concern. It seemed that Babbo couldn't control Rico any better than Mamma could. Everyone else would turn their paychecks over to Babbo and Mamma, to cover the household expenses. Rico kept the money he earned and came and went from our family flat pretty much as he pleased. A lot of times he seemed to use it just as a place to sleep. Mamma prayed earnestly—and often—about Rico. Babbo just shook his head in exasperation. There seemed to be no way to get through to his oldest son, to make him behave as he ought. I know Babbo and Rico exchanged angry words at times because Mamma was upset that they never got along. I never actually saw or heard Babbo and Rico argue. I think Mamma and Babbo tried to hide the conflict from the younger children, yet I always knew it was there. If Rico's name came up during dinner because someone was upset or complaining, Babbo would always say we wouldn't talk about that at the table.

As for the rest of us, we all had our place in the family and unique ways we could each contribute. Babbo added to the family larder by making his own sausage and wine. I was his assistant for the sausage-making, which we did on our big back porch. It's odd to think about it now, but the best view from our home was from the rear of the building, not the front. We could only see the Bay from our place if we were in the backyard or on the back porch. I guess views of San Francisco Bay weren't as important to builders back then.

To make sausage, Babbo would buy a whole pig's head several days in advance. There it would be, sitting on the porch until we were ready to start work. I hated the messy job of sausage-making, but I loved helping Babbo, so it was kind of a toss-up for me. He had a meat grinder that he'd clamp on the edge of the table. Made of metal, it had sort of a cup or funnel on top, with mincing gears hidden inside and a long-handled crank to make it work. Babbo would cut the pig's head into manageable pieces. I'd feed the raw meat into the top of the grinder while Babbo turned the handle. The finely chopped pork would come out the side in a steady stream.

Once that was done, Babbo would mix the ground meat with spices and other filling. For those who aren't familiar with it, sausage is made by stuffing a piece of animal intestine with flavored meat. So I'd hold the guts as Babbo pushed the meat mixture in. Then he would separate it into sausage-length pieces, tying knots between each section. Like I said, I loved working with my father, but I was glad we only made sausage once in a while.

Babbo also put a lot of care into his homemade red wine. Our cellar held wooden barrels and a vat for fermenting. He'd buy grapes by the ton and rent a crusher to begin the process. His best vintages were aged and used only for special occasions. Ordinary red wine was served with every dinner in our house, even after Prohibition was passed in 1920, banning alcohol.

I didn't quite understand what Prohibition was, but I did hear people talking about it. I also saw things in the newspapers about Italians, bootleggers, and the Mafia. That's when Mamma would start muttering about the Southern Italians. But other people seemed to label all Italians as lawless and that confused me. All the Italian-Americans I knew in my neighborhood and family were hardworking, lovable people, including the ones from southern Italy. It seemed to me the whole world was against Italians—which was what I was—and I didn't understand why.

At school I heard the teachers and parents complain about having to pay taxes, and I had no idea what taxes were. It made me worry that my family and I were enjoying life in this wonderful country but somehow not contributing our fair share. It was all jumbled in my mind, but I never talked to anybody about it. I kept it inside me and felt a growing insecurity. Mostly, of course, I simply got on with life the way my family always did.

Although things weren't all that easy, by the start of 1922 three of my sisters were happily married, and our family had settled down to a comfortable routine. After taking a couple of courses in night school, Eda landed a job running a calculating machine in the accounting department of a big department store. Jenny and my other sisters were employed at an Italian cigar factory, rolling cigars. It was steady work and paid better than the cannery. Joe's small grocery never earned enough money, and he had to close it down. But he immediately found a job at a men's clothing store and was earning a good salary. I was the pride of the family for my excellent grades in school, Babbo did whatever he could to add food to our table, and Mamma kept everything at home clean, shining, and running perfectly.

We did have some worries. There had been a flu epidemic in 1918 and a lot of people had died. Even four years later, my parents were afraid something like that might happen again. To protect us, Babbo always kept his homemade brandy-soaked cherries on hand in a big glass jar. He believed that eating a cherry soaked in brandy killed any dangerous germs. He made me take one every morning, to eat on my way to school.

"Per stare in salute"—"To stay healthy," Babbo would say as he held out the cherry jar.

I hated the taste of the brandy, so I'd hold the cherry in my mouth until my cheek went numb from the alcohol. I'd finally give up and bite down, filling my mouth with brandy. I'd swallow the liquid, chew the fruit, then spit out the pit. I thought nothing of it at the time, but now I wonder what my teacher thought when she smelled my breath. Babbo insisted each of us had to eat a brandy-soaked cherry every day, and he ate one too.

Then Babbo caught a cold. He had never been sick a day in his life. Maybe his illness was because of the flu epidemic, but no one else we knew got ill, so that doesn't seem likely. Whatever caused it, Babbo's cold quickly turned into pneumonia. The doctor came to our home and did what he could. There were no antibiotics in those days and no miracle cures. On February 28, 1922, five days after Babbo took sick, I came home in the afternoon and was told he was dead. He had died while I was at school.

He was fifty-seven years old and I was twelve. He had been forced by poverty to live away from our family for most of my life, and suddenly he was gone just as I was starting to get to know him. In many ways I don't have any idea what it's like to have a father. I spent just a few short years with Babbo, and I was so young. I never really understood him as the man he was. I can only remember him as my hero and the handsome genius who helped me with my math problems.

Babbo's sudden death stunned our family and then brought us closer together. Everyone kind of hovered around Mamma. I think my brothers and sisters all realized that we would have to support her from then on—and we did, for the rest of her life. With my sisters' help, Mamma made arrangements for the funeral. It must have been devastating to become a widow so abruptly at age fifty-three, with children still living at home. As always, Mamma did everything that had to be done and didn't show what she was feeling inside.

I don't remember much about the funeral because Mamma thought I was too young to attend. Since my sister Beppa had just had a baby, I stayed with her at her house while Mamma and the others went to church and the cemetery. I do know my sisters said they took smelling salts to the services and used them when they felt faint.

For months everyone in our family wore black. Mamma thought I was too young for full mourning, so she added a black belt on a dress for me and put black stitching around the collar. Besides always wearing a dark black dress, for a long time Mamma put on a big black hat with a heavy black veil whenever she went out. You couldn't see her face at all. Dressed like that—well, to me she looked like death itself. I hated seeing her in that hat and veil. I think just the color black all by itself can make people sad and somber if that's all you see or wear.

I missed Babbo so much. The months after his death are a dark blur in my mind. Our home felt full of sadness. My sister Eda was so upset she was sick for quite a while. I realize now that it was probably emotional. Eda had to see a doctor, but gradually she got better.

Except for the ache of missing Babbo, the routine of my daily life hadn't changed much. I had always been somewhat sheltered, and now everyone in the family seemed to rally around to keep me as unaffected as possible. They tried to make it easier for me, and in many ways they succeeded. I certainly got extra attention, with everyone taking time to chat with me. I think we were all more considerate of each other in reaction to having lost someone so important to our family. It was frightening to realize how fragile life is and how quickly it can end.

Once the funeral was over, I went back to school but it wasn't the same. I wasn't the same. I looked around at the other children and thought, *They have fathers and I don't.* All through grammar school I had felt a little different from the others, and now that feeling was ten times stronger. I kept thinking, *I don't even have a father anymore.*

That June I graduated from the eighth grade. I didn't think it was a big deal, but my family made a real fuss. My brother Joe bought me a beautiful gold-filigree fountain pen. I can't remember if I missed Babbo that day. I think it was still too painful to think about him.

After my graduation, Mamma moved us out of the North Point Street flat. I guess it held too many memories for her. It did for me. Rico got a place of his own. The rest of us—Mamma, Joe, Jenny, Eda, and me—got an apartment on Lombard Street in North Beach, where we went on with life without Babbo.

CHAPTER 5

I could see a lot more of the world from our new home on Lombard Street. The old place had been in a slight hollow. Although there had been a view of part of San Francisco Bay from the back porch, there wasn't much to see out of our old front windows except two houses and a vacant lot across the street. Where we moved to on Lombard Street was on a steep hill with lots to look at from every window. I felt like a bird or something as I gazed out all around us.

The Lombard Street flat was a step up for us in other ways too. The building was newer and the rooms were larger. Lombard Street runs almost the whole width of the northern part of San Francisco, from east to west. When we first arrived in San Francisco, we had lived for a couple of months near the west end of Lombard, in the Cow Hollow area. Now we were on the eastern stretch, in the heart of the North Beach district. Our home was just down the street from what's known as Telegraph Hill, where Coit Tower stands today. Built in the

1930s to honor the city's firemen, the tower looks something like the end of a fire hose, sticking straight up. But when we moved into our flat in the summer of 1922, Coit Tower wasn't there yet, and Telegraph Hill was mostly open space with a few rundown, low-rent bungalows scattered around. Mostly artists lived there.

Our part of Lombard Street was lower down the hill. It was filled in solid with tall, narrow, two- and three-story wooden buildings on both sides of the road. We were on the second floor of a three-story building. Each apartment had two bay windows curving out over the sidewalk. It sounds a lot grander than it was, but I did like the little alcove the bay windows made inside the rooms. There were a lot of reasons why I preferred our new place over the old one.

On North Point Street the linoleum had been so old that the pattern came off whenever we washed the floor. We ended up with dark brown patches in the high-traffic areas where we had to scrub the most. No matter what we did, that floor always looked scruffy and a little dingy. On Lombard Street the linoleum was of better quality, newer, and kept its color when washed. I hated scrubbing the old floor because it felt as if all that work never did a bit of good. At least on Lombard Street the floor looked nice after I washed it. And by this time we had acquired slightly better furniture and more of it. It wasn't fancy, but at least our home wasn't as sparsely furnished as when we first came to America.

The gas jets had been taken out and electricity added to our home while we were still on North Point Street, so it was nothing new to have electric lights on Lombard Street. The big improvement was a little water heater that we turned on for a half hour or so when we wanted to bathe. No more heating water in the kitchen and carrying it down the long hallway—and no more sharing the Saturday night bathwater. Hallelujah!

In other ways the new flat was a lot like the old one. We still used what would have been the living room as a bedroom. That's where Mamma and I slept. Jenny and Eda were in the other front bedroom, and Joe got the middle room, off the long hallway. The kitchen was in the rear, just like our old place, but we also had a nice-sized dining room. There was also a rather large back porch. We put a table there where we could sit and look out at the Bay. We'd often play cards on that table, and it was Mamma's favorite spot for rolling out fresh pasta dough.

After we moved to Lombard Street, Jenny kind of became Joe's personal caretaker. She fixed his lunch, washed his clothes, sewed loose buttons, mended any tears, and ironed and starched his shirts. Jenny still worked long hours in the cigar factory six days a week, but if Joe needed anything done, Jenny did it. In our family men did not have to take care of themselves; women were expected to do it for them. For all her comic brashness and outgoing good humor, Jenny seemed quite content to spend her free time looking after Joe. I suppose it helped that Joe was a pretty sweet and easygoing guy.

Shortly after we moved in we got a telephone—our first—installed in a little niche in the hallway. The phone was tall and narrow, with a conelike mouthpiece and a separate conelike receiver attached by a short cord. There was a little hook where the receiver hung when it wasn't being used. Phone numbers were only four digits long, and you didn't dial or push any buttons. To call someone you picked up the receiver and held it up to your ear so you could hear the operator say, "Number, please." Then you'd tell the operator which number you wanted to call. She'd make the connection for you.

The telephone company seemed to choose operators with the most beautiful voices you could imagine. It was great. With all the buttons you have to push nowadays, I'd love to go back to the operators. As an old lady I'm hard of hearing. When an impersonal voice tells me to push one for this and two for that, I get lost. When that happens I really want those lovely operators back.

There were other changes in my life that summer. I started my menstrual period and felt like a grown-up woman. At age twelve I was sure I was now worldly-wise. Of course I still knew nothing. I never talked to Mamma about what was going on with my body. Sex or anything related to it was a taboo subject. We girls understood quite clearly that we were to have nothing to do with it until we got married. Somehow Mamma made that rule obvious without telling us anything specific or even mentioning the subject by name.

Not that it was any big surprise to me when I started my period; the other kids at school had already told me all about it. So when it happened, I went to my sister Eda and she showed me what to do. In a way, moving to Lombard Street was the start of my friendship with Eda. Mamma still had endless restrictions on where we could go and who we could see. Eda and I ended up spending a lot of time together—practically every night and weekend. Maybe once a month we would have enough money and Mamma's permission to go see a movie. Otherwise we stayed at home. When our chores were done, we'd do embroidery or sewing. Eda and I spent a lot of our time making our "trousseaus"—pillowcases, sheets, tablecloths, napkins, all the traditional items for when we got married and set up our own household. We each had a cedar chest that we gradually filled with our handmade linens.

When we wanted to embroider, we sat by the bay window in Eda's bedroom at the front of our flat. The light was good there. We'd drag a couple of the kitchen chairs into her room and set up a small table between us to hold our supplies. It was convenient and it made it easy to talk as we worked. Other times we would sew. At least Eda sewed and I did my best to help. She tried to teach me, but we both soon gave up. I was obviously never meant to be a seamstress, while Eda was a natural at it. She loved sewing. I suspect some of its appeal was because it let her have stylish clothes even though we couldn't afford to buy them. She would window-shop at all the best department stores to check out the newest looks, then go home and make them herself. They always came out great.

Eda was a natural beauty with what I considered perfect features. Everything about her face was symmetrical and in ideal proportion. Her profile was like a gorgeous sculpture with a small, well-shaped nose and round, full lips. She had beautiful teeth and a dazzling smile, as well as a trim figure. People would often tell her how beautiful she was. Eda enjoyed every word. She loved looking good and spent a lot of time on her wardrobe.

In addition to clothes for Eda, we made lots of outfits for me and for our older sisters when they asked. Eda was generous with her skills—and we didn't have a lot of other things we were allowed to do that we enjoyed. While we worked we talked a lot, mostly about Eda. She was nineteen when we moved to Lombard Street and not very interested in what her thirteen-year-old sister did every day. But I was really fascinated by Eda's life. She was one of six girls working in the bookkeeping office of a big department store. Each girl used a sort of calculating machine called a comptometer—I doubt if they even exist anymore—to add and subtract all the store's daily transactions. The work itself sounded boring and Eda didn't talk about it much. Instead she'd tell me who said what in the office, everything that happened in the store, and all the latest jokes. It seemed so glamorous and made my life feel dull and limited.

School was my only escape from home, but eventually it began to seem like drudgery as well. Starting high school was exciting, of course. We were going to be the first class to graduate from Galileo High, which was one block north of the Ghirardelli Chocolate Factory. The school was only half as big as it is today, but at the time it seemed huge and quite grand. I was keyed up and happy when I went to register for classes.

While waiting in line I started chatting with a friendly looking girl. Her name was Etta Segale, and it turned out her home was only about a block from mine. She was of Italian descent just like me. But while I had Mamma's long nose, Etta's was small and turned up. Where I was thin, dark, and considered fairly tall at five feet five and a half inches, Etta was only five feet tall—but was she pretty and full of life. She was lighter in coloring than I was and much more round and curvy. Etta had big gray-green eyes and chestnut hair. Some people even thought she was Irish. Nobody ever thought I was anything except Italian.

After signing up for our classes, Etta and I walked home still chatting away. Since we lived so near each other, we walked to school together on the first day and met again in the afternoon to come back home. It was about a mile one way to the high school. That gave us a lot of time to talk and get to know each other. It seemed the most natural thing in the world to walk together every day. We soon became inseparable.

As we told each other our life stories, we found out there were an amazing number of similarities. Just like me, Etta was the youngest of eight children, born in a pattern of four girls, two boys, and two girls. Just like my family, her father had died when she was young, and her mother was raising the remaining children on her own. With the complete conviction common to teenage girls, we decided we had been destined to meet.

Of course there were also differences between us. Although Etta's family was Italian-American, her mother, Henrietta, had left Italy while she was a teenager. She met her husband and got married in the United States. All her children had been born here. So Henrietta Segale was much more Americanized than Mamma. And although Etta knew some Italian, her family all spoke English at home. Unlike me, Etta was confident she belonged in this country. After all, she had been born in the United States and was a native citizen.

Even with these minor differences, our similarities made us incredibly comfortable with each other. We could talk about anything—boys, our families, school, and our hopes for the future. Etta became someone special in my life, someone I could always turn to—and she still is to this day, more than eighty years later. Together we've learned a lot about life.

My friendship with Etta was a bright spot in what I sometimes—with the melodramatics of youth—saw as pretty bleak prospects. Compared to what I could see of other students' lives, I felt like a prisoner, stuck within the bars of Mamma's rules. It seemed as if there was an insurmountable wall all around me, leaving me nothing to look forward to except school, studying, and housework—which I hated with a passion.

Mamma and I would argue about this all the time. She always won because I ended up doing my chores, but I brought the subject up frequently, telling her clearly that I hated housework. This really worried Mamma. She thought there must be something terribly wrong with me. Her home was her whole world. Her life was made up almost entirely of cooking, cleaning, shopping, and caring for others. My mother didn't see how I would ever be happy or even survive in the world.

"Come farai quando sei maritata?"—"How are you going to get along when you're married?" she asked me more than once.

I didn't have an answer for her, but I was sure my life was going to be different—somehow, some way. I held tight to the idea that I would find the sugar at the bottom of my cup one day, and it wouldn't include having to wash floors or iron shirts all the time.

Now and then I'd get so frustrated and furious with what I saw as my complete captivity that I wanted to run away. I was sick to death of my mother's rules and all the restrictions that seemed to stretch out endlessly in front of me. I never did run away, but I thought about it a lot. I wanted my freedom—immediately.

I was caught up in my own life and didn't realize how much stress and tension Mamma was feeling—until the night she fainted. It was dinnertime and we were getting ready to eat. Joe, Eda, Jenny, and I were all at home. Suddenly Mamma just fell to the floor, dropping the platter of food she had been holding. We had no idea what was wrong. Joe carried Mamma to her bedroom, then used our telephone to call a doctor—a serious step in our family. At that time doctors made house calls, so he came over right away. We were all relieved when he told us Mamma had a bleeding ulcer that could be easily treated.

"With the right diet, she'll be as good as new," the doctor told us cheerfully.

Mamma started taking a tablespoon of milk every half hour. For the first few days she didn't eat anything else but that milk. It took months for her to get better, but as soon as she could, she got right back into running the household. I understand now that stress and tension contribute to a bleeding ulcer. Back then it was just something that happened. Mamma must have been tied up in knots inside, but we didn't know it.

I desperately wanted to fix what had gone wrong with Mamma's body, but I had no idea what might have caused the problem. So during Easter week in my first year of high school, Etta, Eda, and I started a tradition we kept up for more than ten years. On Good Friday we walked to an odd number of Catholic churches—three, five, or seven, as long as it was an odd number—and lit candles in each one. We'd say an "Our Father" and a couple of "Hail Marys" and then hurry on to the next church. It was possible to visit that many churches in San Francisco, but it was a long walk. We did it because we believed it entitled us to a special benefit. We'd always ask for the same thing: a blessing for Mamma.

Although Mamma's brief illness was upsetting, there were also a lot of bright spots in our lives. Two or three times each summer we'd all go to a Tombola game in Washington Square near our home. Located in the heart of North Beach, the square is just south of Sts. Peter and Paul Church. Today Washington Square is a typical, wide-open city park with a few trees surrounded by a fair amount of concrete. Back then the square was draped with graceful willow trees. You know the kind—the ones with long branches that droop down and wave in the breeze. Eventually they cut down the willows because they couldn't see what people were doing in the park. But when we went to play Tombola, the square was full of all that beautiful greenery. It was a wonderful oasis among all the buildings, sidewalks, and streets.

Tombola is an Italian form of bingo, with cash prizes. People would buy cards and mark off the numbers as they were called out. A platform was set up in the middle of the square. That was where they'd draw the Tombola numbers. There would also be entertainment and music. Everything was in Italian, so Mamma had a wonderful time. Her face would glow with excitement, and she'd chatter away with any friends we might meet. She would buy a Tombola ticket, and I'd mark it for her since Mamma couldn't read the numbers by herself.

"*Speriamo che si vince*"—"Let's hope we win," Mamma would always say. But we never did.

There were other good times. Mamma liked and respected Etta's mother, Henrietta Segale. Under Henrietta's more liberal, Americanized influence, Mama's rules gradually loosened up a bit. She allowed Eda and me to do things our older sisters had never done, such as go places with friends or—after a lot of coaxing—out on dates with boys.

Even before Eda and I were allowed to date, we spent a lot of time at Italian Athletic Club events. My brother Joe helped start the club, coached its soccer team, and was one of its long-distance runners. Etta, Eda, and I went to all the soccer games and the races to cheer Joe on— and to meet all those young, good-looking Italian-American athletes. The soccer club played every Sunday during the season. Afterwards we went out to dinner with the players, and since Joe was the coach, the club paid for the meal. It was great.

The club used to sponsor races, and each year there was a cross-city race, now known as the annual Bay to Breakers event. On race day all the Italian runners would come to our house for an early breakfast. My mother would cook cereal or whatever it was they wanted, and then we'd go watch the race. Oh, it was exciting. I think that's when my life-long love of sports began.

I also learned a lot about my brother Joe by watching him run. At six feet tall he was easy to spot at the starting or finish line. He wasn't a particularly good-looking guy—he had my long, narrow nose, only bigger—but he had a kind heart. If a friend and Joe were running, Joe came in second. If none of his friends were racing, Joe came in first. He was really confident and at ease when he was running or on the soccer field—much more so than when my peace-loving brother was at home in a house full of women.

Soccer games and races weren't the only club activities we enjoyed. There were regular Sunday evening dances in the clubhouse, which was actually a large room above a bank, about a block south of Washington Square. The room had a big wooden dance floor with chairs all around the edges. Etta and I were allowed to attend the dances with Mamma coming along as chaperone. We didn't mind because the room was full of Italian mothers. They sat lining the walls, gossiping while the young couples twirled around the room. There was always a small group of musicians—a drummer, perhaps an accordion, maybe a violin, and usually someone on the club's piano. They'd play a combination of waltzes and fox-trots with something a little faster now and then, like the Charleston. Etta and I thought it was great and went as often as we could.

That's where we met our first loves. Mine was Bill Fossat, who came from the northern part of Italy, near France. I was so smitten. I was sure he was "the man" for me. Etta fell in love with his best friend, Angelo Rampa, and eventually we became a foursome—once Mamma got used to the idea. We dated for a couple of years and then Etta and I broke up with both boys. I have no idea why. I asked Etta about it the other day, and she doesn't remember either. It's funny how life can be sometimes. We loved those boys so intensely—we both remember that part—and we were sure it was going to last forever. Then *poof*, it was over.

Gradually Mamma was becoming more Americanized. Eda and I started saying, *"Mamma, dovresti…"*—"Mamma, you should…" this or that. And our mother was surprisingly willing to try new things. I think she loved what she learned from us rather than resenting it. Mamma wanted to be part of what we were doing out in the world.

Some of the changes showed up in her Italian. She and my older sisters started saying things like *"Si va allo storo"*—"Let's go to the store." Except there's no such word as *storo* in Italian. To this day, I speak Mamma's and my sisters' Americanized version of the language. I never did learn the correct Italian word for *storo*.

And it wasn't just Mamma's words that changed. It was while I was in high school that we ate our first turkey stuffed with ravioli filling, even though we didn't know anything about Thanksgiving. Of course Eda and I explained to Mamma that there were lots of other things she needed to do differently. We never did have mayonnaise or catsup in our house—they were unknown substances to Mamma—but Eda and I convinced her she had to buy Wonder Bread to make sandwiches and not that old-fashioned, crusty Italian-style stuff. My mother loved Wonder Bread in its colorful, dotted package. *"Il pane con le palline"*— "the bread with the little balls on it," she would say.

Our lives were going fairly smoothly, but somehow I couldn't muster the same enthusiasm for high school that I had in grammar school. I did okay in a subject like typing that didn't require any home-work. I also did well in Spanish because it was so much like Italian. I could just skate along on what I heard in class and what I already knew. But for classes like English or algebra, where I really needed to study… Well, I just didn't do it. I think I had burned myself out in elementary school, struggling to earn good grades by working hour after hour at home with no help from anyone. I couldn't make myself do that anymore.

My family thought I was so smart and hoped I would eventually go to college, but I wanted to be out in the world, earning money. I wanted to have new clothes, and we couldn't afford them. I wanted to be able to go out to dinner or go see a show without worrying about the cost, and I couldn't do that. I needed to feel like "the others" and knew I could only do that with money. I didn't have the patience to finish high school. I didn't want to wait another two years until I graduated; I wanted a good job with a paycheck of my own, and I wanted it as soon as possible.

I talked it over with Etta, and she felt the same way. So in the fall of 1924 we decided that instead of returning to Galileo High for eleventh grade, we'd drop out and enroll in business college. We were fifteen years old. We were convinced that we were all grown up and more than ready to make our own way in the world.

I look at the fifteen-year-olds I know today, and I can't imagine them taking on a full-time job. But back in the fall of 1924, I would have argued vehemently with anyone who said I was too young to tackle the business world. I knew I could do it and that was all that mattered.

Etta told her brother-in-law about our plans, and he researched the business schools in the area. Our best choice for what we wanted to learn, he told us, was Gallagher Marsh Business College. So the two of us signed up for the standard six-month course. Since I had no money, my brother Joe paid my tuition. I don't remember how much it cost, but I know it wasn't cheap.

I think it nearly broke Joe's heart, because he really wanted me to be the first in the family to go to college. He was sure I could make it. Joe would have done anything to keep me in high school until I graduated—and he was willing to keep supporting me if I went to college. I had to tell him that I didn't want to do that, that I couldn't do that. I knew paying college tuition would be a tremendous sacrifice for Joe. I also believed I would never fit in at any college and would only feel inferior—the poor immigrant girl with either hand-me-down or handmade clothes and no time or money for having fun. I wasn't willing to do that.

For so long I had been aware of being different. Now I was determined to start being just like everyone else. And I was sure that my best first step out into the bigger, wider world would be through business college, not high school.

CHAPTER 6

Etta and I were required to dress in what was considered proper office attire to attend our business classes. That meant a hat, a long skirt and blouse or a floor-length dress, high-heeled shoes, and gloves—all matching, the whole bit. Back then no one—male or female—went anywhere outside without a hat. Everything had to be just so. Men always wore suits, and they didn't wear wristwatches. Instead they carried a pocket watch tucked into a vest pocket and attached by a fancy chain that draped across the vest. The "casual look" just did not exist. Everybody appeared formal and proper, always.

Business college thrilled me. I worked as hard as I possibly could because I knew these were the skills that could get me a job. I enjoyed typing and shorthand and did well in both. I disliked bookkeeping but threw myself into learning as many basic accounting skills as possible because I knew they were so practical. I was really motivated to start bringing in a paycheck as soon as possible.

My determination paid off: I completed the six-month course in only five months. With all my classes out of the way, the business college sent me on my first job interview in February 1925. My sixteenth birthday was still two months away, but I was thrilled by the thought of earning my own living. Wearing what I considered to be my most businesslike outfit, I headed to the address I had been given. I was eager to tell the interviewer all about my newly acquired skills. My spirits fell when I showed up at the office and found a hallway full of about a dozen women. They all looked a lot more qualified and experienced than I felt.

Finally the man who was doing the hiring came out and had us all line up. He looked us over and without asking a single question about background, skills, or anything, he pointed at me and said, "You're hired."

I was now the sixty-five-dollar-a-month stenographer for the San Francisco sales office of Brown and Bigelow, a calendar-manufacturing company based in St. Paul, Minnesota. Nothing about the interview had gone as I expected, but I was thrilled to have been chosen out of the crowd. It meant I was finally finished with school and on my way in the business world.

I was given an office of my own with just enough room for my desk, chair, typewriter, file cabinet, and another chair for anyone who came to see me. It was all pretty simple and plain. Brown and Bigelow was one of several companies on the third floor of a building on Market Street in downtown San Francisco. Visitors walked into a main meeting room with a large table and chairs. This was where the salesmen would gather if they weren't out making calls. In addition to my small space, there were two larger offices for the top salesmen. That was it. We didn't get many visitors because we sold directly to businesses and retail stores.

My job required me to take dictation from the salesmen and then type up the letters and reports for their signatures. It was harder than I expected because many of the men used words I had never heard before. I had completed only two years of high school, and standard business language was brand new to me. Many of the phrases were completely foreign. One guy in particular was really fussy and liked using what I considered to be obscure, important-sounding words. I did my best, but he wasn't all that happy with the results. He was also one of the people who looked shocked when I innocently explained that my mother and four older sisters didn't speak any English. Many times after that I heard him say loudly to others, "People who don't speak English should leave the country."

He never said that to me, of course—people like that rarely do—but he often said that type of thing when I was sure to hear him. Other people who worked in our building felt the same way he did, and I'd catch muttered comments about "dagos" and "wops." It hurt so much and made me feel terribly confused. I knew how wonderful and loving my hardworking family was. I didn't see how anyone could look down on them.

Yet at the same time I was deeply ashamed of them. I wished they all spoke English and did everything the American way. Then I'd feel guilty for having those thoughts about my family, who had done so much to help me. I also knew that it was mostly a matter of circumstances that I had gone to school in America—that I was the member of my family who was young enough to benefit the most from our move to this country. One of my older sisters might have been me or I could have been her, if you know what I mean. They were as smart as I was; they just never had the opportunities I did. It really was a matter of "there but for the grace of God, go I"—which didn't help my guilt about feeling ashamed of them.

I was too young to realize that it was the prejudiced people who were in the wrong, not me. The people who said those things to me had better jobs than I did, dressed beautifully, and seemed to know all the proper etiquette. I looked up to them. That made their slurs all the more painful.

Of course, not everyone in my office felt or acted like that. Most of the people were welcoming and supportive. Soon I was able to handle everything that came up. The top two salesmen, Jack Etter and John Wade, were just wonderful. They were both older men and very fatherly. My duties included taking shorthand during meetings. When I did a good job, Jack and John would ask me to stand up to be introduced and maybe say something to the group. I was so shy that I'd blush and back out of the room. I wasn't used to being the center of attention. My family had taught me to always do good work, but it was also understood that I would stay in the background the way Mamma and my sisters did. Being publicly praised was a new experience for me—a pleasant one, but it took time to get used to it.

In case you haven't guessed, I'm over my shyness now.

There were lots of new experiences on the job, including glimpses of ways of living I hadn't even thought of. Our building had men's and women's bathrooms on each floor. In the ladies' room and in the hallway to the bathrooms, I got to know people who worked in the other offices, at least enough to say hello and to overhear conversations. One time I was in the bathroom around Thanksgiving or Christmas, and two women were talking about all the work they were doing to get ready.

"I'm beat. I spent all weekend polishing the silver," one told the other.

I was mystified.

"What did you have to polish?" I asked her.

She explained that her sterling silverware and dishes had to be carefully cleaned before being used for special occasions. I didn't understand why on earth she would want to own something like that. Our family had metal dinnerware that we scoured thoroughly. It was practically indestructible. She obviously had nicer stuff than we did, but I couldn't imagine buying something that required so much work. Mamma already had more than enough chores for me to do. I figured I didn't need any new ones, like polishing silver. So I got a glimpse of a finer lifestyle, but I wasn't much interested in that particular type of luxury.

Even before the silverware incident, I experienced other eye-openers at the office. About a month after I started work, the man who had hired me was transferred to the company's head office in St. Paul, Minnesota. He wanted me to go with him.

"There's a great job there," he told me. "Come with me. I'll always take care of you."

Still only fifteen years old, I took his offer at face value and assumed he was just talking about work. I wanted Etta to come with me, but when she told her mother about the "great job," the deal was off. Henrietta Segale understood far better than I did that this married man was proposing a lot more than a new job, and she put a stop to my moving plans. Maybe he picked me out of the line of job applicants because he liked the way I looked—I'll never know. Whatever the reason he hired me, he went off to Minnesota without me.

There were also exciting events in my family. On April 11, 1925, my sister Jenny got married. This brought tremendous joy for Mamma. Relief too. Jenny was thirty-five. Until she met Giulio Nelli, I don't think Mamma had much hope that Jenny would ever get married. Jenny met Giulio while she was visiting friends in the town of Colma, just south of San Francisco. An Italian immigrant, Giulio was working at a vegetable farm on the peninsula. He quit the farm soon after they met and found a new job in San Francisco. Giulio and Jenny knew each other about a year before their wedding, which was pretty much a carbon copy of my other sisters' celebrations. Jenny wore the same type of simple white dress, with orange blossoms on her veil. The small church ceremony was followed by a big family dinner. No honeymoon, of course—that wasn't part of the tradition.

For me the best thing about Jenny's wedding was my new hairstyle: I had my long hair bobbed short just in time for the event. I also wore the latest style dress. I no longer remember what that was, but I know I followed all the fashion trends carefully. Mamma and my oldest sisters stuck strictly to their floor-length, high-necked outfits. But if designers decreed that knee-length skirts were "in," that's what Eda and I wore. If the trend changed to floor-length or mid-length, that's what we did too. At the time of Jenny's wedding I was a few weeks short of turning sixteen years old. I felt daring and sophisticated. To be even more dashing, I started smoking. I figured it was the thing to do, and I didn't want to be left out. Mamma didn't like it, but she didn't stop me.

With Jenny finally in a home of her own, there was a little more room in our family flat. Mamma still slept in what should have been the living room. Eda and I shared the front bedroom, with Joe in the middle room. From time to time Mamma would take one of Joe's friends in as a boarder. He and Joe would share Joe's room, and he would eat with the family. Our boarders were all guys Joe met through the Italian Athletic Club. Mamma liked having them because it helped the family finances. It also meant more people to eat Mamma's cooking. She enjoyed an appreciative audience, and those young men were always enthusiastic eaters.

Once I started my job, my brother Rico began calling me at work now and then, making arrangements to take me out to dinner or a show. He'd call maybe two or three times a month, and we'd agree to meet somewhere. Since Rico was working and doing rather well, he would pay for everything. He seemed to like showing me off as his kid sister. And he had picked up all kinds of manners from working in restaurants—things like opening doors for me or holding my chair as I sat down. Those weren't things the men in my family had ever been taught to do but here was Rico, treating me like a lady. It was fun and made him seem even more dashing to me—my sophisticated older brother.

Every once in a while Rico would introduce me to his new girlfriend—but the girls always seemed to break up with Rico fairly quickly. I think his temper and odd moods always got the better of him. Still, Mamma was glad to hear any news about Rico that I could pass along—even just the fact that he had a girlfriend or had lost another one. Rico didn't keep in touch with the family anymore. He often seemed to be upset if he was around Mamma, Joe, or any of our sisters, but somehow he'd call a truce when it was just me and him, and we'd have a good time. He was a lot of fun when he wasn't angry.

Then something would happen. Rico would get mad at me, usually for a reason I didn't understand, and I wouldn't hear from him for a month or more. Out of the blue he would call again, suggesting that we meet somewhere, without any explanation or mention of what had happened before. We'd go out at least once a week for a while and then settle back into our old routine of meeting every other week. I think taking me out more often was Rico's way of apologizing for his quick temper once he'd calmed down.

The years from 1925 to 1929— when I was fifteen to twenty years old—were definitely a time of discovery for me and gradually increasing freedom. Mamma was still vigilant, but the fact that I was working gave me more time away from home and a wider world to explore. At that time almost every business worked its employees five and a half days a week: eight hours a day Monday to Friday with a half-day Saturday morning. It was a standard practice that didn't change until World War II, when a push to save heating fuel ended half-day Saturdays.

Etta landed a job soon after I did, and we worked near each other. When we were done for the day on Saturday, we'd have lunch downtown and then go shopping for clothes. On Sundays we'd take off together, exploring San Francisco. Sometimes my sister Eda would join us. The streetcar only cost a nickel and if we asked for a transfer—it was just a little piece of paper—we could ride from one end of town to the other and back again. We took full advantage of the system. We loved Golden Gate Park, where we'd visit the Japanese Tea Garden and make a wish as we climbed over its high, round bridge. We'd go as often as we could to Playland at the Beach, an amusement park across from Ocean Beach at the end of the Richmond District.

Etta and I were great walkers too. We'd take off from our homes in North Beach and head out to the Marina, where the sandy dunes were gradually being filled with houses. If we didn't go to the Marina green, we'd walk down to Fisherman's Wharf and get crab or shrimp cocktails served in a paper cup. We'd eat them sitting on a wooden bench and watching the people go by. We also frequently climbed to the open spaces on the top of Telegraph Hill. If we had lots of time and energy, we'd go down the wooden steps on the far side of the hill, down to the docks that lined the city's waterfront. From there we'd head east to Fisherman's Wharf and then back home.

Like any pair of teenage girls, we did a lot of laughing and giggling while we walked. Boys were our main subject. If we had steadies, we'd talk about them. If we didn't, we'd talk about who we were interested in or wish for someone to come into our lives. We never met boys or flirted as we walked—those were different times, and it just wasn't the type of thing we did. Instead we'd people-watch, especially when we went somewhere like Fisherman's Wharf. We'd pick out a group and try to guess what they were thinking and feeling. We never knew if we were right, of course, but it was a fun game.

Sometime during this period—I think it was in 1927—my sister Eda stopped by my office to talk with me.

"Guess what, Elda," she told me happily. "You're two years younger than we thought."

She had found out that I was born in 1911 not 1909. That meant I was only sixteen years old, not eighteen. Eda didn't give me any details about how she discovered this, but I assumed she knew what she was talking about. She was the one who kept track of dates and other "official" information for the family. Her news didn't really surprise me all that much. We never paid attention to family birthdays, and since Mamma couldn't read a calendar or write down notes about when things happened, she was always pretty fuzzy about dates. Time just passed for her and faded into memory. When I told Mamma that Eda said I was born in 1911 not 1909, Mamma just shrugged, said *"Davero?"*—"Is that so?" and went on with her chores.

So I began thinking of myself as sixteen years old again. It made no difference to me. And since everyone in the family knew Eda was exactly six years and three months older than I was, that meant she was twenty-four not twenty-six. No big deal for either of us.

In May 1928, Eda married a man who was four years older than she was: George Parodi, known to us all as Bacci. He was a great athlete who had played soccer in Italy before moving to San Francisco and joining the team at the Italian Athletic Club. Eda met him through the club's soccer games. Bacci was kind of stocky, maybe about five feet seven or five feet eight, and a bit bowlegged—but boy, could he play soccer. He was admired by all his teammates and was always the center of attention. Bacci was great fun to be with, and it felt as if he had a million friends everywhere he went. He had lucrative offers to play with other teams, but he wouldn't leave his friends. In our circle of acquaintances, Bacci was probably the biggest star around. Maybe that's what attracted Eda. Whatever it was, they seemed quite happy together.

Bacci grew up in the northern Italian port city of Genoa. As a boy he earned money for his family by diving for the coins that tourists threw from their luxury ships. Swimming was as natural to Bacci as breathing, so he was appalled to find out no one in our family knew how to swim. I had started teaching myself to play tennis because it looked like a way to "fit in" socially. I decided swimming was another good skill to pick up, and Bacci became my patient teacher. He taught Eda as well, and it didn't take long before we were both moving through the water smoothly and easily.

Bacci wasn't Catholic, so he and Eda couldn't be married in the church. That meant Eda didn't follow the wedding pattern set by our older, more traditional sisters. I think she and Bacci got married at City Hall, but I'm not really sure. Memory has a funny way of saving some details but not others. We did have the usual big family meal as a celebration; then the newlyweds went to Yosemite on a honeymoon—the first in our family. Eda came back from that trip just glowing with happiness. That's one thing I can remember vividly because her face was filled with such beautiful joy.

Eda's marriage left only Joe and me living in the Lombard Street flat with Mamma. I was seventeen years old. For the first time in my life I had a bedroom all to myself. It was great. I was sorry to see Eda move out because she was good company, but I still had Etta to go places with. Now I had my own bedroom as well. And with the household down to just three people, Mamma no longer expected me to help with the housework. I think she began to see me as another breadwinner, like Joe. I hate to admit it, but I thought nothing about hurrying off to the office, leaving my bed for Mamma to make just as she did Joe's each morning. Mamma did all the cooking and cleaning while the two of us were at work, and she had dinner ready when we got home. From my point of view, that certainly went a long way to easing the tension between Mamma and me.

At this point, Joe and I were the only ones supporting Mamma. We made enough to get by, but there was rarely any extra money. Mamma kept taking in Joe's friends as boarders whenever she could. And every penny that Joe managed to put aside was invested in the stock market because everybody said that was the smart thing to do.

Although most things were going well—Mamma had all but one of her six daughters married off—Rico was becoming a real problem. He and I were no longer special buddies, as we had been when he used to take me out on the town. That had gradually faded away. Now he was aggressive and demanding with me, just like he was with everyone else in the family. Nobody seemed special to him anymore. He had been living on his own since Babbo died in 1922. Rico held a series of jobs, mostly in restaurants. Sometime in 1927 or 1928 he moved to Los Angeles for a short while to work in a restaurant specializing in singing waiters. In those days his tenor voice was still strong and sweet.

But that job didn't last long, and Rico ended up moving back to San Francisco, penniless. He would find work now and then, but none of his jobs ever worked out long term. After a while Rico didn't even seem to want to work at all—something almost unheard of in our family. He began living on the streets and expecting us to provide him with food and money. For some reason Rico decided the world should take care of him, and his family was his world. He'd come to one of us begging for money—maybe twenty-five dollars or so—and promised if we gave it to him, he'd go away and never return. We'd give him the money and two or three days later he'd be back asking for more. This happened over and over. He'd also turn up at our flat every morning after I left for work. Mamma would feed him and he'd always argue with her as he ate. I'd hear about their fights secondhand from Mamma and thirdhand from my sisters. Talking directly to Rico didn't seem to do any good.

"Rico, we earn our money by going to work. Why don't you?" I'd ask him. We'd argue about it, but I couldn't understand his attitude at all.

In a way, I think Rico hated having to ask us for things, so when he did he got even more aggressive and demanding. We had no answers for what to do with Rico. Mamma kept feeding him every morning and arguing with him every time. And we all kept giving him money after he wore us down with his begging.

Then came October 24, 1929. Rico was suddenly the least of our problems.

Having lived through what became known as Black Tuesday, I feel like everybody should know that date, but I know that's not true. On October 24, 1929, the American stock market crashed. After riding high for months and months, most stocks were suddenly worthless. It was in all the newspapers, but all you really had to do was step outside, because everybody was talking about it. It was just like there had been an earthquake or some other natural disaster: It was the only thing on anybody's mind.

There was a lot of tragedy. A friend of ours had invested heavily on margin—which meant he had borrowed on credit, a popular method.

He owed far more money than he could ever repay. He killed himself by jumping out of a window.

Fortunately Joe had never bought on margin, so he didn't owe anything. But his entire savings had been wiped out. He didn't have a dime left. We had no other money put aside, leaving us completely dependent on our paychecks to cover the rent and buy our food.

Black Tuesday was the start of what was known as the Great Depression. It might be hard to understand now, but the United States' entire national economy just fell apart. It felt like everything suddenly stood still. Banks and companies closed overnight. People all over were losing their jobs, and the news just kept getting worse. I'd hear every day that someone else I knew was out of work, and I began wondering if it would happen to me.

Finally it did. Early in 1930 we got a letter from the head office saying we had to close our branch to save on overhead. The top salesmen, Jake Etter and John Wade, still had jobs, but they would work directly for the factory. Everyone else in the office was out on the street.

When I heard the news, I was stunned. After such bright, sunny years of prosperity the situation seemed hopeless. Joe lost his job at the same time I did, and suddenly we had no savings, no paychecks coming in, we needed to buy food, and the rent was due in a few days. I had to go home and tell Mamma I had been laid off.

"I don't know if I'll ever get another job," I told her. "How will we live?"

"Guardiamo se qualcuno della famiglia potrebbe auitarci"—"We'll just have to see if there's anyone in the family who can help us," Mamma replied.

That was her instinctive response, to turn to the family for help. I hadn't even thought of it. When they heard what had happened, the family held a big meeting to talk about who had enough room to take us in. It was decided that Joe would move in with Beppa and Giuseppe, sleeping with their son in his bedroom. Mamma and I would stay with Algisa and Lorenzo in their two-bedroom flat. Algisa and Lorenzo were already sleeping in what should have been the living room. Their two children could move into one bedroom, letting Mamma and me share the other.

We moved in a matter of days, quickly breaking up our lovely Lombard Street flat. We gave our furniture to other family members either to use or to store in their basements and closets. We all now had a place to sleep and food to eat, but the abrupt change was traumatic. I think I felt about as helpless as you can get. But after everything settled down my youthful optimism kicked back in. I started thinking it would all work out somehow. I was eighteen, almost nineteen years old, and pretty resilient. Although the sweet sugar seemed far away, I once again believed it would come.

Looking back, I wonder how Mamma made it through those difficult times. She was sixty-one years old, widowed, didn't have a penny to her name, and was forced to give up her home and move in with her daughter's family. If she was feeling panicked or depressed, it didn't show. She just said what she often said— *"Avanti e corragio. Il Signore chudera la porta ma apre la finestra"*—"Let's go ahead with courage. When God closes a door, He opens a window," and got busy doing everything that needed to be done.

CHAPTER 7

*W*ith all my heart I hope there will never be anything like the Great Depression ever again. It was a demoralizing, humiliating experience for everyone involved. Some people my age have told me they were sheltered from the full impact because they lived on a farm where there was plenty to eat, or there was some other buffer between them and what was happening all across the country. In San Francisco the effects of the Depression were all too visible.

Beggars were everywhere in 1930. I saw penniless people daily lined up to get free soup and bread. Sometimes the lines stretched several blocks long. I knew that without our family's help, Mamma, Joe, and I would have been lined up with the others. Part of me still believed that the sweet sugar would come someday, but that belief wavered as I watched the suffering all around us. People really did sell apples or pencils on street corners, desperately trying to earn a few cents. They weren't drifters who had somehow created their own problems. Many of them were ordinary folks who had lost their jobs, homes, and every-thing they owned in a matter of months, weeks, or even days. And usually it wasn't because of anything they had done or not done. It was just something that happened—and to many people. It was a social and financial disaster.

All the stereotypes and images of the Depression are true, but watching them in a movie or reading about them in a history book is very different from living through them. We didn't have any of the government programs people take for granted nowadays—no food stamps, no welfare, no unemployment checks. Everyone was on their own and most people had few resources left.

I was in my twenties during most of the 1930s, and for me those years brought both bad times and good. The decade started off at a low point with the loss of my job and deep worries about the future. Mamma and I were crammed into that small apartment with Algisa and her family, but we considered ourselves lucky to have somewhere to sleep. And because Algisa's husband Lorenzo worked in a produce market, we always had food on the table.

My friends from the calendar company, Jack Etter and John Wade, were still working. While making their sales calls, they always asked if anyone needed temporary office help. If something came up, they let me know immediately. Because of them I sometimes got a job for a week or two. This meant that Mamma and I weren't completely penni-less and could occasionally contribute to the household expenses. It also kept alive my hope that someday I might find another permanent job.

I'm not sure how Rico made out during those hard times. He was probably one of the hundreds of people lined up to get free soup and bread. We had no idea where he was living, although a family friend told me once that he thought Rico was sleeping in a shoe-shine booth downtown. Now and then Rico would show up to eat at the home of whichever sister he thought might have a little extra food. Mostly we were so busy surviving ourselves that we didn't have time to worry about Rico.

I was grateful to Algisa and her husband for letting Mamma and me move in with them, but it meant we had four adults and two children living in a two-bedroom flat. When things felt a little too closed-in for me there, Etta Segale and her family were my salvation. I walked over to their place all the time. Etta, her sister Ena, and their brothers Bob and Henry were still living at home. They had all lost their jobs. Their mother Henrietta had a heart condition and couldn't work. However Henrietta owned the three-story building they lived in, and the rents from the other flats kept them going. If her tenants didn't have all the rent money, Henrietta let them pay what they could as long as it gave her enough cash to buy groceries for her family. Unlike most of the people we knew, the Segales never had to worry about keeping a roof over their heads.

Their place soon became my second home. Often I would sleep over, sharing Etta's bed with her. In the morning, if I was lucky enough to have a temporary job to go to, Etta would make me a lunch that I could take to work. When I wasn't working—which happened far too often—Etta and I spent a lot of time together. Life was a lot more subdued than it had been before 1929, for us and for everyone. There were few parties or dances, and neither one of us had much money. We still occasionally went to a movie because they were so cheap, but mostly we walked and talked, entertaining ourselves. I didn't have a boyfriend then and neither did Etta. We were happy just to be together.

I also spent a lot of time scanning the want ads and applying for jobs—any job, anywhere. A good deal of my life consisted of eating, sleeping, and trying to find work. It's a demoralizing way to live, but I didn't have a lot else to do. In that tiny apartment, Mamma and Algisa easily took care of all the household chores. Even though I didn't have a job and was no longer bringing in a regular paycheck, Mamma wasn't nagging me to help with the housework. I thought that was great, but it also left me with a lot of free time.

Mostly I looked for work. I did everything I could think of to get a job, following up on every possible lead I heard about no matter how vague. Every day I was waiting for a miracle to happen, for someone to offer me full-time work—but it never happened. After a while I felt like I was trying to find something that didn't exist. There *were* no more permanent jobs available. They were all taken and anyone who was fortunate enough to still be working wasn't even thinking about leaving.

The months dragged on. Winter became spring, spring became summer, and summer became fall. Still no jobs. Not for me, not for Joe, not for anyone we knew. I kept my spirits up but it wasn't always easy. I had to remind myself that things would get better—the sugar would come, somehow, some way.

Despite our bleak financial situation, we were able to have a small turkey—stuffed with Mamma's ravioli filling of course—for Thanksgiving 1930. Somehow we always managed, but managing day to day gets old fast. Pretty soon you start feeling helpless and wondering if things will ever change. No one in the family ever criticized me for not finding work, but it was hard not to berate myself or wonder if I really had done all I could. Maybe I had overlooked the one thing that would have landed me a job.

At least we all got along fairly well. It helped that Algisa was a cheerful soul in her own quiet way and a real peacemaker. She still loved to sing, and I enjoyed hearing her beautiful soprano voice come floating down the hallway as she cooked dinner or mopped the floor. Sometimes when I was discouraged about how hard it was to find work, hearing Algisa sing would lift my spirits.

The place was always spotless. Algisa and Mamma saw to that. Fortunately they both had the same incredibly high housecleaning standards. Mamma also helped take care of Algisa's two children, Guido and Olga, which meant Mamma felt useful and therefore happy. The children were a delight and didn't seem to mind the sudden addition of Mamma and me to their home. And Algisa's husband, Lorenzo, was an easygoing guy. Family was important to him, but all his relatives were still in Italy so I guess he didn't object to having his mother-in-law and sister-in-law move in when they had nowhere else to go. As far as I know he never complained. I suppose it helped that Mamma and Algisa kept everything running so smoothly, with dinner waiting on the table the minute Lorenzo got home from work.

But perhaps it was good that none of us suspected how long we would have to live together. The 1930 holidays flew by and suddenly it was January 1931. Still no jobs for us or anyone we knew. I kept looking all the time, but the months crept by with no luck. Winter. Spring. Summer. Fall. In the beginning we had all been sure Joe and I would find new jobs right away so that Mamma, Joe, and I could get our own place again. Joe looked for work just as hard as I did, leaving no stone unturned. Still nothing.

Thanksgiving 1931 marked our second holiday season without jobs, a place of our own, or any prospect of getting either anytime soon. Again we had a big meal, but it wasn't quite as cheerful as in years past. And we welcomed the new year of 1932 with the determined hope that somehow things would get better. Still the months went by without a change. It's difficult to describe how wearing it was to be out of work for so long when all I really wanted was a chance to earn a living.

In the summer of 1932—more than two years after I got laid off—I was finally lucky enough to get an interview for a permanent, full-time job. There was an opening in the collections department at Air-Way, a vacuum cleaner company. They sold most of their machines door-to-door on the installment plan, which was a fairly common way of doing business at the time. They needed someone to handle the constant flow of paperwork as customers made their payments.

Air-Way's San Francisco headquarters was located downtown on Market Street—very familiar territory for me. But I was pretty nervous as I rode the elevator to the second floor and walked into the Air-Way office. There wasn't a single vacuum cleaner in sight, just a front counter with two desks behind it. A young woman was working at one desk, but the other was empty. I assumed it was for the person they were going to hire to handle collections. I hoped with all my heart that it would soon be my desk.

I hadn't brought a resumé, and they didn't have me fill out an application form. None of that was common back then. Instead I sat down with the man doing the interviewing and told him all about my background. It didn't take long: high marks in business college and four years with Brown and Bigelow calendars, followed by being laid off because of the Depression and working in any office that would hire me for however long they needed me.

I got the job at Air-Way.

I was ecstatic. There aren't words that can describe how wonderful it felt to know I would be working full-time again. To make it even better, the salary was about eighty dollars a month, which was more than I had been earning at Brown and Bigelow. That vacant front desk was indeed the one that would soon be mine. I couldn't wait to get home to tell Mamma.

Joe landed a job at a neighborhood market soon after I was hired by Air-Way. Our prospects suddenly looked a lot brighter. Once Joe and I had been on our jobs long enough to be sure things would work out, we started looking for a flat to rent. After staying with our sisters' families for almost two and a half years, Joe, Mamma, and I were going back out on our own. I think our sisters were almost as delighted as we were—maybe even more so. I'm sure that when we made our sudden move into their homes, no one thought we'd have to live together any longer than a few months. It's amazing that we didn't have any big arguments while we were all squeezed in together, but somehow we made it work. Now it was finally at an end.

We decided we needed to stay in the North Beach area, where everyone spoke Italian and Mamma was comfortable. We found a lovely two-bedroom flat on Powell Street, a block south of Washington Square. It was in a nice-looking stucco building. There was a garage on the street level, then our flat, and then another above that. Each apartment had a big bay window in front, looking out over the street. We collected our furniture from the family members who had been using or storing it for us and started setting up our own home.

I was determined about one thing: We were finally going to have a living room, with real living-room furniture. I was twenty-one years old, and I felt everybody I knew had a living room but me. Joe thought it would be nice, but he didn't want to pay for it. Mamma loved the idea of a living room, but of course she didn't have any money. I didn't mind, really, because Mamma and Joe had already done so much for me. Now it was my turn to provide something for our home. I bought our first-ever living-room furniture on credit. Never having bought anything on credit before I was worried they might turn me down. They didn't. As I signed the papers I felt like a real big shot.

Joe and I were at work when the furniture arrived, so Mamma just pointed to show the English-speaking delivery men where each piece went. I was incredibly excited when I got home. It was like getting a fancy new toy, only this was something that made me feel more grown up and more like a real American. There was a couch, which we called a chesterfield, a chair, and a wooden coffee table. I had never selected furniture before, but I was sure I knew just what to choose so that our place would look great. I ordered the couch and chair in a sort of orange-brown thinking it would bring some color and life into the room. It didn't. It was just drab. I got the coffee table in dark mahogany thinking it would look better if it matched our mahogany dining table. It didn't. It just looked dark and massive. I loved that ugly furniture when it first arrived and was so proud of myself for buying it. Eventually I hated it, but we kept it for years and years. It taught me how much I had to learn about decorating a home and that it wasn't as easy as I thought.

The layout of our Powell Street flat was a little different from our previous apartments. In the front was the living room and a bedroom where Mamma and I slept. The dining room and kitchen were in the middle with Joe's bedroom in the back. I was more than willing to share a bedroom with Mamma if it meant we could have a real living room.

I bought two other large items, also on credit. The first was a refrigerator for the kitchen. We'd never even owned an icebox before, and here we were with a refrigerator. Mamma didn't have to shop every day anymore. She could buy things for several days at a time and save any leftovers without worrying about spoilage.

I also bought a big Wurlitzer radio that we put in the living room. We'd all sit and listen to the radio, even Mamma. We would have a nice big dinner on Sunday, and then Joe, Mamma, and I would gather around the radio. We loved Jack Benny and "One Man's Family." You could see it all in your mind, like it was a movie. Those programs were in English and Mamma couldn't understand a word of it, but she'd laugh whenever we'd laugh and she had a great time. We'd translate the jokes into Italian for Mamma, but she would be laughing even before we told her what had been said. There was also a daily broadcast in Italian that she could listen to, so she loved our radio.

She had another form of entertainment as well. Our new flat was directly opposite a fancy restaurant, one that had been a speakeasy during Prohibition. Now it was an expensive, high-class place for dinner. Mamma loved to stand at our front window watching the rich and famous people as they arrived by taxi or limousine. A few people always had money and were able to live the high life even in the heart of the Depression. It gave Mamma a thrill just to see them.

Conditions all over San Francisco gradually improved, especially after Franklin D. Roosevelt was elected president in November 1932 and took office in January 1933. Some of the people I worked with couldn't stand him and were vocal critics, but everyone in my family loved FDR. I wasn't an American citizen so I couldn't vote, but Joe and Eda were citizens already, and they both voted for FDR. I really admired him. My whole family did. So did most of our friends and the people in our working-class neighborhood. To me FDR seemed sincere. He was a human being just like the rest of us, but he was trying to help everybody. FDR got things moving somehow, and the downward spiral slowly started inching back up.

Mostly FDR brought us hope. People adored him. It's hard to

explain, but he was like an idol, a god. He instilled confidence, which had been in extremely short supply before he came along. You just knew he was going to make things better, and slowly conditions began to improve. Agencies like the Works Progress Administration (WPA) and the Civilian Conservation Corps (CCC) gave people jobs, which started the economy going again. FDR also helped push legislation through Congress that created the Social Security program, giving people optimism about the future as well.

Beginning in 1933 the blocks-long bread and soup lines were no longer a daily sight in San Francisco. The apple- and pencil-sellers disappeared from the street corners. Instead of hearing about someone else losing their job, we began to get news of friends finding work. Life started to feel a little more normal.

Our family was still active with the Italian Athletic Club, and we also got involved with the Accordion Club. Algisa's son Guido was an accomplished accordion player and a member of the club. The group's big event was its annual picnic. It was held each summer in a public park in Fairfax, a working-class town in Marin County about seventeen miles inland from the port of Sausalito. We would get up early and—lugging all our picnic supplies—take a streetcar to the ferry building, a ferry to Sausalito, and then a train to Fairfax. All this to arrive by noon at the huge gathering, where there was constant music, dancing, and plenty of Italian food.

The ferries crisscrossing the Bay were a unique feature of San Francisco life in those days. Neither the Bay Bridge nor the Golden Gate Bridge had been built yet, so the ferries were the main way in or out of the city. The ferry building at the end of Market Street was as mobbed as the airport is today except that the airport is spread out in several different terminals. Everything was more concentrated in the ferry building because we all had to funnel through the same place. There were people everywhere.

Since it could take time before you got on a ferry, they showed a silent movie on a screen to watch while you were waiting. There was a flower stand and everybody would say, "Oh, I'll meet you at the flower stand," because that was the only place where you had a hope of getting together. You couldn't meet anywhere else in the ferry building because the place was so huge and so packed, you'd be lost.

Riding the ferry was an experience too. They were all painted white and were rather jaunty-looking. Some of the ferries only carried passengers, while others took both people and cars. Both styles opened at the front and back, for easy loading and unloading. When you were riding on a ferry, you could smell the saltwater and feel the sea. To dock, the ferry had to turn and maneuver between two rows of wooden pilings, which were sort of like bare tree trunks sticking upright a few feet out of the water. The ship would always hit the pilings on one side or the other with a jerk, and the pilings would make a loud creaking sound. All the while the seagulls would be wheeling overhead, crying out…it was really a thrill.

At least I realize today how great it was. At the time I just figured, "Oh, those damn seagulls." And they'd be screaming overhead. In retrospect it was marvelous, but back then I probably just thought they were dirty birds and worried that they might soil my good clothes. How come we only appreciate these things in memory and not when they're happening?

Since life was getting back to normal for us, we found ourselves worried about Rico again. He stopped by our Powell Street flat late every morning, after Joe and I went off to work. Mamma would feed Rico and the two of them would argue. Rico was still angry all the time and quarreled with everyone, especially Mamma.

"Mamma doesn't like me at all," Rico would tell me.

He really believed that even though it wasn't true. Of course Mamma wasn't the type to tell him how she felt. He was her firstborn son and the long-awaited boy in a family of girls. I guess she just took it for granted that Rico knew how much she loved him.

Then one day Rico lost his temper and started screaming at me that he was going to kill Mamma. I was terrified and locked him out of the flat. He calmed down later and showed up as if nothing had happened, but we told him he couldn't come to see Mamma anymore. Instead Beppa, Algisa, and Jenny agreed to take turns feeding Rico. The three of them lived in the same neighborhood, and Rico could easily walk to their homes.

Rico would go to Beppa's every day for a week, then Algisa's, then Jenny's, and then back to Beppa's. They'd give him lunch and something to take with him to eat for dinner. It was hardest on Jenny because her husband, Giulio, came home for lunch every day. Giulio didn't know Jenny was feeding Rico, so when it was her week Jenny had to get Rico fed and out of her house before Giulio came home. It was nerve-wracking. We didn't know what else to do except keep feeding Rico and pray that he'd somehow get better. He was a problem, but he was our brother so he was our problem.

Since we had our first-ever living room, I also insisted we have our first Christmas tree in December and a Christmas Eve party. When we were growing up, the holiday had mostly been a religious one. Our only gifts came in January, in the form of fruit brought by the Befana— an Italian tradition of a broom-carrying witch. So in December 1932 we had a Christmas Eve party and gave each other joke gifts. I remember my bald brother-in-law got a cheap comb.

I also went out and bought special mugs so we could serve trendy hot drinks known as Tom and Jerries. I mixed the batter myself. I wanted everything to be just right. Having a Christmas tree and party was another step toward being more American. I was shaken by what had happened after the stock market crash, but we were all back on our feet and I was determined to stay there. In a way I think I tried to put the Depression out of my mind as soon as possible and get on with my life—although I still carried deep within me the fear that something like that might happen again.

Etta and her brothers and sisters all got jobs once the economy started picking up. As a result, our social life slowly revived. Etta and I would go to parties at friends' houses where we'd all smoke and drink and talk, talk, talk. The hard liquor would flow like you'd never believe. It was just the way things were done. Since no one had a car in those days, many of us would sleep over wherever the party was held. It was all pretty innocent by today's standards—by that I mean no sex, just alcohol and tobacco. Except now everyone knows cigarette smoke is bad for you, and people tend to drink a lot less hard liquor. Back then smoking and drinking a lot was the acceptable thing to do. Nobody thought twice about it.

In 1933, after a year in collections at Air-Way, I was promoted to secretary for the branch manager. I got a little more money each month, and it was a great job. They hired a young woman named Miriam Silverman to replace me in my old job in collections, and we became good friends. I invited her to our house for dinner several times, and since she lived far away from us she'd spend the night rather than trying to go home. Then we'd go to work together in the morning.

Mamma loved having Miriam over for dinner. Every time Miriam spent the night, Mamma would come into my bedroom with holy water to bless us before we fell asleep. The problem was, Miriam was Jewish. The first time Mamma came in with the holy water, I was mortified. Fortunately Miriam didn't seem to mind. The next morning I pointedly reminded Mamma that Miriam was Jewish, but Mamma just waved my objections away. She didn't seem to think that mattered. Mamma loved us both, and she wanted to bless us both with holy water, so she kept on doing it every time Miriam spent the night.

The thing was, Mamma really was acting out of love for us, and I think Miriam understood that. At any rate, Miriam never objected to the holy water blessing and always kissed Mamma good night, just as I did. I learned a lot from Miriam—that people could be different from me and my family and still be good people and that you could accept what people did for you out of love without quibbling over the details of how they did it.

After my long period of unemployment, I was finally back in the business world, making friends and earning that oh-so-important paycheck. After the hard times of the first few years of the 1930s, I was more than ready for a few good times.

CHAPTER 8

The United States was still in the grip of the Great Depression, but things were definitely looking up for me personally. In 1934, when I was twenty-three, I started dating twenty-two-year-old Louis, one of Air-Way's service representatives.

We had been working together ever since I became the manager's secretary. Louis reported to the office next to mine each morning, then went out to customers' homes to fix vacuum cleaners or deliver new paper bags for the machines. He came to my office at the end of the day and turned in any money he had collected. But Louis and I didn't pay attention to each other for the first year we worked together. I always wore a large smock at work to protect my good clothes and Louis told me later that he assumed I didn't have much of a figure. And when I first met him, Louis told me all about his girlfriend back east so I didn't waste any time on a man who was already taken.

Then Louis's brother, who was Air-Way's district sales manager in

Oakland, invited me to a party one Saturday night. I got all dressed up, of course. Louis lived with his brother and sister-in-law in Oakland, so he was there too. I guess he liked the way I filled out a party dress a whole lot more than how I looked in my office smock. He made sure I knew he was no longer seeing the girl in Philadelphia, and then he asked me out.

Louis was of Armenian descent. He was tall with dark, wavy hair and jet-black eyes. When I finally took a good, long look at him at his brother's party, I realized he was a fine-looking guy. And I adored his manners. After spending most of my time with Italian men who seemed to take me for granted, I loved having someone who opened doors for me and showed me all sorts of little courtesies.

We spent a lot of time together. I soon realized that Louis knew all the social niceties I didn't, such as who should sit where at a dinner table or how and when to use each piece of the fancy silverware. I wanted to soak up as much of his style as I could. Although he really didn't have a lot of money and spent every penny he earned, to me Louis was a dashing man-about-town, and I was more than ready for some fun and good times. He had his own car, which added an exciting taste of freedom.

We played tennis in the daytime and at night went out for fancy dinners, dancing, the opera—you name it in terms of San Francisco nightlife and the two of us did it. We went to the opera a lot because Louis loved it, which delighted me. Not everybody likes opera, so it's rare to find someone who loves it the way I do. I'd grown up listening to Rico and Algisa sing arias and hearing my family debate the ins and outs of the plots of all the major Italian operas. I had attended several professional performances with my oldest sister, Beppa, and her husband, Giuseppe, who were both big opera fans. But once I started dating Louis, I went to the opera with him instead. It felt much more glamorous with Louis.

In those days we'd get all dolled up in our best clothes. The opera house was really exciting, too, with lots of beautiful marble everywhere. Louis preferred the German operas. I'd go along, of course, but I never really enjoyed them. For a German production, I'd have to follow the English libretto. In Italian I could understand most of what was sung and I already knew the story lines.

All the famous singers came to San Francisco—people like Ezio Pinza, Beniamino Gigli, and Lily Pons. It was thrilling to hear them. Louis and I always had downstairs seats if we could get them. Sometimes when there weren't any seats available, we stood up to watch the show—with me in high heels. Oh, to be young again and more interested in entertainment than comfort.

Anytime we were going somewhere fancy, Louis would show up with a corsage to match my dress. In those days women wore flowing, floor-length gowns to go out at night. Most women had more evening gowns than daytime dresses, and I soon had my share. They were so much fun, both to buy and to wear. I especially remember a blue one that was formfitting at the top, with a flared skirt. It was rather backless too. Louis's sister-in-law took one look at it and said, "You're really wearing a creation tonight." I was thrilled. I felt I had arrived, that I had finally "made it" in my bid to fit in.

I still shopped at the Emporium, but now I was buying my dresses upstairs where there were lots of salesclerks and real customer service. No more bargain basement for me. Just like Louis, I spent every dime I made. Once the rent and food were paid, I figured out how much was left for clothes and good times and bought everything I could, sometimes on credit.

Being my Mamma's daughter, I still looked for the best deals on my dresses. I couldn't afford top-of-the-line on my salary, but I got some lovely outfits to wear to places like the Fairmont, Mark Hopkins, and St. Francis hotels. Since we had to work five and a half days each week, Louis and I went to those places on Saturday nights. They were always packed with people.

The St. Francis is on Union Square, and the other two hotels are about a mile to the northwest, just outside Chinatown. I thought the Mark Hopkins was the trendiest place—where all the real society people went—but my favorite was the Fairmont. I felt at home there. But Louis and I decided where to go each Saturday based not on the hotel but on which orchestras were playing. Wherever we thought the best music was, that's where we went. We'd drink and dance all night. It was rare that Louis and I sat out a song. Usually we were out on the floor, dancing until late at night when the band quit playing.

Louis was a marvelous dancer and I felt so glamorous, twirling around those elegant ballrooms in his arms. Here was little immigrant Elda Del Bino dining and dancing right next to the best of San Francisco's society, as if I belonged. Louis was so polished that I did feel like we fit in there. It was heavenly.

After we were done dancing, going to the opera, or whatever was on the night's agenda, we'd head over to a place called Joe's on Broadway. It was a hole in the wall, with about fifteen stools maximum, but it was renowned for the best hamburgers ever. We would wait almost a half hour to get in. Everybody waited. At 2 or 3 A.M. there would be a whole crowd of people in full evening dress, all lined up, wanting to get a hamburger at Joe's.

I can still see it in my mind—Joe's, the gowns, the ballrooms, all the wonderful places Louis and I went and the things we did. He opened up a whole new world for me. I was hungry to see everything, and he showed it to me with such class.

Mamma liked Louis and his family, so I was allowed to stay at their house in Oakland on weekends. Although his brother and sister-in-law had school-age children, it seemed as if all the adults did was party the entire weekend. They had a beautiful formal dining room, and Louis's brother John was the perfect host. He'd stand at the head of the table and carve the roast or whatever was on the menu, then serve each of us with a flourish. It was really a production.

Sometimes there would just be the six of us—John and his wife, their other brother and his girlfriend, and Louis and me. Even so, we'd all be dressed to kill and dinner would be completely formal, just as when outside guests joined us. It felt like they led a glamorous life, far removed from anything I'd known before. They had a guest room downstairs where I'd spend the night, and in the morning everyone went off to the public tennis courts for a game. That was a must, that everyone played tennis.

Louis and I saw each other all the time and I really loved him. Nowadays young people seem to jump in bed as part of dating. We didn't do that. Times and attitudes were different, and maybe folks today will find it hard to understand. Men were gentlemen. We'd kiss good night of course and maybe pet a little, but going farther would have meant a commitment neither Louis nor I wanted to make.

But Etta was ready for commitment. Even before I started going out with Louis, Etta had met a fellow named Jimmy Soldavini. I actually don't remember that night at all, but Etta does—for obvious reasons. She and I were invited to a party in Marin County to meet a nice young man that a friend thought one of us might like. After the party Jimmy drove Etta and me back to the Sausalito ferry in his new convertible. Etta thought Jimmy was quite dashing, and they started dating immediately. Like I said, I have no memory of the night we both met Jimmy, but Etta can recite detail after detail.

They were married in December 1934. Etta's sister Ena was her maid of honor for the simple ceremony, and there was a small reception at the Segale family home. Once they were married, Etta and Jimmy planned to move to a small town called San Rafael, in Marin County. That's where Jimmy had grown up, and he had landed a job up there working for the water company.

Etta and I were still the best of friends, but I knew this was going to be a major change. I really felt like I was losing a big part of my life. I was happy for Etta, but I was so sad at the same time. I don't recall this at all, but in later years Jimmy swore I came up to him during the reception and said, "You better take good care of Etta or I'll kill you."

Could be. Sounds like me. I loved Etta with all my heart. Still do. There's nothing like a good friend you can depend on—one who has seen you in every possible mood and circumstance and still loves you.

In between all the partying with Louis, I managed to take care of some important business in 1936: I became an American citizen. I was given time off from my job at Air-Way so I could take the test. My examination was scheduled for April 11, 1936, and was administered by a judge. Nowadays they apparently swear in hundreds or thousands of people all at the same time, but back then it was a one-on-one interview followed immediately by a swearing-in ceremony if you passed.

I had to bring two American citizens as witnesses. So Jack Etter and John Wade, my old friends from the calendar company, went through the process with me and signed the papers after I passed the test. I was glad to have their company. I was pretty nervous when the judge started asking his questions. He was an older man, very distinguished and professional. He seemed quite stern as he offered me a chair in his office, then sat down behind his big desk and began asking a long string of questions.

I'm glad I don't have to answer any of them today, because I don't remember most of it. Back then I could quickly rattle off everything he asked for—all the details of the three branches of government, the length of terms of all the offices, the electoral system, and more. I passed with flying colors, and the judge made me a citizen of the United States of America.

I was so proud. It meant a lot to be able to vote. I felt even more a part of this country than ever before. And Jack Etter and John Wade were beaming when it was all done. I think maybe they were nervous during the test too. They said afterwards that they didn't know the answers to at least half of the questions. The two of them took me out to lunch to celebrate and made me feel so important. I was so happy that I felt like I was flying.

There were a lot of exciting things happening in San Francisco then. The Bay Bridge opened in 1936, followed by the Golden Gate in 1937. My sister Eda and I joined thousands of other people walking across the Golden Gate Bridge on May 27, 1937, the first day it was open. It was wonderful—the views of the Bay and the city are completely different when you're standing on the bridge, and almost no one had seen it from that perspective before.

Eda and her husband, Bacci, were living in the Marina district by then. We walked from her house to the bridge, across the Golden Gate to Sausalito and back, and then home to Eda's place. I think we hiked ten miles that day. It was so much fun; we felt we were taking part in history.

Soon after that we had another wedding in our family. At age thirty-seven, Joe married Annette Biagini on July 27, 1937. Annette lived in the neighborhood and had started dropping by a lot. First she told Mamma that she liked Joe, and then Annette told Joe. Although she was of Italian descent, Annette was born in America, making Joe the first in the family to marry a nonimmigrant. It was maybe the simplest wedding in my family so far. By that time, Joe had opened his own grocery store again and was working long hours every day. So he and Annette got married on a weekend, and Joe was back to work on Monday morning. Annette wore a nice dress but nothing traditional and no veil.

After they were married, Annette moved into our Powell Street flat. Mamma and I were still sleeping in the front bedroom, so Annette and Joe shared the back room, which she soon decorated to suit her more sophisticated tastes.

My whirlwind of parties with Louis went on. We were still having great fun together, but I was aware of a growing feeling that I wanted more in my life. The constant drinking began to seem less exciting and my fairy-tale-like enchantment at being a part of those glamorous good times was slowly fading away.

I didn't like waking up with a hangover all the time. Plus, Etta and some of my other friends said I had changed since I started dating Louis. I didn't think that was true. I was sure I was the same person I had always been. But it did seem like Louis and I spent all of our time with his friends and his family, rather than mine. In a way I was living Louis's life more than my own. It was fun but I wasn't always sure it was what I wanted.

When the Golden Gate Exposition opened on Treasure Island in summer 1939, Louis and I went to check it out. The Army Corps of Engineers had created Treasure Island by dumping sand, rocks, and mud into San Francisco Bay—a pretty impressive feat. Although it eventually became a Navy base, the island was first used to host the two-year fair celebrating the opening of San Francisco's two new bridges, the Bay Bridge and the Golden Gate.

The Golden Gate Exposition was a real sight to see. Everything was all lit up, illuminated like Las Vegas is now. They had shows by big name bands, an amusement park, exhibits of airplanes, and all the latest inventions—something for almost everybody. We enjoyed the Exposition, but just days later Louis casually mentioned that he had gone out on a date with another girl. That wasn't okay with me, but in a way I wasn't surprised. I knew Louis always needed a good time.

You know what? You can get tired of a good time. I guess I did, because I decided to stop seeing Louis.

I adored the more than four years we had spent together, but Louis never once mentioned marriage. I knew we loved each other, but I also sensed he just couldn't see becoming part of my family. I couldn't see it either, I guess. He never did fit in. Louis was high-class and had all the social charms, while my family was strictly down-to-earth. He was polite and friendly and my family loved him, but it was like somebody in a tuxedo mixing with people in overalls. It wasn't something that could work, at least not for the long haul.

It was odd in a way because Louis's Armenian mother had been an immigrant to this country, and she still didn't speak much English. For Louis and his brothers, that was a fact they kind of kept in the background, as if they were ashamed of it. In the end I think my large and obviously immigrant family was too much for Louis.

For me, Louis was freedom. Then I realized freedom wasn't all I wanted. To this day I'm happy I had those years with him, experiencing all those exciting things. I learned so much and gained a lot of poise and confidence. I desperately needed a taste of the fun Louis offered, but then I found myself yearning for something more—commitment, stability, and maybe an end to the late nights and constant drinking.

All the same, I was sad and depressed when we broke up. It felt like a door had shut behind me and would stay closed forever. Now I think it was wonderful I had all those delightful times with Louis, plus the wisdom to know I needed to move on no matter how much it hurt at the time.

CHAPTER 9

*M*y life went on despite what I thought of as my permanently battered heart. Louis transferred to another office so we wouldn't have to keep working together every day. I never saw him again. After the initial shock of the breakup wore off, I sat down and took stock of my life. It was winter 1940. I was twenty-eight going on twenty-nine years old, single, and not dating at all. I was an old maid and I didn't care.

Maybe that was just the way it was going to be. I figured not everyone is meant to get married and have children. I had a good job and a loving family. So I decided to be satisfied with what I had and not look for more. By this time Paolina's son Fred was nineteen years old and his brother Beb was fifteen. Beppa's son Bruno was eighteen. Algisa's son Guido was seventeen and his little sister Olga was eleven. They were practically grown up, and I loved spending time with them.

For several months my life consisted of working at Air-Way, helping Mamma, visiting girlfriends, and being with various family members. It was pretty tame compared to the glamour I'd had with Louis, but I was content, even happy. I always worked late on Mondays, but I didn't mind. All the managers in the area met in San Francisco for the weekly sales meeting, and I'd stay at the office to process their orders. One manager kept telling me about this fine-looking salesman who had just moved to the area from Los Angeles.

"Elda, you've just got to meet Bill Willitts," he told me many times.

"If it happens, it happens," I always replied, keeping my voice carefully neutral.

The truth was, I wasn't at all interested in meeting anyone, but I thought the man might think I was rude if I told him that directly. So one Monday night in spring 1940 this manager introduced me to William Gray Willitts, age thirty-one. Six feet tall. Intense blue eyes, brimming with obvious intelligence. Wavy auburn hair already graying slightly at the temples. I thought the gray made him look distinguished. He really was a dreamboat, but it was Bill's innate good manners that took my breath away. He watched everyone around him and did every little courtesy he could. It was what made Bill a top salesman, but it was also a natural part of who he was.

I had been so certain that I wasn't interested in meeting or getting to know anyone, but Bill just bowled me over with his charm and good looks. He made me want to rethink my position on dating—except I really wasn't interested in getting back into the party-party-party life I'd had with Louis. At home that night I told Mamma all about Bill and asked her what to do.

"Se ti garba, invitelo a cena"—"If you like him, invite him over for dinner," she said immediately.

So I did. Bill agreed to come to our house after one of the Monday night sales meetings to have dinner with me, Mamma, Joe, and Annette. It went beautifully. The meal was delicious. Mamma was a great cook and went all out anytime we had company. And Bill was instantly at ease, as if he had come home. He didn't speak any Italian and Mamma knew very little English, but they seemed to instinctively understand each other. After he left Mamma turned to me and asked *"Quando ritorna di nuovo?"*—"When is he coming over again?"

In the following weeks Mamma was eager to hear how things were going between Bill and me. I'd never seen her like that before. Mamma hadn't asked for progress reports when I was seeing Louis or any of the other men I had dated. Maybe she somehow knew Bill was right for me. Or maybe she thought if I didn't find someone soon I'd never get married. Whatever the reason, she loved Bill from the minute she met him.

The Saturday following that first dinner, Bill called to say he was in town on business and asked me to have lunch with him after I finished my half-day of work. I was surprised because I knew Bill lived in an East Bay town called Martinez and sold Air-Way vacuums door-to-door in that area. I couldn't imagine what he would need to do in San Francisco on a Saturday but of course I said yes. At lunch Bill confessed he didn't have any business in San Francisco; he just wanted to see me. I thought that was so sweet.

He was from Michigan originally, the oldest of five children and the only son. His father was a teacher when his parents met, then a postmaster and storekeeper, next a farmer, and finally a successful real estate agent. The family was quite well-off until Bill's father had a heart attack and died at age fifty-four. Bill was eleven years old. He felt it was his responsibility to help his widowed mother. There was no life insurance and almost nothing left from his father's business. The family was practically destitute.

They rented out some rooms in their large house, and Bill's mother did needlepoint for a local furniture manufacturer. Bill got a newspaper route. He also earned money doing morning and evening chores for an elderly neighbor. The family survived, but Bill swore he'd never be that poor again.

His mother remarried when Bill was fourteen. Although things were a little easier financially, Bill took a long time to warm up to his stepfather. After graduating from high school, Bill enrolled in a two-year course in business administration, working part time to pay the tuition. By the time I met him, Bill had spent several years as a salesman, first in Michigan, then Florida, next Southern California, and finally moving to the Bay Area for the job with Air-Way.

I learned all of this over several months. We spent a lot of time together, mostly talking. Bill was a born salesman, so chatting came easily to him and he enjoyed it. I was immediately comfortable around him, and we were soon comparing our backgrounds. The fact that both our fathers died when we were young was an instant bond. Yet I felt that in some ways Bill had it even rougher than I did. Because he lived in comfort and security until his dad died, Bill went through the shock of losing practically everything all at once and at a relatively young age. It hurt me deeply when Babbo died, but my whole world wasn't turned upside down afterward. My family rallied around me and made me feel protected, while Bill had to immediately shoulder new responsibilities, finding ways to earn money and to help his mother as much as possible.

Bill and I also talked about our dreams for the future. We found we both wanted security and success. I felt we really had a lot in common. It seemed we valued the same things—family, hard work, making a comfortable life for ourselves. Besides his obvious good looks, I felt Bill was intelligent, well-informed, and interesting. He also was ambitious and I realized I liked that. He seemed like somebody who would make things happen and get what he wanted out of life. I liked that too.

Since Bill loved the Mills Brothers' music, he and I became regulars at the Fairmont Hotel anytime they were playing there. I tried to get him interested in opera, but the one time we went he asked me, "What are they yelling about?" So no fancy nights at the opera house with Bill. Except for a few special occasions such as the Mills Brothers, our dates were much more low-key than my time with Louis. My fancy gowns just hung in the closet. That didn't bother me in the least.

I was getting to know—and love—a man I really respected, who was listening and getting to know the real me. I liked Bill's innate good manners when it was just the two of us and the way he acted when we were with my friends and family. Unlike Louis, Bill fit right in. He and Mamma may not have shared the same language, but Bill immediately admired my mother and showed her a lot of respect, which I thought she deserved. It wasn't that Louis had been disrespectful when he picked me up at my family's home. It was just that he was totally focused on us and where we were going that night and what we were planning to do. He was always polite to my family, but it was just a formality before our evening could really begin.

Bill, on the other hand, seemed to really pay attention to Mamma, Joe, and anyone else who was around. He listened to what they had to say and remembered details, such as what they liked or disliked. Bill got along well with every member of my family. He enjoyed them and they enjoyed him. Bill wasn't a "life of the party" type of guy, but if there was a lull in a conversation or someone wasn't joining in, he would always be the one to bring up a topic that got everyone's interest or to make a comment that brought the quiet folks into the discussion. I found myself admiring how he handled himself in any situation. After a couple of months I started thinking to myself that Bill was exactly the guy I wanted to marry—if only he would ask me.

Bill started staying in our family flat on weekends, sleeping on a couch we had in the kitchen. Don't think there was any funny business between the two of us in that apartment. There were always far too many family members around. Bill and I were both too busy working to get together during the week. The weekends were the only time we could see each other. It seemed a waste for Bill to drive back and forth from his place in Martinez.

Having Bill spend the weekends in our flat meant I learned even more about him. He was a really focused guy who did just one thing at a time. Whatever he did, it got his full attention. One day Bill was sitting in our kitchen reading while Mamma and I fixed lunch. I was chopping some tomatoes and accidentally sliced my finger. It was a pretty deep cut. There was a lot of commotion as Mamma and I rushed around trying to figure out how to stop the bleeding and bandage my wound. Once that was done, we finished our cooking chores and put the food on the table. As we sat down to eat, Bill put down his book and joined us.

"What happened to your hand?" he asked me with complete surprise in his voice.

Bill had been in the same room with us during the whole incident but hadn't noticed anything out of the ordinary. Like I said, he focused intently on whatever he was doing and didn't pay attention to anything else.

But when he wasn't lost in thought, Bill could be pretty attentive to details. He used to bring me little gifts—flowers, candy, or maybe a simple piece of jewelry. When he realized we had an old-fashioned toaster that didn't pop the bread up automatically and therefore often burned the toast, he brought us a more modern one as a gift. Then he saw that Mamma still made our orange juice by hand, using a special glass dish. It was a long process and a lot of work. One day Bill showed up with a gift just for Mamma: a hand-cranked orange juice squeezer that he mounted on our kitchen wall. It squeezed out the juice quickly and easily. Mamma was touched by his thoughtfulness and so was I.

I loved spending the weekends together. Bill would come over Saturday morning. We'd go out some place that night and spend the next day together. Either Sunday evening or Monday morning Bill would go back home to Martinez.

We had a favorite place out in the Marina district. It was a little bar with a jukebox and a small dance floor. We would put money in the jukebox, dance, and have a few drinks. Then we'd go parking at the Marina Green by the Bay. This is a circular drive with plenty of fairly dark places to park a car facing the beautiful Bay. You can still see cars of young couples stopped there at night with their windows fogged up from the inside. I guess some things haven't changed.

One night in late summer Bill and I went out dancing at our favorite place as usual. As we sat sipping our drinks, Bill told me he had been married when he was young and divorced when he found his wife with another man. Then he put his hand on mine and looked right into my eyes.

"Elda, my life will never be complete without you," Bill told me. "I want you to be my better half, forever and ever."

"Oh, yes," I told him.

It was so wonderful.

When I got home, I told Mamma everything, even the part about

Bill being divorced. I wasn't sure how she'd react. Divorce was an unheard-of shame in our Catholic household. I didn't bother pointing out to Mamma what she already knew; Bill wasn't Catholic. None of that bothered Mamma at all.

"Quando hai fissato di sposarti?"—"When are you going to get married?" she asked me immediately.

Trouble was, neither Bill nor I had any money. We lived from paycheck to paycheck with almost nothing leftover. A few weeks after Bill proposed, we went shopping for an engagement ring, which he bought on credit. We didn't want to set a date until we could figure out how to get the cash for a wedding plus what we would need to set up housekeeping on our own.

"Perche non stai qui?"—"Why don't you live here?" was Mamma's quick response. She would have been happiest with the whole family living under one roof. But even if we lived in the flat with Mamma, Joe, and Annette, we still didn't have any way to pay for a wedding. So we waited. We saved what we could, but it didn't seem to add up very quickly. Bill was still bringing me little gifts each weekend. I told him to stop but he didn't listen. He got such a kick out of surprising me with something I enjoyed, even if it was small and inexpensive, and he wasn't willing to stop. I loved Bill's thoughtfulness and generosity, but I wondered how we would ever come up with enough cash for our wedding.

The answer came one weekend night in December when an executive from Standard Oil dined in the fancy restaurant across from our Powell Street flat. In the morning we found one side of Bill's Chevy all bashed in. The executive's business card was tucked under the windshield wiper. A note on the card read "I'm sorry I hit your car. Call me and I'll take care of all the expenses."

Bill got a repair estimate and sent it to the executive. Once Bill got the money, he and a friend fixed the car themselves. The whole process took several months, but we ended up with a nice little nest egg of several hundred dollars. By February we had what we needed to get married. I'm still grateful to the man from Standard Oil who paid for our wedding. I don't know what we would have done without him.

Bill and I both wanted to keep things as simple as possible. Even if we could have afforded it, neither of us wanted a big wedding with all that fuss. And we couldn't tell many people about our engagement because Air-Way had a rule against employees getting married. If the company found out about our plans, then one of us would have been required to quit, and we needed both our incomes.

But neither of us liked the idea of a quick civil ceremony down at City Hall. The other option was driving east to the state of Nevada, where we knew we could take care of everything quickly and easily. That meant our choice was between Reno, a northern Nevada gambling town near the California border, and Las Vegas, the big, flashy gambling spot down in southern Nevada. We didn't want to stay a long time in either place, but Bill figured if we went to Vegas we could honeymoon in Death Valley in Southern California.

A place called Death Valley may not sound like a terribly romantic spot for a honeymoon, but the desert is beautiful in February. Neither Bill nor I had ever seen it, but Bill had read about it a lot and really wanted to go there. He made it sound exciting and special. I was easily sold on the idea, so Las Vegas became our wedding destination, followed by a honeymoon in Death Valley.

That meant a long drive from San Francisco to Vegas. Flying was expensive and would have used up most of our bankroll, so the car was the only answer. Back then there weren't interstates and superhighways like there are now. There were a few four-lane highways, but mostly a "highway" was just a narrow, two-lane road passing through small town after small town. Our route would take us south along Highway 99, straight down the center of California's extensive Central Valley. At the farming town of Bakersfield we would head east, through the California desert town of Barstow, and then into the desert and on to Las Vegas.

I arranged for time off work, and Bill simply didn't make any appointments for that week. As a salesman he didn't have to clock in and out like I did. We left around midnight, intending to drive all night. Mamma, Joe, and Annette gathered around our car—Bill's now-repaired Chevy—to see us off. Mamma didn't seem bothered by the fact that we weren't going to be married in church. In fact, she was beaming. She was about the happiest I'd ever seen her. I was her last unmarried daughter and just a few months shy of thirty, which is old for an Italian girl to be getting married. Very old. Maybe that's why Mamma took such a liking to Bill.

Anyway, we were off to Vegas. I didn't know how to drive, so Bill was behind the steering wheel for the entire trip. We kept going all night, through acres of farmland with an occasional small town. We saw almost no traffic on the way. Around dawn we stopped for breakfast in Bakersfield.

"Elda, I'm pretty tired," Bill told me. "Don't you think we should stop here and get a motel room?"

I loved him, but I figured it was high time we were married. I didn't think we should have the honeymoon before the wedding.

"We're going on," I told him. And we drove on.

We found a pretty little chapel in Las Vegas, and they brought out two witnesses to stand up for us. It was February 12, 1941, almost exactly a year from when I had taken stock of my life and decided I was meant to be an old maid. Now Bill and I were married. I was beaming and so was Bill.

We went out afterwards to celebrate. We hadn't slept all night, but somehow we weren't tired anymore. Bill kept looking at me and saying "Elda, I love you so. I'm so thrilled." He told me how beautiful I was and how my brown eyes shone in the candlelight. I ate it up. It was all I longed to hear and to feel.

We spent a night in Vegas and then headed west to the desert. Death Valley was everything we had hoped it would be. We visited places called Stovepipe Wells, Scotty's Castle, and Badwater. I loved it all. The weather was perfect and the desert was in bloom. Everything was rather primitive and untouched, the way it had been when the first pioneers came through.

It rained one night while we were staying in a place with an old tin roof. I still remember the lovely echoing sound of the drops hitting the metal as we lay curled up in bed together, husband and wife. I guess I wasn't destined to be an old maid after all.

CHAPTER 10

After a ten-day honeymoon, Bill and I returned to San Francisco and the usual routine. Our jobs were too far apart to let us live together right away. During the week, Bill stayed in Martinez to work his Air-Way sales territory while I lived in the Powell Street flat with Mamma, Joe, and Annette. As before, Bill and I were together only on the weekends. Of course, since we were husband and wife Bill was no longer sleeping in the living room; Mamma was.

My marriage meant our two-bedroom flat was too small by one bedroom. Joe and Annette were still in the back bedroom; Mamma and I had been sharing the front bedroom. But now Bill and I were in the front room—at least on weekends—leaving Mamma without a proper bedroom.

A friend told me about a marvelous reclining chair that became a bed. Extra-large as a chair, it folded completely flat and was pretty comfortable—although it wasn't very big as far as beds go. That was fine because Mamma wasn't very big either. We bought one of those chairs and put it in the living room. It became a living room chair in the daytime and Mamma's bed at night. She kept her clothes and bedding in the hall closet.

I suppose it sounds terrible that we made my seventy-two-year-old mother sleep on a folding chair in the living room, but Mamma thought it was a great idea. She claimed she didn't need a bedroom of her own. Of course, Mamma always wanted as many of our family members living together as possible. Things were a little tight on the weekends with five adults living in a two-bedroom place, but we made it work.

That summer Bill decided I needed to learn how to drive. I was thirty years old, but I hadn't thought about driving before. It was so easy and inexpensive to go all over San Francisco on the streetcars. I never really felt I needed a car, and who could afford one? But here I was, married to Bill, and he owned a car. I figured he was right and it was time I became a driver. Bill thought it wouldn't take him any time at all to teach me himself.

What a mistake. Don't ever let anybody you love try to teach you how to drive. Bill took me out to the Sunset District, which at that time was just a bunch of empty roads between sand dunes. None of the houses had been built yet. It seemed the perfect place for a driving lesson.

My husband was a wonderful man, but he had a short fuse. He'd tell me to stop or go, and I'd try, but I wasn't always sure what to do. Back then cars didn't have automatic transmissions. You had to really work the clutch and the brake and lord help you if you mixed up which was which. It was tricky, especially on San Francisco's steep hills. And at that time cars didn't have turn signal indicators or brake lights. Those wonderful devices hadn't been invented yet, so it was up to the driver to make hand signals out the window before turning or stopping.

Bill would tell me to turn or to do this or to do that. He seemed to expect me to do everything perfectly, immediately, and almost before the words were out of his mouth. The more he barked out orders, the more confused and agitated I became and the less I could remember. It was a disaster. I started crying because I was sure this was going to destroy our marriage. I thought we'd be divorced before our first wedding anniversary if we continued the driving lessons. On the way home I hesitantly told Bill I wanted to hire somebody to teach me to drive. I think he was relieved because he agreed immediately. I went to one of the regular driver-training companies, and I did beautifully. I had no problem at all passing the test and getting my driver's license.

There was something else Bill began teaching me that summer. One day he sat me down and said, "Elda, you've got to learn to love yourself."

"Who, me?" was my startled reply.

I wasn't even sure what he meant. Loving myself sounded so selfish. I had been brought up to believe you were supposed to do everything for everybody else. Then if you had time, you did things for yourself. And if there wasn't any time left for the things you wanted, that was just how things were.

"Don't worry about everybody else," Bill told me. "Take care of what you need."

It was a strange concept. It was almost as if Bill were talking to me in a foreign language. I loved what he was saying but I couldn't really take it in and apply it to my life. I understand it now, but I sure didn't back then. It took years before I realized he was right. It took even longer to actually love myself.

Bill also taught me to be comfortable with my family and not get embarrassed about what they did or didn't do. I'd say something full of shame about Mamma not knowing English, about her and my sisters not being able to read and write, or simply that they didn't do things like "other people."

"So what?" Bill would say. "There's a lot of people who don't speak English. Why should you worry about it? Look at this wonderful family you have."

And I realized I had it all wrong. The bigoted people who had embarrassed me and taught me to look down on my immigrant family had been mistaken. Here was this wonderful man, this polished, well-mannered American who grew up with what I considered a "normal" life telling me that my family was great.

"Be happy with what you've got because you've got a gold mine here," Bill told me. "Your family's got such beauty, such love, such values. Enjoy it."

That helped me so much and was easier to understand than Bill's advice about loving myself. The part of me that had always fretted about being different began to relax and gradually faded away. There was nothing wrong with me, my family, or anyone else being different. In fact those differences could be beautiful. I loved that idea and gradually was able to apply it to everyone I met, simply accepting them as they were.

In the fall Bill quit Air-Way. I had been after him for some time to get a "nice, steady job" with a regular paycheck. He had worked on commission for years and was used to its ups and downs. I wasn't. There would be a lot of money coming in one month and none the next. We never knew if we'd be broke or flush. I couldn't stand it. I needed to be on a budget. I wanted the security of a steady paycheck, and I was sure Bill would be better off living that way.

So after months of my telling him he should get a "regular" job, Bill started work on the sales floor at a Goodyear Tire store. That meant he reported at the same time every morning, left at the same time each night, and always made the same amount of money. I was so sure this was the right thing for him to do.

I was so wrong. I could see right away that it wouldn't work. Bill was an excellent salesman with an uncanny understanding of people. But he didn't fit into a routine job with a boss watching over his shoulder all the time, telling him exactly what to do and when to do it. Bill was trying hard, but he was miserable. I realized then that it was possible for me to be absolutely positive I was right about something and be totally wrong.

It was a good lesson to learn but a hard situation to fix. Here was Bill doing what I had asked him to do—maybe even nagged him to do—and I could clearly see that it was a total mistake. But he couldn't go back to Air-Way; the company now knew we were married, plus another salesman had already taken over his territory. And he couldn't just quit Goodyear Tire because we needed his paycheck. The only good part was that Bill's new job was just over the Bay Bridge in Oakland and a pretty easy commute from San Francisco. Bill was able to give up his apartment in Martinez and move full-time into our Powell Street flat.

The first thing Bill did was install a gas heater in our living-room fireplace. Up until then the only heat in our entire two-bedroom flat was the woodstove in the kitchen. That stove was just powerful enough to heat one room. In the winter we'd keep the kitchen door shut to hold the warmth in, which meant the rest of the flat was ice cold. Once he moved in full-time, Bill quickly got tired of freezing his fanny off. So he added the gas heater and did it all himself. Mamma thought Bill was a genius both for thinking of it and for doing it. She was warm and toasty even in cold weather, and to Mamma that was a miracle.

Except for Bill's unhappiness with his "nice, steady job," things were going well. We had a big family Thanksgiving complete with Mamma's usual ravioli-stuffed turkey. (We didn't switch to the more traditional bread stuffing until years later, when Eda and I took over responsibility for cooking the bird.) Bill and I went shopping together and bought a few Christmas gifts. I was really looking forward to the holiday, my first as Bill's wife. Then came Sunday, December 7, 1941. I was taking a shower at about 10 A.M. when I heard Bill calling through the door.

"Elda, guess what? The Japanese have bombed Pearl Harbor in Hawaii."

I was stunned. I suppose I'll always remember the shock of that moment. We had been following the grim news about the fighting in the Far East and in Europe. I knew immediately that the attack on Pearl Harbor meant our country would declare war. America was now part of World War II.

Some of the Christmas gifts Bill and I had already bought were stamped "Made in Japan." We threw them away because we knew we couldn't give them to anyone. It wouldn't have been right. Japan was now our enemy.

Everyone we talked to was sure San Francisco would be the next bombing target. Over the next couple of months antisubmarine nets were laid across the Bay, and guns were mounted at the entrance near the Golden Gate. Air raid sirens were installed, and volunteers were recruited for a civilian defense corps. A complete blackout was put in place. Everyone hung black sheets over their windows so there wouldn't be a even glimmer of light that a Japanese pilot could use as a target. Hardly any restaurants were open and few people went out. We did nothing, every night.

With rare exceptions, people were completely gung ho about the war. Patriotism was the most important thing. There was a togetherness then that I have never experienced at any other time. The country was united in a common cause, and it seemed as if everyone believed in it 100 percent. Everything was seen in black or white, right or wrong. Just like the presents we threw out because they were marked "Made in Japan," every detail counted. Most young men were going into military service or finding some way to help the war effort. Those who didn't were ostracized.

Bill started taking early morning welding classes before Goodyear Tire opened so he could get a job helping the war effort. As soon as he completed his training he went to work at the Moore Drydock in Oakland, doing welding on the big warships being built there.

After a few months, Bill found a better-paying job closer to home in San Francisco, also as a welder for a company producing war materials. He worked the swing shift from four in the afternoon until eleven at night. Bill was asleep when I left in the morning and off at work when I came home from my job. The only person he ever saw awake in our household was Mamma. I'd get home from work, and Mamma would give me a verbal message from Bill—that he was coming home at a different time than usual or something like that. Since neither spoke a word of the other's language I have no idea how the two of them managed to communicate—but they did.

Starting in February 1942, all the Japanese people living in California were rounded up and sent to relocation camps. The news made me sad and confused. I was all for winning the war and "teaching Japan a lesson," but my heart went out to those who were being forced to leave their homes. Many had been in this country for years, and some of the younger people had been born here. I was sure most of them were innocent of any spying or wrongdoing, that it was all a matter of circumstances. After all I had been born in Italy, and Italy was now our enemy too. I knew it could have easily been the Italians who were rounded up. In fact I found out only recently that some outspoken Italians were sent to the relocation camps as well. That was something I didn't hear about back then.

Even though I empathized with the people who were being forced out of their homes, at the time it didn't occur to me to think that our government was doing the wrong thing. After all, we hadn't started the war. I felt sorry for the Japanese-Americans who were being carted away to the relocation camps, but I didn't say anything against it. Nobody did. Back then it was second nature to simply follow the rules and assume that those in charge were doing what was best for everyone. That was the downside to the country's 100 percent unity.

More and more companies were converting to wartime production. Air-Way made the switch early in 1943. They eliminated my job, but I quickly found another one as a secretary at a company that made patriotic souvenirs. It was known as Charles Davis and Company. In private we employees referred to it as "Uncle Charlie."

Algisa's accordion-playing son Guido entered the Army Air Corps. He was eventually stationed in Europe. He took his accordion with him and in his off-duty hours formed a small band that entertained the troops all around them.

Paolina's son Beb was drafted into the Army infantry as a foot soldier and also shipped to Europe. His brother Fred signed up with the Navy's Coast Guard branch and was assigned to the USS *Liggett* in the South Pacific. Only Beppa's son Bruno failed his physical and was classified 4F, so he wasn't drafted. We supported the war with all our hearts, but we worried about our three family men who had joined the fight. Joe and Rico were too old, but I was starting to fret that Bill might be drafted at any moment.

We had other problems as well. Beppa, Algisa, and Jenny came to me all upset and saying Rico was out of control. I figured my sisters were probably exaggerating. My husband had lunch with Rico occasionally, and Bill considered Rico a street-smart, intelligent guy.

"Let me handle him," Bill told me. "You people are all too involved. Don't worry, Elda. I'll have a talk with Rico at lunch and straighten him out."

I was so relieved. I knew that if anyone could handle Rico, Bill could. Except that Bill came home shaking his head in defeat.

"There's nothing anyone can do for your brother," he said.

Bill wouldn't give me any details about what had happened at lunch. He just kept repeating that there was nothing that could be done. My heart sank. I had figured that with Bill being a salesman, he could deal with Rico when no one else could. I mean, salesmen have psychology coming out of their ears. It's how they make their money. So when Bill said there was no reaching Rico, I knew it was hopeless. With no other options that we could see, my sisters went on feeding Rico daily, and we all kept praying he would somehow change. We didn't know what else to do, so life just went on.

Worried that he might be drafted into the Army, Bill volunteered for the Navy's construction battalion (CB), known as the Seabees. We figured Bill's welding skills would get good use with this group, and at least he wouldn't be fighting on the frontlines. I tried to be upbeat when Bill left, but the future seemed pretty grim. Once he finished boot camp, Bill was sent back east to Providence, Rhode Island, for more training. I arranged to take some vacation time so I could go see him.

I traveled cross-country by train. It was the first time I had done that since my family had arrived in America twenty-seven years earlier. I had never met Bill's mother and sisters, so I stopped off in Michigan for a few days. Bill's family was delightful and the visit went quickly. In no time at all I was back on the train and heading to New York City to see Bill. He had managed to get a weekend pass and was standing in Grand Central Station when I arrived. He had slept all night on one of the station's benches, waiting for me.

I felt such love for him. It was almost overwhelming.

We checked into a hotel and spent the weekend playing tourist. We stood on the top of the Empire State Building, walked through Times Square, saw the Rockettes dance—everything that was typical New York. When Bill's weekend pass ended, I went back to Rhode Island with him. We had about a week left before I had to go home. Bill rented a room for me near his base in Providence. He wrangled a couple of one-day passes before I left, so we visited Boston and also took a trip to Narragansett Bay along the East Coast. We tried to spend as much time together as we could. A few nights we had to sleep apart because Bill was required to be at the military base.

I wasn't alone, though. There were other women all around me, in the same situation I was. When we couldn't be with our husbands, we turned to each other for companionship and support. We were all strangers, but we were all friends too.

Bill and I were both aware that he would be shipping out soon, but we never talked about it. Instead we kept things as upbeat as possible and tried to enjoy the time we had together. We went to see the movie *Pennies from Heaven* with Bing Crosby. I remember it clearly because it thrilled both of us. Even the movies were lighthearted, so when you left the theater you felt good.

We both believed that Bill's going off to war was the right thing to do. Even so, when the time came for me to leave, it was hard to say good-bye. According to the news reports the war wasn't going well. It seemed like it might last for a long, long time. We had no idea if we would ever see each other again. Bill was on duty that day, so he couldn't come with me to the train station. We had to say good-bye in my rented room. Neither of us made much of a fuss. I think we felt too much to try to put it into words. We simply kissed quickly, said a quiet good-bye, and went our separate ways.

I was like a zombie on the train trip home. I was numb inside. I had no idea how to feel or what to think, so I just gazed out the window and watched the scenery go by as the train took me farther and farther away from my husband.

Bill's ship sailed to the war in the Pacific shortly after I left Providence.

CHAPTER 11

I spent a lot of time writing letters during World War II. We had no cell phones, e-mail, or faxes to provide instant communication, and there certainly weren't any standard telephone lines out to the battle zones. Instead we poured our hearts onto a thin piece of paper, slipped it into an airmail envelope, and slapped a stamp on it. That was the only connection we had with anyone overseas.

I wrote Bill every night, without fail. I told him everything I had done that day and how much I missed him. He was building airfields on islands in the Pacific: on Tinian and then on Guam. I kept reading in the newspapers that the Japanese were bombing the heck out of those airfields. I was full of worry, but I tried to keep that out of my letters to Bill.

I also wrote several times a week to my nephews Beb and Fred. They were the sons of Paolina, the fourth of my four older sisters. Her husband had died of cancer when the boys were quite young, and

Paolina had raised them herself. She did all the housework as well as holding down a job in an Italian-owned factory. As a result Paolina still didn't speak a lot of English—everyone she worked with spoke Italian—and she hadn't learned to read or write in any language. She was too busy making a home and earning a living to try to overcome the handicap of her complete lack of schooling as a child.

Fred and Beb wrote to their mother in English. I would read their letters to her, translating into Italian as I went. I'd take notes on what Paolina wanted to say and then write a reply in English. Algisa, my third-oldest sister, was able to write directly to her son, Guido, who was an Air Force crewmember in Europe, but Paolina needed my help to keep in touch with her boys. Beb was an Army infantryman in Europe, and Fred was on a Coast Guard ship in the Pacific. The letters I read and wrote were Paolina's only link to them. My heart ached for her, and I did my best to write down everything she wanted to say to her sons.

I couldn't write letters all the time, so I tried to find other ways of keeping busy. My office was on Montgomery Street, across from the elegant Palace Hotel. It was such a fancy place that I figured I had to go there at least once. I gathered together some friends from the office, and after we finished our half-day of work on Saturday, we went to the Garden Court in the Palace for an extra-special lunch. The bill was terrible—sky high—but the experience was wonderful.

There were humongous chandeliers hanging everywhere, a huge glass dome, and a marble hall with pillars. It was a beautiful sight. We went in our best outfits, trying to look as if we belonged. I'm sure we were overdressed, and I'm equally sure the mâitre d' and waiters knew immediately that we were just a bunch of secretaries. I bet they had us pegged before we even walked in the door, but they treated us wonderfully. We probably overdid the tip because we were trying so hard to belong. Even so, it was one more piece of the good life that I got to experience for myself. I enjoyed every minute of it.

Other events weren't as happy. Algisa, Beppa, and Jenny came to me again, even more frantic about Rico than before. They just couldn't take his ranting and raving any longer. Whatever Rico wanted, be it food, money, or anything else, he was sure we all owed it to him. Even while our sisters were taking turns letting him into their homes, feeding him, doing his laundry, and packing more food for him to eat later, Rico complained bitterly that he was neglected, overlooked, and unappreciated and that none of us liked him. More importantly, Rico kept insisting that Mamma didn't love him. It was a belief that made him furious. His anger was now a constant state, and my sisters were terrified he might hurt somebody. They were especially worried about Mamma, who was the main subject of Rico's verbal tirades.

"Something has to be done," my sisters told me over and over. "Something just has to be done."

With Bill gone, coping with Rico seemed to be my problem. My brother Joe worked from 4 A.M. to 8 P.M. and wasn't around to see what was going on or to handle anything. Besides, Joe was a sweet guy who never liked confrontation or taking action. I felt it was all up to me.

I decided we needed outside help. Back then there weren't any twenty-four-hour crisis lines or support groups for every possible problem. We had no knowledge of psychology or counseling. If other families had trouble with someone like Rico, no one talked about it or shared information about what could be done. So I went to the only place I could think of—the police station. I hoped they could arrest Rico as a vagrant who had no place to live.

The officers were polite but said they couldn't do that. Instead I had to sign a warrant for Rico's arrest for intimidating and threatening

Beppa, Jenny, and Algisa. A cop told me to find out exactly where Rico would be and when and then come back to the police station.

Locating Rico was easy. Late each morning he was at one of my sisters' homes, eating and complaining. I checked with my family to see who was feeding Rico that week and then returned to the police station with the information.

I had to go along with the officer who was going to make the arrest because he needed me to identify Rico. That was the hardest part. I got into the patrol car and gave the officer directions to Jenny's house. She lived on a quiet San Francisco residential street. Two- and three-story buildings lined both sides of the road. Each building held a number of flats, and each flat was some family's home. I had been there many times before to visit Jenny. Everything looked exactly the same as it always had, only now I was sitting in a police car outside Jenny's place, waiting to have our brother arrested.

It wasn't long before Rico came out. I'm sure the cop wouldn't even have stopped him for questioning if I hadn't signed the arrest warrant. Rico didn't look homeless or at all dangerous. His clothes weren't fancy, but they were clean. Beppa, Jenny, and Algisa saw to that. He ate regularly—also courtesy of our three sisters—and he looked healthy, even handsome. He didn't talk to himself, hunch his shoulders, or wave his arms wildly as a known "crazy" person was supposed to do. Although he was always angry at our family, Rico was smart enough to act more normally around other people. But everyone in our family was afraid of Rico. We had run out of excuses for his behavior and no longer had the strength to cope with his unpredictability.

"That's him," I said in a low voice as I pointed to where Rico was walking along the sidewalk.

Then I got out of the patrol car and walked away. I was aware that after a brief pause the policeman drove after Rico and stopped him. I never looked back. I couldn't bear to watch Rico being arrested. He was my oldest brother. I had looked up to him when I was little. For years I had thrilled at the sound of his tenor voice. He had helped instill my deep love for Italian opera. After I grew up and started working, he escorted me around the city, giving me my first glimpse of a wider, more glamorous world. We had been so close once. We had so much fun together. That was all gone and had been for years. Now there seemed to be no way to reach him and we were all at our wits' end from trying to cope.

Rico was arrested by the police officer. My task completed, I went back to my office. I had arranged to take a couple hours off, but I hadn't told anyone where I was going or what I was going to do. When I returned to work, I acted as if I had done nothing out of the ordinary that morning. All day long as I typed, filed, and answered telephones, I kept wondering how my oldest brother was doing and what he was thinking.

The police took Rico to jail and then to San Francisco General Hospital, where he was admitted to the psychiatric ward for observation. The official process of deciding what to do with Rico seemed to take a long time. I kept worrying about what might happen if he was released after a couple days or even after a week or two. What if they didn't find anything wrong with him? What if there wasn't anything they could charge him with? If that happened, Rico would be so angry with us all—with me, especially, and with Mamma. It was hard to sleep at night and hard to keep going to work, where I had to act as if nothing unusual was going on in my life.

There were two hearings, both at the hospital. Rico wasn't present at either one. My sister Eda and I took time off work, and together we represented our family. For the first hearing Eda and I met with a panel of doctors who told us they had diagnosed Rico's problem as schizophrenia.

"What's that?" I asked. I had never heard the word before.

"It's a mental disorder," one of the doctors explained.

I understood that. Even though it had taken a while for our family to admit it and accept defeat, it had been obvious for a long time that something was wrong with how Rico thought and felt.

The doctors were extremely gentle with Eda and me. They patiently answered all our questions even though we weren't entirely sure what to ask. I think they could see we were pretty naive and not at all experienced in dealing with this type of situation.

The second hearing was held in late summer 1943. Its purpose was to officially commit my forty-six-year-old brother to Napa State Hospital. We all knew what Napa was: a place for crazies. If you wanted to say someone was loony, you told them "you belong in Napa." Now Rico was going to Napa.

It sounds sad to say this, but we were all incredibly relieved once we knew Rico would stay locked up in a psychiatric ward. When I heard the news, I said a heartfelt prayer of thanks to God. I felt like a weight had been lifted off me. For Algisa, Beppa, and Jenny, it was as if they had been handed brand-new lives. That was especially true for Jenny, who had been feeding and caring for Rico without her husband's knowledge.

The task of coping with Rico now belonged to people who had been trained to deal with that type of behavior. I was still a bit shaky from the strain of having Rico arrested, but my sisters all thanked me for what I had done. We hadn't told Mamma anything about what was happening because we didn't want her to worry. When it was all over, I told her that Rico had to go to the hospital and while he was there they decided he was mentally ill. I said he had been taken to Napa

State Hospital. Like the rest of us, Mamma knew what that meant. Rico was now one of Napa's "crazies."

Mamma didn't show what she was feeling, but I think she was relieved, just like the rest of the family. We all knew how uncontrollably angry and scary Rico could be. Now we could tell ourselves that he was getting the help he needed. At the very least he would get more help than we had ever been able to give him. But the news had to have broken Mamma's heart, because Rico was her treasured, firstborn son.

Each month everyone in the family chipped in to pay for Rico's care at Napa. No one ever complained about the cost. Rico's behavior had become so alarming that I think my sisters would have paid almost any sum of money to have him taken care of somewhere far away from them. I visited Rico in the hospital once a month. One of my sisters would go with me, and occasionally Mamma came along. At times Rico was his old, lighthearted self. Other times he was completely out of control, and they wouldn't let us see him.

That isn't the whole story. For most of my life I haven't told anyone everything that happened. A lot of it is too painful. The reason I remember so clearly that our flat had gas lighting when we first moved to North Point Street is because Rico tried to use the gas to kill himself. He wasn't successful, but it was one of many early signs of his inner torment and the difficulties that were to come. I can recall how pretty those gas lights were, but that memory sticks in my mind for a very sad reason.

And remember when my sisters agreed to take turns feeding Rico? He had started screaming that he was going to kill Mamma, so I locked him out of our Powell Street flat. There was more to that incident too.

It was after I got the job at Air-Way but before I started dating Louis. Rico knew the building where I worked and was often standing on the sidewalk at the end of the day. That particular time I froze when I first saw him because it was obvious how angry he was. Almost mechanically I started walking to where I always caught the streetcar. Rico followed, yelling at me. He got on the car with me, still shouting. There we were on a crowded streetcar with Rico ranting and raving.

"I'm going to kill Mamma. She doesn't love me and she never did," he shouted at me. "I'll kill her!"

I was petrified. I had never seen him so completely out of control. By instinct I got off at my usual stop and started walking home. Rico went with me, still yelling. It was only a half-block walk to our flat. Our building had two outside steps leading up to a wide entranceway. I climbed the steps with Rico right next to me, still shouting in my ear. Before we reached the doorway I jumped in front of him and turned to face him. I knew I couldn't let Rico get anywhere near Mamma.

"Rico, you are not coming into this house," I told him as firmly as I could. "You are not getting in."

He hit me hard, right in the middle of my face.

Poor guy, I think as soon as he did it he regretted it. He ran away immediately. I'm sure he wished he hadn't done it. I'm sure he wished that.

Holding my head with one hand, I rang the doorbell to have Mamma let me in. My key was still in my pocket, but I was too stunned to fumble for it. If it had been hard for me to think straight when Rico was yelling at me, it was even worse now. Mamma opened the door and I kind of fell into her arms. As best I could, I told her about Rico's threats and how he hit me. My face didn't look too bad at first, but after a few hours I had two big black eyes. Both of my cheeks were puffy and swollen.

I didn't tell anyone what had happened. Mamma and Joe knew, of course, since we lived together. But I told nobody else. Not any of my sisters. Not even Etta, my best friend. When I went to work the next day, I explained my bruises by saying I had walked into a door. It felt like such a disgrace to be hit by a family member. I was ashamed to admit what Rico had done to me. Mamma and Joe reacted the same way, as if it was something deeply embarrassing that had to be hidden from the world. Mamma always said that what happens in the family should stay in the family.

It may seem odd, but for years I was perfectly willing to tell people that Rico had been committed to a psychiatric hospital, yet I never said a word about him hitting me. Even when my husband was trying to help, when Bill ate lunch with Rico to try to clear things up—even then I didn't explain that years earlier Rico had hit me. I didn't tell Bill for a long time. Somehow I just couldn't get the words out until years after Rico was locked up in Napa State Hospital.

Rico's illness seemed like an act of God that none of us could avoid; it wasn't our fault. Being struck by a family member was somehow much more disgraceful and too terrible to talk about. I know that won't make sense to a lot of people, but it's how I was raised and it's how I am deep inside.

From the moment he hit me, I was afraid of Rico. Sometimes my body would shake at the mention of his name. He had been my buddy, my "date," my friend. Once he seemed so proud that I was his little sister. Then he terrified me. I'm only talking about this because I hope I can help someone else who has to struggle like I struggled. It was so hard deciding what to do about Rico. I kept putting off taking action until I just couldn't delay anymore.

Things are much better nowadays. People talk about mental illness, and there seem to be more drugs and treatment for someone like

Rico. But there's still a lot of family shame, and I know many people keep silent.

Don't.

When I finally started talking about what really happened with Rico, I felt lighter inside, as if I had dropped a weight I had been carrying for a long, long time. And if my honesty can help just one person feel less alone or convince someone to get help with this type of problem, breaking my silence will be worth it. Maybe in a way that could be kind of a memorial to Rico. His life was tormented, and it would be wonderful if something positive could come from it now.

Occasionally I still wonder if I let Rico down by going to the police. I don't know. All my family and I could do was give Rico what he demanded. We did that for years and years, and it didn't do any good. Maybe Rico never really intended to hurt Mamma or the rest of us. Maybe he just wanted to scare us into doing what he wanted. For all his threats, Rico never hit anyone but me.

At least I think that's true. I can't be absolutely sure. I assume that if Rico had physically harmed Jenny, Algisa, or Beppa, they would have told the rest of the family. But then again, I never let any of my sisters know that Rico hit me. So who knows what else he did or what he was capable of?

And yet I still believe he didn't really mean to hit me. Things just got out of control, and when Rico realized what he had done, he ran away. It may seem like I'm making excuses for Rico's behavior and being pretty easy on him instead of blaming him for what he did. You have to remember that he was my brother. Family is family, and we were trained from a young age to take care of each other. Rico might not have treated us very well, but that didn't lessen my instinct to take care of him and protect him.

I guess I'll always wonder if Rico's problems were made worse by living completely on his own in a strange city when he was fifteen. I went to work at age fifteen too, but it was my choice and I was still surrounded by my loving family. Rico wasn't just expected to live alone and support himself at age fifteen. He also had to help save enough money to bring the rest of the family over from Italy. I have no idea what that isolation and responsibility did to him inside. I still wonder if that situation added to—or perhaps created—at least some of his problems.

Whatever the causes of his disease, each month when I went to visit Rico at Napa State Hospital, I felt a deep fear. At first I went anyway because he was my brother. Then my visits got farther and farther apart, until eventually they stopped. I just couldn't do it anymore. Even today, long after Rico is dead, I don't like going to the Napa Valley. It's a beautiful place, but I can never enjoy it. It holds too many sad memories.

I guess some things simply have to be. You can't avoid them and you can't change them. You have choices, but not the choice to have those things *not* happen. I couldn't make Rico better just by wishing or praying. I simply had to put my hand in God's and go on. At least that's what I did with Rico. That's what I've done all my life.

There were happy events to balance the sad ones. In November 1943, Joe's wife, Annette, gave birth to twins, Jon and Joanne. Since space was already tight in our flat, Jon slept in a crib in his parents' bedroom, and Joanne ended up in a crib in my room. I would get up every morning at 6 A.M., prepare a bottle for her, and then feed her before I left for work. Mamma was still sleeping in her folding chair in our living room. She and my other sisters cared for the twins during the day since Annette went back to her department store sales job as soon as possible.

By 1943, some of the hysteria generated immediately after Pearl Harbor had died down, and San Francisco was no longer under black-out conditions. However ration books were a fact of life. There was very little sugar, meat, or butter. Gasoline for cars was hard to come by because most of it was being shipped to the troops overseas. You had to have a ration coupon to buy any of these scarce items. But rationing wasn't hard for my family. We were experts at making do with what little we had. We'd had years and years of experience doing that, so rationing wasn't a problem for us.

But the war was always in our thoughts. I kept writing to Bill daily and to my nephews Fred and Beb anytime Paolina asked me. I also got updates about my nephew Guido from Algisa and Lorenzo. I listened avidly to the news reports on the progress of the U.S. and Allied troops. Sometimes I would talk back to the radio as if it were a person who could hear me. If the news was vague, I'd demand more details. If there was a story about a victory, I'd tell the radio, "Great, that's just great," as if encouraging it would make it want to give me more good news.

And the reports did get better. Nowadays I have to look up the dates to remember what happened when, but back then I knew the details of every battle—from the landing on Sicily in July 1943 to kicking the Germans out of Rome on June 4, 1944; to D-day, the Allies' massive invasion of Europe only days later on June 6; and the battle of the Philippine Sea that same month. We were glad when Allied troops entered Paris in late August and again when the Japanese were driven out of the Philippines that October. Our hopes were buoyed by the first B-29 raids on Japan in November and the hard-fought victory in Europe's Battle of the Bulge in December 1944.

And still I kept demanding more even information from the radio—details no one could give me. Because the enemy might be monitoring the mail, U.S. troops weren't allowed to write home with any specifics that could give away where they were or what they were doing. Censors read everything sent back to the states and often cut big holes in soldiers' letters to remove what might possibly be critical details about the war effort. Sometimes there were so many holes that it was impossible to make any sense of the letter at all.

So we had no idea exactly where Bill, Fred, Beb, or Guido were, or if any of them were involved in the battles being reported on the radio. Despite my frustration, I kept listening intently as the announcer talked about our troops winning the bloody battle for the Pacific island of Iwo Jima in February 1945; U.S. forces landing on the island of Okinawa in early April; and Soviet troops capturing Berlin in mid-April.

On May 8, 1945, Germany officially surrendered. Peace was declared in Europe. Our family was happy and excited because we knew Beb and Guido were safe. But Fred and Bill were still in the Pacific, and judging by the news reports about how determined the Japanese were to fight to the last man, it looked like that war might go on for years. So although the news in Europe was good, we were still praying for Bill and Fred.

In early August, the United States dropped the atom bomb in Japan, first on the city of Hiroshima and then on Nagasaki. I think it surprised everyone. I know it surprised me. I remember feeling awed by the inventiveness and sheer ingenuity of it. At the time I had no idea of the devastation it caused. Now I'm sorry they ever dropped it. I can't imagine what it was like for the people in Hiroshima and Nagasaki. I also hate and fear the stockpiles of terrible weapons that have been built up since then. But when I first heard about the bomb, I welcomed it as a way to quickly end the fighting in the Pacific. And it did.

I was at work on August 14, 1945, when the news came that Japan had surrendered. There would be no more killing. World War II was over. The whole city rejoiced. Everybody was out in the streets, laughing and using noisemakers. True pandemonium and pure happiness. People were just wandering around in a state of joy. We knew there would be no more fighting and no more need to worry about someone we loved being killed in combat.

But our family's relief was quickly replaced by grief. On August 17, just three days later, my nephew Guido was a crewmember on a routine airplane flight in Europe. It crashed. There were no survivors. Guido was twenty-three years old. The official notification of his death came by telegram. It was followed by a letter from Guido's commanding officer, Major Frank Klappas. He wrote about how well Guido had done his duty as crew chief on a C-47 Skytrain, carrying troops and cargo.

Guido had been a sergeant and part of the first wave of airplanes on D-day when the Allied forces landed in France. He was in one of a long line of planes flying through rain and then through antiaircraft flak in order to drop paratroopers into battle. Although his airplane was hit by flak many times during that invasion and later missions, Guido was never injured. Then came a standard trip hauling air freight to Germany, months after the Nazis had surrendered. Peace had been declared in both Europe and the Pacific; World War II was over. Guido and his crew were simply flying supplies from one spot to another to support the troops in occupied Germany. The day was extremely cloudy with heavy fog. Their plane smashed into a wooded hillside. The major's letter explained that Guido wouldn't have suffered because such accidents happen so quickly and unexpectedly. The wording was a bit stilted, but it was a heartfelt attempt to comfort Guido's family.

"Words cannot express to you what your son's passing has meant to the officers and men in this squadron. Your son, together with two officers and one other enlisted man, had organized a four-piece band and were playing nearly every night either at the officers' club or in someone's tent. He was one of the best accordion players and one of the best musicians we had in this squadron. On several occasions he played at the officers' club for us, and his playing and personality held the entire group spellbound just listening."

The major praised Guido's work and listed the medals Guido had been given for his many missions. The letter ended with a hope for peace.

"We pray to God that He will look after your son, together with the other men who have given their lives to rid the world of the Nazi aggressors. We pray that it will never again be necessary for our boys to lay down their lives to squelch the greed and lust of another nation."

Our family sent four men off to fight in the war to end all wars; only three would be coming home. I read the major's letter and tried to take it all in, but I couldn't stop crying. Guido had been a handsome young man, just over six feet tall with curly brown hair. He had a small mustache and was always smiling. He was like sunshine; he'd walk into a room and brighten it up. He was engaged to marry a wonderful young woman named Dianne, but now she would never walk down the aisle and into his arms. She would never see him again. None of us would.

As time goes on and I reflect on things, I have very different viewpoints than when I was young and naive. Guido died in one of the "wars to end all wars." It didn't work. It just didn't work. Wars kept on coming. So many wars came afterward that it's almost as if we've had a century of combat. To me war is absolutely evil and has no reason and no purpose.

Guido's death tore apart Algisa's family. She and Lorenzo still had their daughter, Olga, but Guido was their only son. Olga was able to go on with her life and was always there to comfort and help her parents.

But it felt like Algisa and Lorenzo were never the same. Algisa used to sing so beautifully. Just hearing her had cheered me up when I was unemployed and feeling sorry for myself during the Great Depression. After she got the news about Guido, I never heard Algisa sing another note.

Lorenzo appeared to be in shock for the rest of his life. It was as if he was stunned somehow and never able to get over it. It was a complete personality change for both of them. Up until Guido's death, they were outgoing people and loved to entertain. After that, except for small family gatherings they never hosted another party. At the time everyone thought you were a real hero if you died for your country. Now I don't feel that way at all. I still love this country deeply, but I don't understand why a twenty-three-year-old should have to die in a war. There has to be a better way to settle disputes between countries. Maybe someday we'll figure out what it is. I hope so.

Somehow our family kept going and welcomed our other returning heroes. Bill came home on December 3, 1945. What I had been constantly praying for since the day he left finally came true. My husband came back to me, whole and healthy. I was still grieving for Guido, but I was also ecstatic. Bill was home.

He and I immediately went out barhopping. We had to do something to celebrate. We kept running into friends whose husbands had also just returned from the war. They were out partying just like us. Everywhere we went everybody was rejoicing. Despite our sadness over Guido, it was our best Christmas ever. We were eager to get on with our lives and to put the war behind us.

CHAPTER 12

Our baby was born nine months and three days after Bill got home. I had a lot of company on the maternity ward. Everywhere you looked in 1946 you saw pregnant women. I guess those hundreds of couples we saw out partying the night Bill got home did *all* the things we did to celebrate. My obstetrician had so many patients ready for labor that he was given his own hospital room where he could nap when he wasn't delivering babies.

Of course there were other things happening in our lives between Bill's return home and my going into labor. We lived in the Powell Street flat for several months. Mamma still slept on her folding chair in the living room. Joe, Annette, and their son Jon were in the back bedroom. That left just Bill, me, and Jon's twin sister, Joanne, in the front bedroom. Home sweet home.

In February the doctor confirmed my suspicions—Bill and I were going to be parents. Like most of America after World War II, we decided we wanted a place of our own. We could finally afford it.

While Bill was overseas I had saved as much of my salary as I could. Bill had arranged for the Navy to send part of his salary home to me, and I put that aside as well, so we had a nice nest egg. As soon as he got home, Bill landed a job supplying information about prescription drugs to doctors, dentists, and veterinarians in San Francisco and the East Bay. As always, Bill charmed everyone. Having gone back to working independently, earning sales commissions rather than on a boss-looking-over-his-shoulder salary, Bill was doing great and bringing home quite a bit of money. I wasn't about to bring up the idea of a "regular job with a nice, steady paycheck." That didn't work for Bill, and now we both knew it.

The combination of the cash in our savings account and Bill's high income meant I could afford to become a full-time expectant mother and housewife. Bill and I had always wanted children. After our long wartime separation, I was eager to make a home just for us. As soon as I knew I was pregnant, I quit my job and started looking for a suitable apartment. In early April we rented a flat on Taylor Street, about three blocks west of Washington Square in North Beach. I was almost thirty-five years old, and this was the first time I had ever lived anywhere without my family. I loved them and they were still within easy walking distance, but this was going to be our home, Bill's and mine. I felt liberated. And although he loved Mamma and my family, they were awfully Italian for Bill. He had grown up with a typical midwestern American lifestyle. Once we had a flat of our own, I happily learned to do things his way. I wanted that American lifestyle as much as he did—if not more.

Before we moved I worried a lot about how Mamma would get along without us—without me. I shouldn't have wasted my time. Joe moved Annette and the twins into a comfortable two-bedroom flat right next door to Jenny and Giulio's apartment in the Cow Hollow district, then asked Mamma to live with them to help take care of the twins. It was perfect. Mamma had young children to tend to and was surrounded by her family. More importantly, she was still living with her son. Mamma needed a man as the center of her life, and Joe always had a special place in her heart.

So we all settled happily into our new homes. There was only one worry—in the spring we were notified that Rico had escaped from Napa State Hospital.

"Don't worry, I'll take care of it. I know exactly what to do," Bill told me.

What wonderful words. I had always been the family's translator; the go-between with doctors, clerks, or officials of any type; the person who had to decide what to do and how to do it. And I usually ended up doing things the hard way. With Bill around, I no longer had to do everything myself. It felt great.

Rico made a beeline for familiar territory in San Francisco, and Bill was able to tell the police exactly where to look. My brother was easily caught and sent back to Napa. Bill also got the government to pay for Rico's care from then on because Bill and two other family members were military veterans.

I put Rico out of my mind once again and got busy with happier details. I loved our one-bedroom flat, Bill's and mine. We had a living room, of course, and we decided the dining room would be the baby nursery. There was enough room in the kitchen for our table, so that wasn't a problem. I bought baby bottles and other supplies and lined up all the services I thought we would need, like diaper delivery and pickup. I also tried to learn how to cook American-style. One night Bill asked me to make scalloped potatoes. I'd never even heard of the dish. Bill bought me the *Betty Crocker Cookbook* thinking that would do the trick. I'm not good at learning how to do things from a book, but I tried my best. The results were less than spectacular—in fact they were less than edible.

Cooking failures aside it was great to finally begin our married life. Of course it wasn't always sugar and honey. Bill and I had never spent so much time together, just the two of us. We loved each other, but we both had strong personalities and didn't always see eye-to-eye. After Bill and I fought one day, I headed straight home to Mamma. I didn't get the welcome I expected.

"Non venire qui a lamentarti, se hai bisogno di sfogarti ritorna a casa capire al tuo marito"—"Don't come complaining to me. Go back home to your husband," Mamma told me.

I was shocked. I figured, *Ohhh, I don't even have Mamma anymore.* That was hard at the time, but now I realize what a favor she did for me. Mamma hated to see any of her children get married because it was painful for her to say good-bye. But once we were married she would never interfere. I went home, Bill and I made up, and life went on.

William Guido Willitts was born in the early morning hours of September 6, 1946. I went into labor the night before while my husband was out on the road making sales calls. My nephew Fred drove me to the hospital, and Bill showed up as soon as he could, even though he wasn't able to do anything except sit in the waiting room and wait. In those days fathers weren't allowed anywhere near the delivery room.

Holding my son, Billy, was the single biggest thrill of my life. I felt truly blessed, as if God had given me a gift with His own hands. Nothing compares to that feeling. It's a miracle. There you are in all that pain, and suddenly they present you with a beautiful, perfect baby. I immediately counted his ten fingers and ten toes, all in perfect working order. They were so tiny. Billy had lovely blue eyes just like his father's. As he got older they changed to kind of a gray-blue, but as a baby Billy had the most true-blue eyes you could imagine. Our son also had a deep dimple in the middle of his chin.

"Dimple in the chin, rascal within," was the first thing my husband said when he saw Billy. I thought the dimple was adorable. I was convinced our son was the most beautiful baby God had ever given to any couple.

I hadn't decorated the nursery ahead of time because I wanted to follow the American tradition of pink for girls, blue for boys. When Billy and I came home from the hospital, I made sure his room was filled with lots of blue—blue paint on the walls, blue bedding, blue everything. I thought it was just perfect.

My husband was often traveling on sales trips, but when he was home, Bill always liked to put Billy down to sleep at night. Bill would hold the baby and sing to him. I can still hear the sound of my husband's voice, drifting down the hallway—"Tura lura lura, tura lura lei. Tura lura lura, that's an Irish lullaby."

For Christmas 1946 the three of us—Bill, baby Billy, and me—joined Eda and Bacci for dinner at Beppa's home with Beppa's husband, Giuseppe, their son Bruno, and his wife, Virginia. This was the first of more than twenty Christmases that our three families spent together, all of them at Beppa and Giuseppe's place. We didn't get the entire family in one place for a holiday dinner for a simple reason—none of us had enough room. There were too many of us. We kept in touch and would visit one family or another throughout the year, but we had to spend Thanksgiving or Christmas in more manageable-sized groups.

Eda and I were comfortable with Beppa and Giuseppe, so it was natural for us to go there. Algisa and Jenny were such good friends, and their families always spent the holidays together. Mamma, Joe, Annette, and the twins joined them, sometimes at Jenny and Guilio's San Francisco apartment and sometimes at Algisa and Lorenzo's home. Paolina and her sons, Fred and Beb, had their own celebration at their home, with their friends. In the late 1940s, Algisa and Lorenzo built a lovely custom home in Marin County, giving them much more space. After that if the holiday was at Algisa's, then Paolina and her sons would join them.

Paolina still lived in her house in the Cow Hollow district. After the war ended her boys lived with her and took care of her. Fred got married and started a plumbing company while Beb studied business at the University of San Francisco. After he graduated, Beb became Fred's partner. They were a real success. Fred remodeled Paolina's house from a typical drafty old San Francisco home into a modern, comfortable place for the four of them—Paolina, Fred, Fred's wife, Norma, and Beb.

We all had come a long way from cold-water flats and flour-sack underwear. Except for Rico, all of Mamma's children had good homes, good families, and were doing well financially.

From that point on, everything seemed to just fly by. In 1947 Bill changed jobs and began selling for Primrose House Cosmetics and Toiletries. He'd call on small drug, department, and specialty stores all up and down the West Coast, selling face cream, lipstick, powder, and similar items. His sales territory included seven states: California, Oregon, Washington, Nevada, Montana, Wyoming, and Idaho. Bill was on the road seven to eight weeks at a time, traveling by car. He ended up being away from home at least half the year.

I hated it. Bill wanted to be a good husband and father, but he was

Sometime in 1913, Mamma sent Babbo this photograph of me (left) and Eda to show him how his youngest girls were growing up.

Babbo is on the right in this photo of him and a friend at Asti, California. He sent the photo to Mamma in Italy.

Mamma had this photograph taken in Lucca around 1914, to send to Babbo in California. I'm the youngest, holding the hoop. The others, from left, are Jenny, Eda, Joe, Mamma (seated), Paolina, Beppa, and Algisa.

Reunited in San Francisco, Mamma and Babbo, seated in front, had this family portrait of all ten of us taken in 1917. I'm standing next to Mamma and Babbo. Behind us are, from left, Eda, Paolina, Jenny, Rico, Joe, Beppa, and Algisa.

Sometime around 1917, when I was about eight years old, a neighbor lady Mrs. Casassa gave me a book to read and this lovely, lovely dress, which I adored.

I don't know how Mamma and Babbo came up with the money for my store-bought First Communion dress, but I felt so wonderful wearing it.

Employed as secretaries in the late 1920s, my lifelong friend Etta, left, and I spent a lot of our leisure time together, and followed all the latest fashion trends, from clothes to hairstyles.

On the town—I'm on the right in this picture of Eda and me walking in downtown San Francisco in the late 1920s. It was taken by a sidewalk photographer. They'd snap your photo and then sell it to you.

Bill and I posed for this wedding photo in San Francisco, after we got back from our honeymoon in February 1941.

Hoping to capitalize on his welding skills, my husband, Bill, joined the Navy Seabees in 1943.

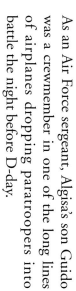

As an Air Force sergeant, Algisa's son Guido was a crewmember in one of the long lines of airplanes dropping paratroopers into battle the night before D-day.

Getting together during World War II are, from left, my niece Olga, Algisa's daughter; me; my sister Eda; Beppa's son Bruno; and Eda's husband, Bacci.

Our fighting men,—from left, my husband, Bill, with Paolina's sons, Beb and Fred,—shown in 1943 before they all shipped overseas.

My rambunctious son gets the drop on the photographer sometime in 1948, when Billy was about two or three years old.

With World War II behind us, once again Bill hit the streets as a salesman, as shown in this snapshot taken by a street photographer in downtown San Francisco.

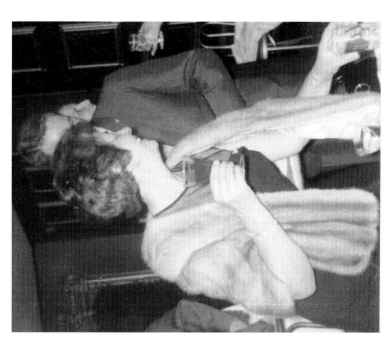

Once I got used to the idea, I loved the fur stole my husband insisted on buying me.

This picture of our son, Billy, was taken in the late 1950s, when he was about thirteen or fourteen years old. Isn't he handsome?

Gathered at a family wedding in the early 1970s are my sisters and me, from left, Algisa, Jenny, Paolina, me (peeking from behind), and Eda.

My son, Bill, took this photo while on vacation with his family sometime in the 1970s. That's Greg on the right, Shannon climbing on the redwood tree sign, and Patti holding Jason.

My son, Bill, and daughter-in-law, Patti, relax sometime in the 1980s.

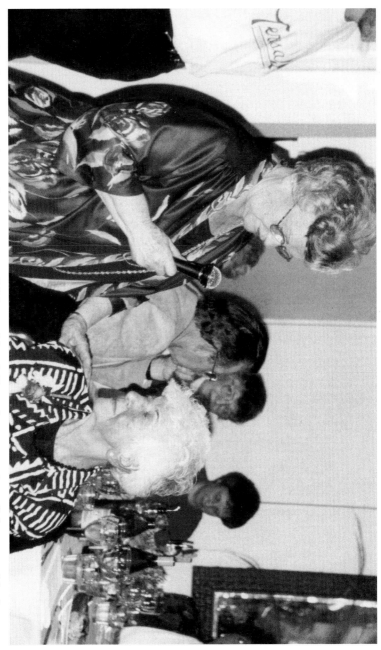

At a family party in the early 1990s, my lifelong friend Etta shares stories of the past. Notice my white hair after chemotherapy.

My family gathered for Christmas 1999: front row from left, Greg's wife, Debbie, holding their son (my great-grandson) Gabe; my grandson Petey; me; my great-grandson Max (Shannon's oldest); my granddaughter Shannon; and her youngest, my great-granddaughter Zoe. Back row: my grandson Greg holding his son, my great-grandson Sean; my grandson Riley; my son, Bill; my daughter-in-law, Patti; Jason's wife, Shelby; my grandson Jason; Shannon's stepson Jonathon; and Shannon's husband, Michael.

I can't describe how amazing it felt in 2000 to return to my home town of Lucca, Italy, and find the house where I was born.

totally devoted to his career. His family's poverty after his father's death had scarred Bill deeply. Many times he told me, "I'll never be poor again." He was determined to be a financial success as soon as possible—if not sooner. He was always pushing for the next sale, the next goal. I didn't set my sights as high as Bill did, but we were in complete agreement in terms of what we ultimately wanted. We both came from poverty. He needed success and I wanted security. For us, they went hand in hand.

So I understood why Bill pushed himself so hard. I was honest enough to admit to myself that if our roles had been reversed I probably would have worked the same long hours. Once he started selling for Primrose House I knew Bill had found his niche. He loved what he was doing and he was great at it. Bill said he was gone so much because he wanted to give his family the best he could. I found it hard to argue with that. I craved financial security, and here was my husband trying to give it to me. And Bill did his best to keep in touch. His schedule was uncertain, but he'd phone me at least every other day to let me know where he was and where he was going next. He'd give me the names of the stores he was planning to call on. That way I could leave messages for him if I needed to. The store owners all liked Bill and seemed glad to help us.

Even so I was terribly lonely when Bill was on the road. I wanted financial success with the stability and comforts it would bring, but I also wanted to share my life with my husband. There I was in "our" one-bedroom San Francisco flat, with a beautiful blue nursery and a beautiful, blue-eyed baby boy. It was our home; we weren't sharing it with any of my numerous family members. But it felt empty. I didn't want to go back to living with Mamma or anyone else. I wanted my husband at home with me and our son, like a normal, all-American family.

I wrestled with my unhappiness for many long, frustrating, and lonely months. Eventually I realized I either had to accept Bill's frequent traveling or call it quits. I wasn't willing to leave him. I decided to accept my life as it was, not as I wanted it to be. I figured that when Bill was home, I'd make sure we had a good time together. When he was gone, I'd take care of Billy and be reasonably content. Maybe it wasn't all that I wanted, exactly as I wanted it, but I loved them both and was willing to work at being happy with what I had.

Of course this meant that my husband got to do exactly what he wanted. However all three of us—Bill, Billy, and I—ended up with some pretty happy times because I was willing to bend enough to make things work. Bill and I tried to have a second child, but I never got pregnant again. It was disappointing, but I also felt I had my hands full just keeping up with Billy and Bill.

Very quickly Bill's long hours and determination meant we began enjoying the good things in life. In summer 1948 we took a train trip to visit his family in Michigan. We traveled in our own first-class roomette. Each day we would saunter into the dining car, which was set with gleaming silver and sparkling crystal on crisp white linen. It was a whole new form of luxury for me, and I was a bit awed by it. Bill took it all in stride.

We had a great time in Michigan, and I even got some cooking lessons from Bill's mother. She was so sweet. I described my failed attempts at making scalloped potatoes. "We'll make them together," was her quick reply, and we both headed into the kitchen.

Her version of scalloped potatoes included butter, onions, thinly sliced potatoes, and milk, with pork chops baked on the top. Today I figure it's amazing that the cholesterol and fat didn't kill us immediately, but back then all I understood was that it came out tasty and delicious. I finally knew how to make scalloped potatoes. I felt one step closer to being a real American.

About this time my sister Algisa and her husband, Lorenzo, decided they wanted to become U.S. citizens. They hadn't recovered from their son's death, but I think they were trying to get on with their lives. With prompting from their daughter, Olga, they began reviewing the extensive information that was covered by the citizenship exam. It helped that they could both read and write English fairly fluently. I think their children had taught them a lot, and Algisa always had a sharp mind, eager to learn new things. So Olga drilled her parents on the questions they would have to answer.

Algisa and Lorenzo made an appointment to take their exam with a judge. Before starting the test the judge asked them about their family. As soon as he learned their son had died while serving in the Air Force during World War II, the judge told Algisa and Lorenzo that they didn't have to answer any questions. They had already done enough for their country. He immediately swore them in as U.S. citizens. His gesture meant so much to my sister and her husband. And Olga still gets tears in her eyes when she talks about it, even today. So do I.

In spring 1949 Bill and I were finally able to buy a house of our own. Like many of our friends we decided it was best to live in the suburbs outside the crowded city. Since Bill was familiar with the East Bay, he wanted to live there. I hated that area. I wanted Marin County, north of San Francisco. I felt comfortable in Marin because of the accordion picnics we had attended in Fairfax for so many years. And by this time Algisa and Lorenzo had built their own home in Fairfax, which meant I would have family living nearby. I told Bill no East Bay; only Marin for me. It was one of the few times Bill gave in without any argument.

"I'm not home much and you are, so we'd better go with what you want," he said.

We bought a cute two-bedroom cottage for $12,950 on Rutherford Avenue in San Anselmo, an attractive little town immediately east of Fairfax in the gorgeous Marin County hills. Our small bungalow wasn't new, but I thought it was perfect for us. It had a high, peaked roof and looked like a thatched cottage out of an old fairy tale. The attic room had sharply slanted ceilings, but there was enough space for a pool table and a guest bed up there. There was also a large backyard where Billy, now almost three years old, could play. The neighborhood was full of young families just like ours, starting out in their first homes. The children all played together, which made it easy to get to know their parents.

Once Bill and I bought our home in San Anselmo, Eda and Bacci began sleeping at our house on Christmas Eve so they could share in the joy of watching Billy open presents Christmas morning. Eda and Bacci never had children of their own, and I think Eda thought Billy was kind of her son too. She loved showering attention on her nieces and nephews, but she never once said anything about wanting her own child. Certainly they couldn't have had the antiques and precious items that filled their home if they'd had children running around. And Eda loved her department store job—with its access to the latest fashion trends—too much to give it up and spend several years at home changing diapers. So instead Eda spoiled her nieces and nephews, spent Christmas Eve at our place, and got to share Billy's excitement each Christmas morning.

The years sped by. Bill was focused on work and success, and I was focused on Bill and Billy. With Bill often out of town, Billy and I spent a lot of time together. He was a sweet boy but an active one and kept me pretty busy. Bill agreed I could raise our son as a Catholic, so I took Billy to Mass with me each Sunday. At some point in the service he'd always start squirming. If I didn't watch him closely, he'd slide off his seat and crawl under the pew. One time I gave him a little pinch on his arm to remind him to behave.

"You pinched me," he cried in a loud voice, startled that I would do such a thing. He was shocked, but he soon got over it and went back to crawling around the pew.

After several years of ever-increasing financial success, Bill began insisting he wanted to buy me a fur coat. For the life of me I couldn't see why we should buy such an extravagant item. Bill was out of town most of the time, so we weren't attending events that required a fur coat. We weren't even going out all that often. A high-quality wool coat looked great and was enough for me. This was long before animal rights activists made it unfashionable to wear real fur. Back then, mink or other fur coats were considered stylish and real status symbols. I think Bill wanted to buy me one as a sign that he had "made it" and could cover me with fur. Only I was having none of it. I didn't want a fur coat, I didn't need a fur coat, and that was that.

Then one day Bill and I went shopping together in downtown San Francisco. He somehow maneuvered things so we ended up on the sidewalk in front of a furrier at precisely the time Bill had scheduled an appointment.

"Guess what, we're buying you a fur coat," he told me cheerfully.

"Guess what, I don't want a fur coat," I told him, absolutely furious at what he had done. "I'm not coming in."

I turned and stalked up the sidewalk in grand style. I was sure Bill would have to follow me in defeat. When I was about a block away I slowed down and looked back over my shoulder. Bill hadn't moved an inch. He was still standing on the sidewalk in front of the fur store, waiting for me. I stopped and turned around. We stood there looking at each other, one block apart.

Bill always told me I was stubborn while he was simply "determined." Like I said, except for choosing where we were going to live, my husband always got his way eventually. I loved my fur, and once I calmed down I had great fun picking it out. I chose a stole rather than a full coat. It was so soft and beautiful; both elegant and luxurious. I felt wonderful wearing it—as Bill had known I would. I don't wear it now that I understand the cruelty of using real animal fur, but I sure enjoyed it back then.

Soon Billy was five years old and ready to start kindergarten. On the first day of school, I was sure Billy wouldn't want me to leave him. I almost wished he would make a fuss so I'd have to stay or even take him back home with me. Not my Billy. He said a rather offhand good-bye and trotted off to play with his new classmates. My baby boy was growing up. I was crushed, but then I told myself, *At least he's happy*, and I went home.

CHAPTER 13

*W*ith Billy in school, I looked around for something to do with my extra time and energy. I wanted it to be engaging and profitable but still give me the time I needed to take care of my family.

In 1952 I qualified for my real estate license and started selling houses part time. That way I could be there when Billy got home in the afternoon. It was a real boom time for real estate in Marin County, and I did well. I treated my clients the way I would have wanted to be treated—I tried to figure out what sort of house would make them happy, and I never pushed to make a sale. Selling real estate gave me outside contact with the "adult" world while still leaving me time for my son. It was a good balance for me.

By 1954 Billy was almost eight, and it was time for him to start catechism. Bill decided he should join Billy and me at Mass. Bill hadn't attended church with us before, but now he felt Sunday morning should be a family time. Since he was gone on sales trips more often than not, this was one more thing the three of us could do together when he was in town.

Unfortunately the local Catholic church was in the middle of a big fundraising drive for a new building. That's all we seemed to hear about on Sunday—money, money, money.

"Forget it," Bill told me. "I'm talking money all week. I don't want to go to church to hear the same thing. I go to church to for inspiration."

I had the same reaction, but I still wanted the peace and comfort of going to church to talk with God. So we came up with what I thought was a good compromise: We agreed to go to church after the last Mass. There's usually nobody there then, either people or priests. You can light candles and pray or meditate, and you can talk with God on your own. Nobody lectures you, nobody bothers you, and you can feel the full impact of that sacred place without distraction. So that's what we did, and that's what I still do to this day. On special holidays I'll go to Mass, but mostly I go on my own, between the services.

At the time, I thought Bill and I had worked out an original approach to religion. It wasn't until recently, when I started recalling my family history, that I remembered all those years when Mamma would skip Mass but go light candles and spend a little time talking directly with God. I've been following her example for decades without even realizing it. I bet this isn't the only area of my life where, without knowing it, I've done the same thing Mamma did. We all think we're so different and independent from our parents, but that's not always as true as we'd like to believe.

The other big event in 1954 was that Primrose House was bought by another company. All the Primrose salesmen suddenly lost their jobs, including Bill. My husband was determined to never let that happen to him again. Instead of finding another job with just one company, Bill set himself up as an independent representative for several different manufacturers of cosmetics, toiletries, related accessories, and gift items. Bill was selling to all the same small mom-and-pop drug and gift stores he'd been working with for years, so he was able to build on the great reputation he'd created while selling for Primrose House.

Eventually Bill was representing a dozen manufacturers, selling to stores all over the West. I kept his books for him and handled any office-type chores. It worked well. I was still selling real estate now and then, but mostly I handled Bill's office work. However, I did have a couple of extra-special real estate clients in 1957: my sister Eda and her husband, Bacci.

"Get a good house for us," Eda told me.

I did. It was in San Anselmo, less than two blocks up the hill from our little cottage. As soon as I saw it I knew it was right for Eda and Bacci. That took a leap of imagination because the fad right then was to paint each room of the house a different color. The people who owned the house had done that with a vengeance. I think one room was chartreuse and the next bright orange or purple. It was almost physically shocking as you walked from one hideously colored room to another. But the price was right, and I felt the house had real potential. Eda agreed, and she and Bacci bought the place immediately. By this time she was working in bookkeeping at Gump's, a really fancy upper-class department store in San Francisco. Eda soon had her coworkers giving her tips on the best remodeling designs and furniture selections. Her place was picture-perfect in no time. But of course Eda kept improving on it for years because she enjoyed decorating so much.

By spring 1959 Billy was twelve; I was forty-seven, almost forty-eight; and Bill was fifty. Things were going well and we were in a mood to celebrate. We invited Eda, Bacci, Mamma, Joe, Annette, and the twins over for Easter dinner. We held an Easter egg hunt for the kids and then ate a huge meal. After everyone left and Billy went to bed, Bill and I cleaned up the house and washed the dishes. To relax we decided to have one of our favorite drinks, hot milk laced with brandy.

While Bill fixed the drinks I went into our bedroom to slip into my nightgown and robe. When I came out, Bill was sitting on the couch, sipping his drink. I joined him and as we talked I slowly stretched, getting the stress and tension out of my body. I had spent the whole day cooking and cleaning; it felt great to stretch my arms high overhead, loosening the muscles in my neck, shoulders and back. Feeling much more relaxed, I slowly brought my hands down to massage my neck and then let them sort of drop down into my lap. As I did this my hand lightly brushed my right breast. I quickly brought my hand back up to my right breast, to double-check that I really had felt something there. The lump was maybe three-quarters of an inch long and about the size of a date pit.

I went cold inside. I told myself it was nothing. Bill hadn't paid any attention to what I was doing, and I didn't say a word to him. He and I talked a little more, and then we went to bed. I knew that if the lump was still there in the morning, I needed to call my doctor. I didn't want to think about it until then.

After Bill had left for work the next morning and Billy went off to school, I took a bath. The lump in my right breast was kind of an elongated shape rather than round, and it hadn't gone away while I slept. I called my doctor, and he had me come to his office immediately. My big fear, of course, was that it could be cancer. My doctor referred me to a surgeon. When Bill got home that night, I told him everything.

"Let's not panic," he said immediately. "Let's wait and see what it's all about."

His words calmed me down a bit, but in my heart I was still worried. The operation was scheduled for one week later. The surgeon explained that they would put me to sleep, remove a piece of the lump, and have it tested, a process known as a biopsy. If the tissue was benign, they'd let me wake up and that would be that. If it was malignant, they'd operate immediately, removing the breast and any nearby tissue that might be involved. It was a one-step thing: I wouldn't know what they had done until I woke up. If only a few hours had passed, I would know the lump was benign. If it was late in the day, I would know the lump was malignant and my breast was gone.

It was a pretty scary proposition and seemed totally out of my control. Nowadays they do a biopsy and then discuss all the options with the patient, who decides what she wants done. In 1959 there were no options. It was all left up to the doctors. They told you what would happen, and you just listened and nodded. Even Bill, who was a real take-charge, give-me-the-answers type of guy, didn't ask much more than, "What are her chances?" Doctors were godlike figures in crisp white, and patients followed their orders.

I didn't tell Mamma. When Paolina's husband died of cancer years earlier, Mamma just referred to it as *"la malatia brutta"*—"that ugly sickness" or "that." She couldn't say the word *cancer*. To her it was a punishment God gave you. Since Mamma lived in San Francisco and rarely came to Marin, it was easy to keep her in the dark about what was going on. We talked on the phone often, but I never let her know I had "that sickness." I did tell Joe and my sisters. Algisa confessed that she had a similar lump in her breast but was afraid to go to the doctor. I urged her to have it checked immediately, and she said she would.

We didn't let many other people know. Back then if you said you had breast cancer, people assumed you were going to die. When I told someone, I could almost hear them thinking, *Oh, I'm looking at somebody who isn't going to make it.* So I tried to avoid that reaction as much as possible by not talking about my illness. Except for family members and a few close friends, we kept the news pretty private.

My operation started at 8 A.M. on April 3, 1959. As I went under the anesthetic, I prayed I would wake up in just a few hours, which would mean the lump had been benign. If the surgery took longer, than meant it was malignant and they would have cut off my right breast.

When I regained consciousness, I immediately asked the nurse to tell me the time. It was 5 P.M. My heart sank. I reached up and touched my bandaged chest where my breast used to be. I felt shock and then defeat. I was in physical pain, but the emotional agony was even worse. I felt like half a woman, as if I didn't have a real body anymore.

They had butchered me, really butchered me. It seemed as if they had scraped away the right side of my body. They cut so much away that to this day you can see my ribs. Doctors hadn't yet learned that it's not necessary to remove absolutely everything. The surgeon cut off all of my right breast as well as the lymph nodes and the muscles under my arm.

It didn't help my stunned emotional state that I felt almost completely on my own. Even though I shared my hospital room with another woman, I still felt isolated. The setting didn't help. The hospital was a two-story stucco building, fairly modern and kept spotlessly immaculate. It was clean but not very comforting. You sort of got the feeling you should whisper when you walked down the hall. The nurses all wore severe-looking white uniforms with those awkward starched caps on their heads. They were friendly in a sort of regimented way, but there never seemed to be time in their busy schedule for listening to me talk about what had happened to my body, my fears, or my emotional turmoil.

Visiting hours were severely limited. My husband could only come to see me for short periods of time. My twelve-year-old son couldn't get in at all because no visitors under sixteen were allowed. I had a room on the second floor and could see the hospital parking lot from my window. Once a day Bill would call as he and Billy left the house. I'd go stand at the window, and when they arrived I'd wave to my precious son. He seemed so small and far away. Then Billy would have to wait downstairs while Bill came up to talk with me for a few minutes.

I was scared I'd die before Billy could grow up, and I wanted so much to see his face. How could they have such stupid rules? How could they keep an ill mother from seeing her son? It was ridiculous. After a while my husband got fed up. He dressed Billy in a shirt, tie, and jacket to make him look older and snuck him in. Bill didn't tell me when they were coming because he knew I'd worry about it.

A twelve-year-old boy in a jacket and tie still doesn't look anything like a sixteen-year-old, but I didn't care. I don't have the words to explain what it was like to see my son's face, to touch him. As soon as he walked in the door I stood up and hugged him tight against me. We didn't say anything. We just stood there holding each other. It had been a little over a week since I'd entered the hospital for my surgery, but it seemed like forever since I'd been with Billy. My son told me years later that he looked at me that day and figured I was going to die. His father had been pretty honest with him about what was happening, and Billy held me tight because he was worried he might not have many more chances to hug me. I was kind of worried about that too.

Our moment of togetherness didn't last long. A nurse came bustling in and insisted that Billy leave immediately. It was heart-wrenching to watch him walk out of the room. I imagine the nurses spotted him before he even entered my room and felt they were doing us a favor by letting us have even a brief time together. It doesn't matter. I'm still furious that they made him leave. How could anyone do that to a mother and son? Bill had to take Billy back down to the parking lot. I stood at the window, and when they got outside I waved to Billy again. It felt like I was waving to a stranger. He seemed even farther away than before.

A few days later I was allowed to go home, but I wasn't healing properly so I had to go back to the hospital. They took skin from my stomach and grafted it onto my chest, then treated everything with radiation. Finally my body started healing, and I got to go home again.

Algisa had kept her promise to me and went to her doctor about the lump in her breast. Her operation was done two days after mine, with the same result. It was malignant, so the doctors did a radical mastectomy, cutting everything out. Algisa didn't tell Mamma either. I attempted to talk with Algisa about cancer, but she wouldn't discuss it. She had absorbed Mamma's attitudes, and it was a taboo subject even between the two of us.

I don't know how much I could have helped Algisa even if she had been willing to talk because I was a mess, a real mess. I felt unbalanced, both physically and emotionally. I tried wearing a prosthesis, but it was so heavy and awkward that I hated it. I felt so negative about my "mutilated" body; I was sure it had to be disgusting to Bill. I didn't want to undress in front of him. I didn't want him to see my scars. The only person who saw my chest was my doctor.

"Elda, you haven't changed, I haven't changed," Bill told me. "I love you, you love me. What difference does it make?"

I was sure it had to make a difference. If I raised my hands while wearing short sleeves I was convinced everybody saw my long scars. Bill was patient with me and simply accepted everything I did and felt.

His gentle understanding helped a lot, but it wasn't enough. According to the doctors we had to wait five years before I could consider myself cancer-free. Five years was a long time to have that worry hanging over my head. I couldn't stop thinking about cancer, death, and what might happen to me. I kept wondering who would take care of Billy if I died. My doctor assured me everything would be fine.

"Don't worry, Elda. We got it all. I know we did," he told me over and over. "You don't have to worry about a thing."

But I did worry, all the time. I was forty-eight and my world had fallen apart. I was no longer certain that everything would work out. I doubted that one day there would be sweetness in the bottom of my cup because I wouldn't be around to taste it. After several months of being an emotional basket case, I called my doctor in desperation and asked him to prescribe something—a tranquilizer, anything. Fortunately for me, he was not the tranquilizer type.

"I tell you what I want you to do, Elda," he said thoughtfully. "I want you to have a glass of port at noon before your lunch, then a glass at night before your dinner, and another one before you go to bed. Go relax, sit in the sun, read a good book."

It may have been an unorthodox prescription, but it turned out to be exactly what I needed. I followed his advice, and over the next few months I began to slowly unravel the emotional cage I had built for myself. I started noticing a few of the pleasant details of my life, like the beauty in our large backyard. Bill always planted wonderful gardens full of flowers and vegetables, and then I kept everything watered. Our yard got a lot of sunshine, which I loved, and there was a big plum tree when I wanted to rest in the shade. I got in the habit of sitting in the garden around noon, sipping my port. I brought out a comfortable chair so I could relax and soak up the sunshine. I would kind of meditate or pray, but mostly I just thought about all that had happened and might happen.

One afternoon the weather was just gorgeous. It was a perfect Marin County, northern California–type day—warm but not too hot with a gentle breeze and a blue, blue sky. I settled myself in my chair and closed my eyes. I kept saying to myself, "I hope I can live to see Billy grow up. I hope I can live to see Billy grow up."

All of a sudden I felt like I was floating. It was as if my soul had come out of my body. The physical me was still sitting there, but "I" had somehow drifted away. I've never had a near-death experience, but I think it must be kind of like what happened to me that afternoon in our garden. In a way it felt as if somebody had taken control of my thinking. My soul was simply doing as it was told. I don't know "where" I went. I didn't see lights or a tunnel or anything like that. There were no buildings or paths or other details. I was just somewhere other than in my body.

"You don't have to worry," a wonderful voice told me.

I felt the truth of those words with my whole heart and soul. It wasn't a voice, exactly, but something deep within me, an inner occurrence that's difficult to put into words. The whole experience was beautiful, blissful, intense, and vivid. I've never forgotten that feeling. I truly believe it was God speaking to my inner self.

I have no idea whether this all took a minute, a half a second, or an hour. I had no sense of time left. When I "returned" to my body, I was kind of in a stupor. I sat there for long time, getting my wits back and smiling. My heart was rejoicing from the experience. Every inch of my body was rejoicing. I felt completely calm and at peace, yet at the same time I was euphoric. Everything was going to be all right. I was going to be all right. I was going to live.

CHAPTER 14

There's an interesting thing about sugar: Even though it settles to the bottom, it still sweetens everything in the cup, at least a little. When you watch and wait for the sugar, you can also taste it as you go along. One of my sweet moments was on a summer day in 1959 when Bill and I got married for the second time.

I hadn't told Bill or anyone else about what had happened to me in the garden. It was too precious, too personal. It was years before I was willing to talk about that incredible experience. So although I was convinced I would survive, Bill had no reason to share my belief. One day he turned to me and asked a surprising question.

"Elda, would you like to get married in church?"

"I sure would," I answered quickly, touched that he would even think of such a thing. I knew Bill suggested it just to make me happy. It did. It was such a loving gesture on his part.

We decided on a simple ceremony held on a Saturday in our local

Catholic church. Twelve-year-old Billy was part of the service as Bill and I renewed our vows. Bill and Billy wore suits and ties, and I wore a nice dress, nothing formal or bridelike. My best friend, Etta, and her husband, Jimmy, stood up for us. The only other people present were Eda and Bacci. I was still fragile emotionally, and we didn't want anyone making a big fuss about what we were doing. We didn't even tell Mamma and the others until after it was over.

"For better, for worse, in sickness and in health..." Bill's voice was strong and confident.

My words were equally clear when it was my turn. I felt wonderful as the priest blessed us. It was if Bill and I were making our commitment to each other all over again. It didn't change anything, but it put a warm glow in my heart.

I needed that warm glow. My life hadn't suddenly become perfect just because God told me I wasn't going to die. I was still walking around feeling lopsided and extremely insecure about my appearance. For instance, swimming had always been part of our annual family vacation, but in summer 1959 I refused to get into my swimsuit. I thought everyone would stare at me because I only had one breast. Bill tried to reason with me.

"Do you think people are spending all their time looking at you?" he asked.

My answer was yes. It wasn't at all reasonable, but I was obsessively certain everybody was staring at me. Of course they weren't, but I couldn't see that then. With complete patience, Bill talked me step-by-step into putting on my swimming suit and getting into the water. Bill's acceptance of me as I was—irrational fears and all—helped me start adjusting to my new body.

I hated the heavy prosthesis I had been given to wear in place of my missing breast. It was a small, thick plastic bag filled with some type of liquid. It seemed to me the prosthesis weighed a lot more than my remaining breast. I was never big-breasted, and wearing that thing made me feel uneven. Plus it was covered with a sort of sweaty material. I didn't like touching it, much less wearing it every day. I just hated it in general. When we got home from vacation, I went shopping at Woolworth's and found a soft, lightweight piece of padding about the same size as my remaining breast. I threw the prosthesis out and wore the padding in my bra instead. It felt a lot better.

Bit by bit I regained my positive outlook. I started to believe once again that the sugar would be in the bottom of my cup and that I would be around to taste it. Financially things were going well. Bill's dedication to his career was really paying off. In 1960 we sold our little cottage on Rutherford Avenue and moved about eight blocks away into a three-bedroom, multilevel showplace on Woodside Drive. We deliberately chose to remain in San Anselmo so Billy could stay in the same school with his longtime friends.

The Woodside Drive house was custom-built to Bill's specifications. Only the best was good enough for him. Besides top-quality wood and other materials, we had all the latest household appliances. And since wall-to-wall carpet was trendy at the time, every square inch of that place was covered with the best carpeting available. We also had fancy drapes for each window and brand-new furniture. Bill and I picked it all out together. There was an imposing living room set as well as a massive mahogany table and chairs for the dining room. Everything was new in the master bedroom too. Instead of the old but serviceable double bed we'd slept in on Rutherford Avenue, we now had a stylish set of twin beds with matching dressers, all in the best workmanship and design. We had custom-built closets, of course. Bill needed even more hanger space than I did for all his fancy suits, shirts, ties, and such.

Our new house hugged the side of a hill. It had a wraparound deck and huge glass windows everywhere. On a clear day we could see the Bank of America building across the Bay in San Francisco. It was a spectacular house, built on two levels. On the bottom was a two-car garage, a guest bedroom, and a huge recreation room running most of the length of the house. We figured that was where Billy could entertain his friends.

The staircase from the basement to the main level was located near the wide front entrance area. Off to one side was the kitchen, dining area, and large living room. On the other side of the stairway and entrance was a long hallway leading to our TV room, Billy's bedroom, and our swanky master bedroom. All the windows on the downhill side of the house had breathtaking views. Unlike all the places I grew up in, this was a house that just screamed "success."

If it had been up to me, we would never have left our cute little cottage on Rutherford Avenue. I was content with what we already had; owning a home was enough of an achievement. But Bill always had to have more, bigger, and better. He needed to immediately go on to the next challenge, and he liked visible signs of his accomplishments. So we moved into our fancy new home. Don't get me wrong—the house was really gorgeous and I loved every inch of it. But it took Bill to make the change. It never would have occurred to me to move.

Mamma also moved in 1960, but it wasn't a happy event. After years of living with Joe and Annette in their two-bedroom flat on Union Street, the place was just too small. The twins were growing up. To ease the crowding, Joanne slept next door in the home of Jenny and Giulio, who both adored her. But Joe and Annette wanted their daughter to live with them. Plus Mamma was getting older and wasn't able to get around as well as she used to. We all figured it was best to find another home for Mamma.

Algisa and Lorenzo had plenty of room in their custom-built house in Fairfax—their daughter, Olga, had married a Navy man and moved back East—so it made sense to everybody for Mamma to move in with them. We figured Algisa could take care of Mamma and everyone would be happy. None of us realized how crucial it was for Mamma to feel needed. All of her adult life Mamma's world had revolved around taking care of other people. Now she was the one being taken care of.

We also didn't understand that it was important for Mamma to have a male to care for. First she had Babbo, then Rico, then Joe. Now Babbo was dead, Rico was locked away, and Joe was fifty-four years old with a family of his own. Mamma was ninety-one. Other than a couple of years during the Depression, this was the first time since he was born that Mamma didn't live with Joe. Even though Algisa did everything she could think of to make Mamma happy, Algisa couldn't be the son Mamma yearned for. And there were no young children for Mamma to care for, to let her feel useful. The only man in the house was Algisa's husband, Lorenzo, and he didn't need Mamma to care for him—Algisa did that.

Since Algisa and Lorenzo lived near us, I was able to visit Mamma several times a week. I was surprised to find her sleeping whenever I dropped by, no matter what time of day it was. Mamma had been a strong, vital woman all her life, and now she seemed to be withdrawing from the world. She was disappearing right before our eyes, but none of us could think of anything that would stop her decline. As we had done with Rico, we just prayed and hoped and went on with our lives.

One night in 1961 Bill came home, talking as he often did about the problems of the many small, mom-and-pop stores that were the majority of his customers. For each of the dozen manufacturers Bill represented, a store had to order a prepaid minimum of thirty or thirty-five dollars, or else pay shipping costs. That may not seem like a lot of money, but today's equivalent would be five hundred dollars or more. This made things difficult for Bill's smaller clients. They couldn't place prepaid minimum orders with all the companies because it tied up too much of their cash in merchandise that might not sell quickly. And yet without a minimum order, the freight charges were killing them. Bill had heard all about it for years.

"Elda," Bill said suddenly, "Let's start our own business."

His idea was that we would order merchandise from all the companies and let the small stores put together a minimum order from any of the items we carried, regardless of who manufactured them.

"Let's do it," I told Bill.

The idea excited me. Bill could handle the sales and I could run the office. It felt like a tailor-made business, perfect for us. As always, Bill was up for the challenge, and for once I was equally excited. I was fifty years old and Bill was fifty-two. Billy was fourteen and fairly self-sufficient. He no longer needed—or wanted—his mother around all the time. I was still occasionally selling real estate, but my heart wasn't in it anymore. So that's how William G. Willitts and Associates was born.

Of course, it wasn't quite as simple as it sounds. There were an incredible number of details to iron out. At first we thought we could run the business from our home, using the huge family room on the bottom level of our house as a warehouse to store our inventory. But San Anselmo zoning laws wouldn't allow that. We started hunting for a warehouse to rent and found one in nearby Fairfax. It was a long, narrow, white building, old but in good repair. We could afford the rent, and it was a short drive from our San Anselmo home. There was plenty of storage space for our inventory and enough room up front for an office for me. So we signed the lease.

I immediately went out and had a great time selecting secondhand office furniture and equipment. I bought two desks and chairs—one for Bill when he was in town and one for me—plus a typewriter, a filing cabinet, and a small mimeograph machine to print flyers about our sales or other special promotions. Bill built us a bunch of shelves in the warehouse area, and that was it. We were in business for ourselves.

Opening day was so exciting. Bill had already been out on the road selling, so there were orders I needed to ship out immediately. We quickly settled into a routine, and neither of us had an idle moment. Bill made the sales calls; I'd pack and ship the orders. I also did all the ordering, billing, general ledger work, invoices, and payments. Plus I typed any letters that needed to go out and tried to collect from the overdue accounts. Things started hopping right away.

Of course ours was a far cry from the modern high-tech office with computers, copiers, and fax machines to do most of the work. My accounts payable system was a cigar box full of three-by-five-inch cards. If we wanted a copy of a letter, I put a piece of carbon paper between two pages of typing paper. If we needed a lot of copies of something, I'd have to type it more than once because the image got too faint if you used a lot of carbons. It was time-consuming, but it all worked.

William G. Willitts and Associates soon became more than a full-time job for both Bill and me. We worked Saturday, Sunday, and late every night. There never seemed to be enough time to get everything done. Bill lived the business twenty-four hours a day. It was exciting to be running our own company and to have it be such an immediate success, but it was also exhausting. Bill was still telling me to love myself and to put my own needs first, but he was also calling in furious because an order hadn't been shipped on time or demanding to know why something else hadn't been done.

One of the reasons for Bill's success was that he was a perfectionist who really wanted to provide whatever his customers needed. Unfortunately, he had a quick temper when things went wrong. I was trying to be warehouse manager, office clerk, and secretary all rolled into one at work and then wife and mother at home. I also served as hostess, cook, and tour guide whenever Bill entertained business clients. I had a housekeeper who came in once a week to keep up with the cleaning, but I still did all the shopping and cooking. So here was Bill telling me to love and take care of myself and to put my needs first, yet at the same time he seemed to expect me to anticipate everything he needed and to do it perfectly. I tried—I really tried. When Bill was upset or angry about something, I wouldn't argue back. I'd just work on fixing whatever was wrong. But the frustration kept building inside me.

I'd blow up every six months or so, and it would all come tumbling out at once. Bill seemed to have a sixth sense for when I was close to the breaking point. Instead of berating me as usual for something that had gone wrong, he'd start backing out of the room, saying we'd talk about it later. That made me even angrier. There I was, with enough steam built up to give him what I felt was a well-deserved piece of my mind, and he would cut and run, leaving me fuming. I'd calm down after a while, and we'd go right back into the routine that had me running from task to task, trying to anticipate everything Bill or Billy might need done for them.

I was all mixed up inside. I was delighted at how well the business was going and really enjoyed my role in making it all work. In most ways my life seemed picture-perfect. At the same time, I felt a growing inner turmoil. How dare Bill tell me to take care of myself when he was the one expecting the most of me? But I didn't tell him that. I just fretted and worried to myself, trying to figure out how to make everyone happy, including me. I felt like a failure each time that proved to be an impossible task.

And that wasn't my only source of tension. Even though our son, Billy, was smart and his teachers said he could do well if he would just work, he had never been much of a student. The older he got, the less time and attention he put into his classes and the worse his grades got. He was a talented artist, and his art teacher said he could easily earn an A for the quality of his work. But Billy never did any of the class assignments, so he ended up with a D in art.

There was no way our son could go on to college with such low grades. That didn't bother Billy at all, but it did worry his father. Bill had worked long, hard hours to pay for his own education after high school. Now he was all set to send his son to any university he wanted to attend, but Billy wasn't the least bit interested.

Their verbal arguments over Billy's grades and possible college career got pretty explosive. A typical teenager, Billy wasn't interested in anything Bill had to say. Unfortunately, both father and son were stubborn, and the arguments kept escalating. I'd sit down at the dinner table with my husband and son and would have indigestion in less than five minutes from listening to the two of them go back and forth about any issue that came up. I didn't have any answers, and I couldn't seem to change either of them.

Here I was with everything I had thought I wanted: a husband, a son, a gorgeous home, and the financial stability I had craved since childhood. I even had someone to come in once a week to clean my house—my teenage goal of avoiding endless housework had come true. But I still had troubling problems and no solutions.

My son and I had always been pretty close, but Billy was starting to distance himself from me as well. That hurt. He didn't constantly disagree with me the way he did with his father, but we sure didn't have the same companionable times I remembered from when he was young. He was pulling away from both Bill and me. I knew it was normal teenage behavior, but it still worried me.

Things were happening quickly in our lives, and I didn't have a lot of time for reflection. I was also concerned about Mamma. By this time she refused to get out of bed at all. Algisa had taken her to a doctor, but he couldn't find anything physically wrong. Mamma was almost ninety-three years old. She had given up on life.

One night in early December, Algisa called to say that Mamma was having trouble breathing. I called Eda and we agreed to meet at Algisa's. As I drove the short distance to Algisa's home, I thought about Mamma. Our fairly tense relationship when I was in high school had eased as soon as I started work. The freedom of going to the office every day and the confidence I gained from bringing home a paycheck made it easier to accept Mamma's many rules. Plus her restrictions eased up a bit once I was employed and contributing to the household. I guess Mamma started seeing me less as her little girl and more as a young woman. When I was about seventeen or so, Mamma and I talked about how she felt when I was born. After Eda's birth, Mamma was convinced she couldn't have any more children. She didn't want any; she had her hands full as it was. Then six years after Eda was born she realized her eighth child was on the way.

"Poco dopo che sei nata sentivo come piangevi pensavo fra me, se avessi il coraggio di strozzala non dovrei allevarla"—"When you were born and I heard you cry, I said to myself, 'If I had the courage to strangle her I wouldn't have to bring her up,'" Mamma told me. *"Eppure, dopo tutto*

questo tempo lo fatto conto che sei stata la piu amabile"—"And yet what I realize after all this time is that you've become my most lovable child."

It was a wonderful moment and led to what became a real friendship between us. We had a lot of good times together. I remember once, shortly after World War II, Mamma and I went out for a Mother's Day dinner with Paolina and her sons, Fred and Beb. We ate at a buffet restaurant. Mamma had never been to this type of all-you-can-eat place before, and she was overwhelmed. She had spent years struggling to put food on the table, and now here was this long counter full of all kinds of dishes, starting with salads and ending with desserts. Mamma had never seen anything like it. Never.

Faced with all that abundance, she refused to pick and choose. She was going to taste everything. We were each given a huge dinner plate, but Mamma's almost wasn't big enough for her. By the end of the buffet, Mamma's plate was piled several inches high, like an edible little mountain. She had stacked pickled pigs feet on top of Jell-O, mashed potatoes on fried chicken. Mamma was so happy; she was just in heaven. We all laughed at her, but she laughed at herself too. She thought it was funny, just like the rest of us, but that didn't stop her from tasting every single item at that buffet.

Now it was December 1961, and Mamma had lost her zest for life. I still remember the click of my shoes on the marble-like terrazzo steps leading to Algisa's beautiful home. Eda was already there, visiting with Algisa. The three of us went into the bedroom to check on Mamma. We stood quietly at the foot of Mamma's bed for a few minutes, watching her sleep. Her skin was ashen and looked as if it had been drawn too tightly over her face. Her breath sounded loud and harsh. I thought Mamma looked fragile, like a china doll that might break if you touched her too hard. Algisa had crocheted a lovely white bedspread of delicate squares for Mamma's bed to make everything as beautiful as possible. Now the wide expanse of white spread, white sheets, and white pillowcases just made Mamma appear tiny and lost.

I sat on the edge of the bed and took Mamma's hand in mine. I started talking softly to her, telling her who I was even though I doubted she would hear me. Mamma slowly opened her eyes and looked up at me.

"Elda, come sei stata fortunata d'avere Bilone e Bilino di sostenere la tua vita"—"Elda, you're so lucky to have Bill and Billy in your life," she whispered.

I hope she's right, I thought to myself, *because right now they're really kind of a lost cause.*

All my anxieties about my husband and son flooded my mind. I hadn't told Mamma any of it. I figured it was better if she didn't know. So I just patted Mamma's hand and went out into the living room with Eda and Algisa.

Her words about Bill and Billy were the last thing Mamma ever said to me. A few days later, on December 10, 1961, I went to Algisa's in the early evening. My sisters had each taken a turn sitting up all night with Mamma so Algisa could get some sleep. Even though I had worked all day, it was my turn to stay the night. I visited with Algisa for a few minutes. She wanted to go out and run some errands but went into the bedroom to check on Mamma before she left. I looked up as Algisa came quietly back into the living room.

"Mamma's dead," she told me softly.

My first thought was that it was a blessing Mamma wasn't suffering anymore. I knew she was in heaven and it was a better place. I walked back to say good-bye. The room was peaceful now. No more labored breathing.

All of a sudden Mamma's statement about my being lucky to have Bill and Billy took on a new significance. I realized it was her final blessing to me. With all the turmoil in my life just then it seemed hard to see the truth in Mamma's words, but I still treasured them. Mamma had come to this country forty-four years earlier with everything she had in life: her family. She was one tough lady. We all knew she loved us, but she wasn't much good at saying those words. Instead she fussed about and cared for us all her life. Her saving grace was her sense of humor—and that carried her through a lot.

She never learned English and never became an American citizen, but she loved this country. In the 1950s, Eda and her husband, Bacci, decided to vacation in Italy. They invited Mamma to go with them. She was delighted that Eda was going to see Italy again and gave her lots of advice about what to see, but Mamma refused to go along.

"Non lasciavo se avevo l'intenzione di ritornare"—"I wouldn't have left if I was going to go back," Mamma replied firmly, ending the conversation.

America was Mamma's home and she saw no reason to leave, even for a short trip. I thought about Mamma's family back in Italy, who had disowned her for marrying the gardener. Her only link to them had been her brother, Father Luigi. He kept writing letters to Mamma until his death in 1940. I was responsible for reading them to her and then writing back to him in Italian. He was disappointed when we all left Italy because Mamma didn't tell him or anyone else that we were going. He never got to tell her good-bye in person. His death meant Mamma had lost her last link to Italy, yet she didn't show any emotion when she heard the news. As always, she went on with her never-ending chores without giving any hint of what she was feeling inside.

But in many ways Mamma had a great life. Except for Rico, her children all had nice homes and good families. And all of us loved Mamma deeply and tried our best to make her happy. She never had a place of her own so she always had to depend on her family, but we were always there, willing to help.

Algisa and I took turns on the telephone, calling to let everybody know that Mamma had died. Besides Joe and our sisters, we had to notify the doctor and the funeral home. I picked out a dress for Mamma to be buried in, and the next day all six of us sisters went to choose Mamma's casket. We decided to hold her funeral Mass in Sts. Peter and Paul Church in San Francisco, where she had gone so many times to light candles and talk with God. That neighborhood was where all her friends lived—those who were still alive. Plus all our friends growing up had known Mamma and wanted to pay their respects to the family.

The church was full. Mamma's pallbearers were her grandsons, including Billy. Each one wore white gloves and a white carnation in his lapel. At the cemetery after the Mass, one by one they dropped their gloves and flower on the casket. They were all so somber and so young. Mamma was laid to rest in the Italian Cemetery in South San Francisco, in the family crypt that already held Babbo. When the services were done, the family went out to lunch together. Since Mamma had no money, we had all chipped in to pay for the Mass and burial expenses.

Our mother never had a nickel to call her own. When she got older, each of us gave her a little cash every month. Several months before she died we found out that as a widow Mamma qualified for about forty dollars a month from Social Security. We applied on her behalf because we figured it would give her the first "paycheck" of her life. It would have been her own money and not a gift from anyone in the family. She said the first thing she was going to do was to give five dollars to each of her seven grandchildren, which would have taken most of the money. But the paperwork hadn't gone through in time, and now Mamma was gone.

She worked so hard to bring us up after Babbo died. It was only after I had a family of my own that I really appreciated all she went through. I'm not sure I could have done what she did and started life over in a brand-new country in my forties, with eight children. Yet I benefited the most from the family move—even more than Mamma ever knew.

I always say that when I get to heaven I'd like to tell her, "Mamma, I know what a hard life you had, and I really do love you." I wish I had said that to her while she was alive, but I never did. There was so much I didn't understand until long after she was gone. It took a lot more living before I was able to realize all the valuable things my mother had taught me.

CHAPTER 15

*I*n the months following Mamma's death I threw myself into my work—which was fortunate because there was always too much to do. The orders just kept pouring in. It was more than one person could handle; I decided I needed help. So in 1962, just one year after we started our business, we hired Jeannette Turrini as our first part-time office employee. It was a big step, but right away she started making my life more bearable. Jeanette was a lot like me—fast, highly accurate, and a hard worker who did whatever was needed to get the job done.

Jeannette and I are still friends. I think those early years forged a bond that will never be broken. We helped build a business together, and even though we worked long, hard hours, we both look back and say that it was the happiest time of our lives. We had a clear goal—making William G. Willitts and Associates a success—and the skills to put it into action. In retrospect it was wonderful. At the time it just seemed like never-ending work.

Also in 1962 we began dividing up our territory and taking on salespeople as independent contractors. The business was getting larger than one sales rep could handle, even one as good as Bill. Once we got salespeople in place, the orders just kept coming in. Within a year Jeannette went from part time to full time. Even with Jeannette on board I was still working long hours. Somehow the workload expanded to include Jeannette's efforts without leaving me any less to do. At least I no longer felt alone as I struggled to cope with everything.

Bill and I were both living the business twenty-four hours, seven days a week. Even if he was in town, I didn't see him much during the workday because he'd be out making sales calls or on the phone with customers. If we had important decisions to make or there were problems to be ironed out, we thrashed out our options during dinner, as we got ready for bed, and while we ate breakfast in the morning. Often our "leisure" time meant entertaining people involved in our company, from clients to representatives of our various manufacturers to our own sales reps. Many out-of-town guests stayed in our home. I thought nothing of picking them up at the airport, providing them with dinner and breakfast as well as a place to stay, and giving them a quick tour around the San Francisco area. One gentleman from Japan even went grocery shopping with me because he was fascinated by our American supermarkets. That was all in addition to my working my usual full day at the office.

Things were a lot different in our "showplace" home on Woodside Avenue compared to our little cottage on Rutherford Drive. At our old place we knew all the neighbors, and a group got together occasionally for dinner on Saturday nights. The people living around us were our social life. On Woodside Avenue everyone kept to themselves, each family tucked into its own fancy house. We knew each other by sight, enough to say "Good morning" or "Hello," but that was about it. Any socializing we did, especially inviting people into our home, was connected in some way with William G. Willitts and Associates. Our business was our life, and I have to admit we both loved it. Bill thrived on the new challenges, and I felt like I was helping to create something lasting. For the first time I had complete control of an office and could set everything up as I thought best. I was in my element.

By this time Billy was in high school. He turned sixteen in September 1962 and immediately got his driver's license. Bill and I bought him a car—this was what Billy had been living for. Even today my son can quickly rattle off the details of that automobile without giving it a moment's thought: a 1957 Plymouth Fury two-door with a 318 engine, which he and his father bought in a gas station parking lot for $250.

It never occurred to me not to give our son a car as soon as he could drive. From the time he was fourteen, it was almost all Billy could talk about. All his friends were getting cars on their sixteenth birthday. It seemed to be almost an American rite of passage. And it was something my husband really wanted to do for his son. Bill would have loved to have been given a car when he was a teenager. I suspect we both desperately wanted Billy to have so much more than either of us did when we were young.

Once that kid got an automobile, we almost never saw him. If he wasn't out joyriding with his friends, Billy was in the garage, tinkering on his car. When I called him for dinner, he'd come into the house with grease coating his hands and arms all the way up to his elbows. Even if he had a date, Billy was still apt to be fussing with the car. School and homework were even less likely to be on his mind than ever before. Billy wasn't interested in books or anything academic, and he still didn't see any reason why he should care about college or want to go there. He was just crazy about cars. He loved them and everything about them. Eventually Bill gave up on getting his son to agree to go to a university or even a local junior college. And it was clear to both my husband and me that Billy had no intention of working in our business.

"I don't care if you don't go to college, but you have to get some kind of training somewhere," my husband told our son. But Billy didn't seem to have any idea at all about what he wanted to do with his life.

Starting in 1963 Billy did have a girlfriend, Patti O'Rourke, a fifteen-year-old freshman at his high school. As a prank, one of Billy's friends telephoned Patti and pretended to be Billy. He told her how pretty she was and how much he was looking forward to going out with her. Billy knew nothing about it. He and Patti were in the same drivers' training class, learning the basics before getting behind the wheel of a car.

All during class the day after the phone call, Patti kept turning around, trying to make eye contact with Billy—who didn't respond at all. When the class ended, Patti marched up to Billy and demanded to know what was going on. They quickly sorted it out and Billy realized his friend had been right; Patti was pretty. They started dating and soon were going steady.

My husband and I both liked Patti a lot. We had her over for dinner a couple of times. She wasn't much more than five feet tall, while Billy was a hair over six feet. Patti had short brown hair that she wore in a puffy bouffant style, which was popular at the time. She was outgoing with a great sense of humor and seemed to speak right from her heart. I enjoyed that about her. She always had something to say, and it was always positive. While I thought Patti was a great girlfriend for Billy, I didn't take the relationship seriously. After all, they were both just kids. Patti was fifteen and Billy was seventeen, almost eighteen. I figured it was just puppy love.

About this time I had an upsetting experience. In a rare bit of relaxation, Bill and I decided to go see a movie in San Francisco. Afterward we went window-shopping along Market Street. I was staring intently at a dress on a mannequin, trying to decide if I liked it or not, when suddenly I noticed the reflection of a man standing just behind me. It was my brother Rico.

I didn't know what to do. I didn't know what to think. It had been years since I had visited Rico in Napa State Hospital or even had any news of him. I had dismissed him from my mind. It was startling to have him suddenly appear like this. He looked older, but he was still the handsome brother I remembered. Yet I hadn't lost my deep-seated fear of him. I turned around, looked Rico in the eyes, and then I walked away. I don't think I even said hello to him. I just had an overwhelming urge to get away. I couldn't stop myself.

As we drove home I kept asking Bill how this could have happened. My husband calmed me down, but he didn't have any answers as to why Rico was walking around downtown San Francisco. The next time I got together with my family I asked if anyone knew anything about Rico. It turned out he had been released from Napa State Hospital as part of then-Governor Reagan's cutbacks. Rico was living in a halfway house in San Francisco. He was on medication and appeared to be calm, almost docile. Joe visited Rico from time to time, making sure he had everything he needed. Knowing how much just the thought of Rico bothered me, Joe hadn't told me about his release. I guess Joe decided that since I lived in Marin County and not San Francisco, I'd never find out.

Rico was still my brother, but there was no way I could get past the terror he evoked in me. I had lost my love for him. There was just fear left. Apparently Joe was the only family member who was still in touch with Rico. None of my sisters were willing to deal with him again either. I don't think any of us could forget the anguish Rico had put us through.

Maybe we should have behaved better. Maybe I should have somehow found the strength to reach out to Rico one more time—but I couldn't, I just couldn't. With a heavy heart I decided that Rico was no longer my problem, and I threw myself back into the usual routine of work, work, work, both at home and at the office.

The twenty-four-hour-a-day seven-day workweeks were beginning to take a toll on me. It was 1963 and we had been in business a little over two years. We had three employees in the office and three in the warehouse, plus two sales reps. Bill and I were still living the business all day, every day. Our hectic pace was fine with my husband, who seemed to live to work, but I wanted to work enough to live and then enjoy life. There never seemed to be time for us to just relax. There was always something more to be done for the business, one more piece that had to be put into place. I thought our success was wonderful, but when would we get to enjoy it?

And I was worried about Billy's lack of direction. He graduated from high school in June 1964 and landed a job at a gas station. It wasn't exactly what Bill and I had dreamed of for our only son. Billy seemed to be just drifting along without any goals or ambition. It was hard for me to accept and even harder for Bill, who was all ambition.

Our son was a puzzle to us, one we couldn't solve. He seemed to live in blue jeans and T-shirts. And he kept his hair slicked back with oil in the "greaser" look. I hated it. He was always a fairly clean kid and would often shower twice a day because he got so dirty at his gas station job. He scrubbed his hands carefully after he'd been working on cars to get rid of any speck of grease under his nails. Yet he almost never washed his hair. Instead he'd shower without shampooing and then comb his hair back with more oil. He looked like a punk.

Billy's gas station work hours were erratic. I was never sure when he would be home. One day I needed something at our house so I decided to drop by on my lunch hour, which I rarely did. I pulled my car into the garage and climbed the stairs up to the main level. I turned to walk down the long hallway that led to the bedrooms only to be met by Billy, clad only in a towel. He had heard my car and rushed out to meet me.

"Patti's in my bedroom," Billy told me. "Please don't make a scene. Please don't embarrass her."

I realized that Patti must have cut her high school classes in order to be alone with Billy. Back then things weren't like they are now, with all kinds of people sleeping or living together and most folks not thinking twice about it. Casual sex just wasn't accepted. I was shocked and deeply embarrassed—almost as embarrassed as my scantily clad son standing in front of me, red-faced and pleading.

I turned around and left. I guess I didn't want to make a bad situation any worse than it already was, and I didn't know what else to do. But the next time I saw Billy I gave him a piece of my mind.

"You're both too young," I told him. "You're going to get Patti pregnant, and then what are you going to do?"

But Billy just waved my question away, as if he knew better. So all I could do was worry and throw myself into my work once again. I kept thinking of my mother's last words to me, saying how lucky I was to have Bill and Billy in my life. To tell the truth, right then that was pretty hard for me to see. Everything was all mixed up. I had all the things I thought I wanted in life—success, financial security, a wonderful home—but both my husband and son were almost strangers to me. Billy was all wrapped up with Patti even though I considered them much too immature for a real relationship. And Bill and I had grown so distant that the business seemed our only connection to each other.

I felt that my mother's words had been her final blessing to me, and I desperately wanted them to be true. What I didn't realize was that things were going to get a whole lot worse between all of us before they got any better.

CHAPTER 16

There are times in everyone's life that simply have to be gotten through somehow. There's no other way to get to the good stuff on the other side. That's how I feel about most of 1965. To say it was a difficult year for me is a huge understatement. I didn't lose my faith in God that year, but I did wonder quite a bit if things would really turn out all right in the end. I know that other people have gone through much worse things in their lives than I did in 1965. I knew that even back then. But when your life is falling apart, it doesn't matter how it compares to what might be happening to someone else. It simply hurts and you keep trying to find a way out even when it feels like all the pathways are blocked.

The first bad news came in early March. On a cold and gray afternoon Billy called me into his bedroom.

"Patti's pregnant," he said quietly, not meeting my eyes. He was eighteen years old. Patti was sixteen, just a few weeks short of her seventeenth birthday.

"Oh, Billy," I said with a long sigh as I sat down on the edge of his bed. I couldn't think of anything else to say. I would have given anything *not* to be in a position to think, *I told you so*. Of course I didn't say that aloud. I was too crushed. All my worst fears had come true. I wasn't sure what was going to happen to my son, his young girlfriend, or my unborn grandchild.

Nowadays couples live together all the time without getting married, and almost nobody looks twice at an unmarried mother. It wasn't like that in 1965. Back then, having an illegitimate child on the way still felt shameful. It was something you didn't want the neighbors to know. It's true that attitudes were starting to change. The development of birth control pills had sparked what some were beginning to call the sexual revolution. Values were shifting. But for most people things hadn't changed that much, not yet.

A lot of girls who got "caught" back then with an unexpected baby on the way and no wedding ring on their finger found a way to get an abortion even though it was illegal. Of course "nice folks" didn't talk about such things, and people lied through their teeth if it happened in their family. A girl would go off to visit an aunt, a sister, or some vague relative who supposedly lived far, far away. The girl would come back after a while. She might look a bit pale or sad, but no one would talk with her about what had really happened.

Patti's parents were devout Irish Catholics, so they weren't about to whisk her away for a quick operation. A baby was coming into this world, and that was that. I agreed with them completely. Which left the question of what to do during Patti's pregnancy and after the baby was born. It was hard to think of Billy and Patti as parents. They seemed just children themselves. It's true that with his slicked-back hair and greaser attitude my son didn't look much like a little boy anymore. But with her baby-faced good looks, Patti didn't appear to be much older than twelve at the most.

My husband was out of town on sales calls, so I told him the news when he got back home. Bill accepted it like any other challenge and immediately started talking logically about what to do. I suspect his attitude might have been different if it had been our daughter rather than our son, but I don't think the situation fazed Bill. His response was to look everything over and say, "What's next?"

Both Bill and I sat down and talked with Billy, telling him he had to face up to his obligations and take care of Patti. I will say this for our son—he appeared to take the situation seriously and understood that he needed to act responsibly. In that day and age, being responsible meant getting married.

Billy had always loved children, and he seemed enchanted with the idea of being a father. He promised Patti's dad that he'd contribute some money every month for Patti's expenses during her pregnancy. And even though he didn't earn much money at the gas station, Billy always came through with the agreed-upon cash.

Patti's parents really disliked Billy—dislike is an understatement—and I couldn't blame them. If the tables had been turned and it had been our daughter and their son, I'd have felt the same way. There was Billy, looking like a greasy punk, working as a gas jockey, hardly making any money and with no sign of any ambition to do anything better with his life. His friends had all headed off to college, and there he was just hanging around home with a nothing job. At the same time, he was my son and I was proud of the fact that he wanted to marry Patti and raise their child together.

Patti's parents didn't see it that way. They wanted to hide the pregnancy and the birth, then put the baby up for adoption. Patti had been adopted as an infant and her parents thought that was the best solution. They forbid Billy and Patti to see each other. Of course that didn't work. It just meant Billy and Patti did a lot of sneaking around in order to be together.

Watching it all, I felt pretty alone. The only thing Bill and I talked about anymore was William G. Willitts and Associates. Our only other connection was our son, and that wasn't exactly a positive topic of conversation right then. We were in agreement that Billy needed to act responsibly. Other than that and various business items, Bill and I didn't seem to have much to say to each other.

By May Patti's pregnancy was beginning to show, and she had to drop out of high school. Her parents shipped her off to visit her sister in Hawaii. Billy was beside himself. He was desperate to keep in touch with Patti, and now she was hundreds of miles away.

When our next telephone bill arrived, it was apparent that our son had found a way to bridge the gap. The long distance charges totaled more than three hundred dollars, all of them to Hawaii (and remember that in 1965, a three-hundred-dollar phone bill was a *lot* more than it is today). Billy had neglected to mention to us that he was talking to Patti daily. Apparently they had a lot to say to each other. To top it off, Billy was furious with us that we didn't understand his point of view or his overwhelming need to keep in touch with Patti.

"I just have to talk with her, Mom. I just have to," he told me.

Bill and I told our son in no uncertain terms that the long distance phone calls had to stop. Billy stormed off in anger. We thought that was the end of it. Then the next phone bill came, just as high as the last one. There was a lot of yelling back and forth between my husband and son. Bill couldn't believe Billy could be so irresponsible. Billy couldn't believe his parents were being so unreasonable. Billy figured we had more than enough money to pay the long distance charges, so why shouldn't he talk to Patti as much as he wanted? In his mind, this was a desperate situation and his Dad and I just weren't cooperating. In his dad's mind, the daily calls to Hawaii needed to end immediately.

Bill contacted the phone company and had some kind of limit put on our telephone. I don't remember the details, but the result was that our son couldn't call long distance without our approval. Billy couldn't believe how stingy and unfair his parents were on such a crucial matter. He figured this was his entire life on the line here and we should be supporting him instead of stopping his attempts to keep in touch with his pregnant girlfriend. The tension in our household was pretty thick, but the phone bills dropped back to their normal amounts.

I did sympathize with Billy's longing to talk with Patti. He was frantic about her parents' plans to put the baby up for adoption. They wanted to make sure Billy and Patti never saw each other again. The situation bothered me too because it meant I might never see my first grandbaby. That thought alone could make me cry.

As worried as I was about Billy, Patti, and the baby, I still had to face up to my main problem: Bill. Although he never had much to say to me, he sure seemed to have a lot of time to chat with one of our sales reps, Alice. That wasn't her real name, but even after all these years it's probably best if I just call her "Alice" and leave it at that. She was the first salesperson we hired and was the same general age as Bill and me, maybe a few years younger.

Alice had been a big success selling for a competing company. Bill was overjoyed when she agreed to work for us. He said she was really top-notch. And as a saleswoman Alice was one of the best. You have to have a certain charm about you if you're selling. Bill and Alice both had it coming out of their ears. She was always well-dressed, very feminine while also professional. Her appearance was part of her job, and like I said, she was great at her job. She wasn't very tall—only about five feet or so—but she wore her clothes well and they were always of top quality. I was pretty sure her curly, always-perfect hair came from a bottle of permanent wave solution, but maybe that was just cattiness on my part.

Alice was good not only at selling but also at training others on how to close the deal. That's why Bill said she was such a "wonderful catch" for our fledgling company; she could help all our sales reps be as good as Alice and Bill. But from the very beginning I felt the two of them were working together an awful lot.

"Don't you think you're spending a little too much time with Alice?" I asked Bill.

"Oh, it's just business. She's doing such a good job," he said.

Bill pointed out that he often took other sales reps and lots of clients out to lunch or dinner. Alice was just one of many, he said. But I wondered if that was true. I knew Bill really thought Alice was the best of the best and wanted her to be happy working for our company. Sometimes I wondered what else he thought.

For most of our marriage, Bill had traveled a lot. He called me, let me know he was thinking of me, and brought me presents when he came home. It was just that sometimes, when I was alone and he'd been gone for a long time—well, I'd wonder. I didn't know for sure what he did when he was on the road. He was a handsome man and a traveling salesman. So I'd wonder. But I never asked him and I never tried to find out.

I didn't want to know. Thinking about it made me crazy. Early in Bill's career I decided to trust him and to depend on how good things were between us when he was home. I guess I also put my faith in Bill's ambition. It was obvious to me that most of his energy was going into the business, and I thought he wouldn't do anything to upset the lifestyle he had worked so hard to create. I figured his wife and son were part of his hard-won success, and he wouldn't risk losing that.

But month after month of watching as Alice and Bill took customers to lunch or had a dinner meeting—well, trusting got more and more difficult. Still, I ignored the situation for quite a while. It hurt too much to admit to myself what might be going on right under my nose. Although some of my anxieties about my appearance had eased, I still felt like less of a woman because I only had one breast. That made it even more painful to think about my husband making love with someone else.

Bill always told me I was beautiful just the way I was. He seemed to genuinely mean it. But what if he was bothered by my scarred body and simply wasn't telling me? That thought hurt so much that I just kept pushing it away.

The situation affected my behavior. When Bill and I made love, I couldn't respond freely, the way I had before. A voice in the back of my head kept wondering how long it had been since he had made love to Alice and how I compared to her. I wondered if he did the same things with her that he did with me or if they did something different—and if so, what? A part of me stayed withdrawn from our lovemaking, wondering.

By June 1965 I couldn't take it anymore. Want to know what the final straw was? One day I realized that if Alice was around, my workaholic husband had more time for her than for the business. That was something that had never, ever happened before for anyone, not even me. Alice was more important to Bill than work. Up until then, business always came first. Bill even helped entertain Alice's sister when she came for a visit. That's when I couldn't ignore my hurt and pain any longer. I told Bill that Alice had to stop coming into the warehouse and office. She could phone or mail in her orders—whatever she wanted to do, as long as I didn't have to see her. Still denying that there was anything for me to worry about, Bill agreed.

I wanted to get Bill to admit that he was having an affair with Alice, but I didn't know how. I kept looking for the "right" time, but there wasn't any right time. Then one day in late June Alice came waltzing into the office on business. I couldn't stand the sight of her, and I knew I couldn't wait any longer. I decided to confront Bill that night.

Our son wasn't home for dinner—he often wasn't—and it was just Bill and me. I wasn't angry, just determined to get it all out in the open and to stop living such a strained, unnatural life. I had learned early on in our marriage that yelling didn't do much good in arguing with Bill. He only responded to logic and a straightforward approach. So we had a fairly controlled conversation about what was then the most important topic in my life.

"Alice came into the warehouse today," I told Bill calmly, almost conversationally. "You have to stop her from doing that."

"You know she has to do her work," he protested.

I put down my fork and looked directly across the table at him.

"Bill, I know you're having an affair with Alice. I won't put up with it anymore. I want you to move out."

That was probably the last thing my husband expected to hear from me. For both of us marriage was "till death do us part." Bill wouldn't admit anything was going on between him and Alice. He also wouldn't promise to stop seeing her. He believed everything could go on just as it was—me at the office and home, Alice for business lunches and whatever else they were doing. I guess somehow Bill thought he could have us both, keeping the successful lifestyle he had built up and adding something a little extra as well.

No more. Not for me. I loved Bill, but I had reached the end of what I could tolerate. Without admitting he'd ever strayed from his marriage vows, Bill agreed to look for somewhere else to live. The decision made, we finished dinner and got ready for bed. We had almost nothing to say to each other. We followed our usual nighttime routine and turned out the bedroom lights just as always. While I lay there trying to fall asleep, the gap between our twin beds seemed enormous, as if nothing could ever bridge it.

For the next few days Bill and I lived side by side in that big house even though in some fundamental way we were no longer together. We had been married for so long that we just continued doing what we had always done even though all of it felt empty. Finally Bill told me he had rented an unfurnished apartment in San Rafael, not far from our Woodside Drive home. I agreed that he could take the spare bed out of the guest room and the old couch from the downstairs rec room. We also decided he'd use a few of the extra plates, pots, and things from the kitchen, as well as a couple of other items. It was all extremely civilized and cool. Once everything was set, I let Billy know what was happening.

"Your Dad's moving out," I told him. "I asked him to leave because of Alice."

Billy didn't say much but just gave me a quick hug. I knew he understood. He had been in the office a lot; he had seen Bill and Alice together. He told me years later that he had known what was going on, and the whole situation just made him disgusted with his father.

My husband packed up his things while I was at work. Bill came back for one last load just as I got home. We said hello and he told me what he had accomplished as far as moving out. We talked quietly, as if this were an everyday event. Finally Bill carried the last of his things downstairs to the garage and put them in his car. I heard the engine start up and the sound of him driving away.

I walked into the master bedroom and saw that Bill's custom-built closets were empty, stripped of his expensive wardrobe. Billy wasn't home, so I was all alone in that beautiful, gorgeous house with its spectacular views and expensive furnishings. Even without Bill there I knew I still had financial security. I would never want for material things the way I had as a child. But I was empty inside. I felt nothing. I had nothing. It seemed as if my world had come grinding to a halt.

CHAPTER 17

I kept going, of course. I had learned that from my family. No matter what life hands you, trudge on.

At work I made sure I saw Bill as little as possible and Alice not at all. I told no one on the warehouse or office staff that Bill had moved out. I think Jeannette had a good idea of what was going on, but we never discussed it.

Now there was just Billy and me at home. In a way it brought us closer together. He was caught up in his worries about Patti and the baby, while I was preoccupied with my problems. It gave us a bond. Billy started bringing his friends over to the house a lot more often, just to hang out. Maybe without Bill there to argue with him Billy felt more relaxed. It's also possible that my son sensed that a little extra noise and young-man liveliness in my house helped me feel less alone. I was operating on emotional autopilot, but I liked having Billy and his buddies around.

I knew my son needed a better way to earn a living, so I called up my nephews, Fred and Beb, who had a successful plumbing business. Billy loved cars and I thought Fred or Beb might know a mechanic who would give Billy a job. Instead they agreed to take my son on as a plumber's helper and train him if he showed any aptitude for the business.

I was so grateful to Fred and Beb. Even an entry-level plumbing job paid a lot more than pumping gas and meant working regular hours, so Billy was willing to give it a try. Fortunately my son's appearance had improved a bit. He'd gotten tired of the greasy hairstyle, stopped using so much oil, and started shampooing like a normal person. Billy had lost some of his punk look and attitude—which was good, because I don't think Fred or Beb would have put up with it.

For the first few days on the job, all Billy did was wash toilets and bathtubs so they would be clean when they were installed.

"Oh God, Mom, I just hate it," he told me after his first day of work.

But he hung in there. I will say this for Billy, he always was a good worker. Whether he was repairing his own car, tinkering with his friends' vehicles, or filling up tanks at the gas station, he didn't tend to slack off. Even if he was just cleaning a car windshield at the gas station, Billy would make sure that glass was immaculate when he was done. Like his father, Billy would focus in on whatever task was at hand and be almost unaware of other things happening around him. If he was going to do something, then he was going to do it right.

I suspect that's what Fred and Beb were trying to find out by having Billy wash those toilets and tubs. After several days in which a thoroughly miserable Billy did exactly what he was told to do, Fred started taking Billy along on various plumbing jobs to show him the ropes. Even though Fred and Beb had known my son all of his life, I bet those first few days were a test to find out if their young nephew was serious about the job or just looking for an easy ride.

Their company handled mostly commercial jobs, installing all the plumbing in new buildings, especially high-rises. Billy got really interested. He asked Fred lots of questions and began taking pride in the top-quality work they did.

With Billy on a slightly firmer footing in life, I decided it was high time I did something nice just for me. Ever since the Ford company had come out with their Mustang cars I had been telling my husband I wanted one. I knew they had a lot of power under the hood, but mostly I just liked the looks of those cars. A lot. I felt they were classy and sporty. I wanted one. Bill would just wave the idea away because I had a perfectly good car already. Somehow I don't think a Mustang fit his image of what his wife should be driving.

Maybe that's why I decided to buy myself a Mustang. Billy was all for it. He loved cars and he thought the Mustang was great. So one Saturday summer morning my son and I drove to the local Ford dealer. I still remember how excited Billy was. I don't think he ever expected his mother to do something so spontaneous or cool.

In the past, whenever Bill and I wanted to buy any kind of big-ticket item, my husband the salesman did the dickering. Bill was a natural at it; it was his line of work, so I just sat back and let him do it. Even though I had my son by my side, this time it was all up to me. When it got down to the closing details and contracts, I tried to play it the same way I thought Bill would have, to get as many concessions from the salesman as possible. In fairly short order I had traded in my old car. Billy and I drove out in a 1965 light blue Mustang.

It was gorgeous. I loved being behind the wheel. I had paid about $2,700 for the car. I knew my husband probably could have gotten a better price for it, but I didn't care. If I was living on my own and figuring out my life on my own, at least I was doing it driving the

Mustang of my choice. Best deal, phooey. It was my car and that was all that mattered.

That summer I also went out on a couple of dates. An old friend of ours, a woman who had lived across the street from us on Rutherford Drive, was divorced and dated quite a bit. We had always been friendly. When Bill moved out, she was definitely sympathetic and understood what I was going through. After giving me a little time to get over the shock of being on my own again, she suggested we double-date.

"I've met somebody I think you'd like," she told me.

I gave it a try a couple of times, but dating felt pretty strange after so many years of marriage. And this was the start of the sexual revolution, when everything was loosening up in terms of what "respectable" people might be willing to do. Guys no longer seemed to think a gal's company for an evening was enough, as they had when I was a young woman. I didn't find the men she set me up with to be even remotely interesting or attractive, so when they started making moves on me I figured it was time to call it a night and go home alone. I still felt married, and I sure wasn't ready to jump into bed with someone I had just met.

And every single time I got home from a date Billy would tell me, "Dad called while you were out."

My husband and I were still working in the same building every weekday. If Bill had something to say to me, he could and did do it at work. He almost never called me at home. But the few times that I actually went out on a date with another man, Bill called the house asking for me while I was gone. Maybe he was watching the house or keeping an eye on me; I don't know. But when it happened the third time, I thought it was pretty odd and no coincidence.

We hadn't talked about a divorce. In fact, the idea never entered my mind. It was too ingrained in me that marriage is forever. I had asked Bill to move out because I couldn't stand the situation any longer, but I didn't want to *not* be married to him. I just wanted him to straighten up and stop the affair with Alice, even though he never, ever admitted anything was going on between them.

Bill was living by himself in a small apartment. I'm sure he was spending a lot of time with Alice. After I thought it over, that didn't seem like such a bad idea. I never expected the relationship to last. The two compliments Bill always gave me were to tell me that I was beautiful and—when I had worked out something particularly complex or difficult for the business—to praise me for being so smart. When Bill was encouraging me to value myself more, he would always mention my good looks *and* my intelligence as if those were the two most important attributes a person could have.

Alice was beautiful, but in my opinion—which of course was biased—she was an airhead. Her outfits were always perfectly put together and she was a charming saleswoman, but that's about as far as it went. I could see this clearly, of course, and suspected Bill would get tired of her once he figured out there wasn't much under the surface.

And I had spoiled Bill pretty thoroughly, both at home and at the office. He was used to having a woman support him in everything he did. A salesman needs someone to back him up by bolstering his confidence and taking care of all the petty details. I had done that and more. Somehow I couldn't picture airhead Alice doing the same for Bill. In fact, I figured that she was enough like Bill to unconsciously expect him to bolster and support *her*. So I had a fairly strong suspicion that the more time Bill and Alice spent together and the more they really got to know each other, the less likely it was their relationship would become anything permanent or lasting. But I couldn't depend on that happening, and I had no idea how long it might take for Bill to wise up—if he ever did.

I dropped by Bill's apartment once. We had been somewhere nearby on a business matter, and he suggested I stop and see his place. It was sparsely furnished, mostly with our household leftovers. It looked highly temporary, as if he didn't expect to stay long. While we were there, Bill took me in his arms and kissed me. It felt right and wonderful. But later on when I was alone, thinking about our brief closeness brought back all my pain and despair. I decided I wouldn't go over to Bill's apartment again, and he never invited me. I think the emotional turmoil was too much for both of us. We needed some distance.

I started looking for a job and searching for someone to replace me at our business. Neither proved as easy as I expected. I applied to be a secretary at a local school, but they wouldn't even interview me, saying I was way overqualified. I'd been running a rapidly growing business for several years, and I think everybody but me realized I had become much more than a secretary.

At the same time, I didn't see how we were going to find someone who could take my place. The business had sort of grown up all around me. Bill was in charge of the sales force, but I kept tabs on everything else in the office and warehouse. Jeannette could have done the job, but she wasn't at all interested. I couldn't blame her. It was a lot of work. I had been willing to take it all on only because it was a labor of love. But it was too painful for me to stay at the company Bill and I had built together—I needed to get out. So I kept applying for likely sounding jobs for myself while Bill and I interviewed candidates to be office manager in my place.

The trouble was that no matter who we talked to, I just never felt we had someone who could run the whole business. I know it might sound like I was torpedoing the idea of anyone being able to take my place to prove I was somehow indispensable to Bill. I don't think that was it at all. I loved that company. I had nursed it along for years, and I didn't want to see it go on the rocks. And as one of its owners, I had a financial stake in its continued success. I really did want to find someone to replace me who I felt could do it all and do it well.

That person was proving hard to find. Maybe we were expecting too much. I was well aware that Bill demanded perfection in our deliveries and customer service. He also took a smoothly running office and warehouse for granted. He credited his great sales team for our company's success, but I knew it was equally crucial to always have the stock on hand, to get it to the customers exactly as ordered and on time, and to tactfully clear up any of the inevitable mix-ups.

In a way, I think Bill knew that too, because he agreed with me that none of the women who had applied for the job had enough experience and executive backbone to pull it all together. So we kept looking, just as I kept searching for a job to give me some income and something to do all day long after I left the company.

In late August, Patti came home from Hawaii and moved into St. Elizabeth's, a home for unwed mothers in San Francisco. Patti, now seventeen, got tutoring so she could keep up with her high school classes and not fall behind. The place had a dedicated social worker who met several times with Billy and Patti to talk about what might happen after the baby came. In addition to the counseling sessions, Patti snuck out of St. Elizabeth's a number of times to see Billy. No matter how hard the officials and Patti's parents tried, they just couldn't keep those two apart. But as an unwed father, Billy had absolutely no legal rights and no say in any decisions. Patti's parents and the authorities at St. Elizabeth's were pushing heavily for adoption as the best option for the baby. Billy, now nineteen, desperately wanted to get married so that he and Patti could raise their child together. Patti's parents wouldn't hear of it.

On October 19, 1965, my granddaughter was born at St. Elizabeth's. Patti managed to call me right away, to give me the happy news.

"I had a baby girl, whom I'm going to name Shannon, and she has a dimple in her chin just like Billy," Patti told me.

I was deliriously happy that Patti and the baby were well and fearfully anxious about the future all at the same time. Billy got to go see his daughter. He told me later it was love at first sight. Patti's parents, the O'Rourkes, also got to visit their granddaughter, but Billy asked me not to go, as the situation was too complicated. What he didn't tell me was that the O'Rourkes had demanded that I not be allowed to see the baby.

After a few days, Billy and Patti spent one final hour with their daughter at St. Elizabeth's, and then Shannon was whisked away to a foster home. Patti went home to live with her parents, who still insisted she not see Billy at all. The O'Rourkes were convinced that without contact Patti would forget Billy and get on with her life. Patti had exactly thirty days from when she surrendered her baby to decide whether or not to put her daughter up for adoption. A big part of that decision depended on the O'Rourkes, who were still convinced that adoption was best for the child.

Patti had agreed to follow her parents wishes, but she wasn't at all happy with her decision. And she really wasn't happy about the idea of never seeing Billy again. She kept insisting she had an undying love for Billy. That statement only made her parents more confident that their young-looking daughter was immature and would get over it.

There was definitely a negative attitude toward unwed mothers at the time, but Patti never appeared to feel she had done anything wrong. She loved Billy. What had happened between them felt natural to her. Although their baby had been sent away and her parents were keeping them apart, both Patti and Billy seemed optimistic that things would work out.

For me it was an extremely painful situation. I had a beautiful, wonderful granddaughter and I couldn't go see her. If she was adopted, I might never see her at all. That thought tore me up inside. I would watch a woman walk by with a tiny baby in her arms and think, *That could be my grandbaby. Maybe she looks just like that.* Then my eyes would fill up with tears, and I'd have to go off and find a place to have a good long cry.

I kept trying to place my trust in God and know that things would work out, but it was hard to do. I ached inside. I couldn't bear the fact that my flesh and blood could be somewhere in the world and I might never know where. I wanted to hold her. I wanted to see her smile and cry. I wanted to watch my first grandchild grow up. So it was a long thirty days as we waited to see what the O'Rourkes and Patti would do. It appeared more and more likely that Shannon would be put up for adoption.

In early November we finally found a woman whom Bill and I both thought might be able to take my place at William G. Willitts and Associates. She wasn't perfect, but I felt she had enough on the ball to give it a good shot. I hadn't found a job for myself yet. We hired her anyway and agreed she would start in mid-December.

Bill was out of my house, I would soon be out of the company, and it looked like my infant granddaughter could be heading off to an unknown future where she would be forever out of my reach. Everything seemed bleak. I kept trudging through each day, going ahead the only way I knew how. There didn't seem to be much sweet sugar in my cup at all. Then just a few days before the end of the thirty-day decision period, Billy phoned me. His voice was filled with joy. The O'Rourkes had finally relented. He and Patti were going to get married and keep Shannon.

Hallelujah.

I said a quick prayer of gratitude and repeated it continually over the next few days as we got ready for a quick wedding. It turns out that every time Mrs. O'Rourke had tried to talk with Patti about giving Shannon up for adoption and options for Patti's future, all Patti would talk about was Billy and how much she loved him. Patti also kept talking with Billy on the phone every chance she got and sneaking out to see him.

"I give up!" Mrs. O'Rourke finally said. "You can't seem to get over him, and you'll probably just get pregnant again. You might as well get married."

It may not have been a very romantic sentiment, but it was exactly what Patti and Billy wanted to hear. Once they made up their minds, the O'Rourkes moved rapidly. They arranged for a wedding in their local Catholic church on the day before Thanksgiving. In addition to the bride and groom, there were only about a dozen people at the marriage ceremony. The O'Rourkes attended along with a couple of Patti's aunts. My sister Eda and her husband, Bacci, came, as well as my nephews Fred and Beb and their wives, plus Bill and me.

Bill and I sat side by side for the service, but I didn't pay much attention to him. I was focused on the joy of Patti and Billy finally saying their wedding vows. Afterward the O'Rourkes had us all over for champagne at their house. Bill was courteous as usual, staying by my side and acting the role of a gentleman. I had eyes only for the happy bride and groom. My baby boy had become a handsome young man, a husband and a father. Soon I would be able to see my precious grand-baby, Shannon, who would grow up as part of our family instead of with strangers. All I could think about was how wonderful it was after so many months of confusion and worry.

The next morning was Thanksgiving Day. I woke up as usual and started getting ready to go over to Eda's house for Thanksgiving dinner. The phone rang and I answered it, figuring it was Eda asking me to bring something she needed or to stop at the store for a last-minute item. Instead of Eda it was Bill. He spoke intently, as if he had been thinking about what he was going to say and wanted to pick just the right words.

"Elda, I can't go on this way," he told me. "I haven't slept all night because I've been thinking about you. I just can't live like this anymore."

My heart sang. It was like sunshine and a rainbow after a storm.

"I need you, Elda," Bill told me. "I want you back in my life. I want to be back in your life."

I had been waiting for him to say those words. I had been hoping that he would smarten up and realize what a precious thing he was in danger of losing—me. We had been separated more than four months, and I had pretty much given up hope. This call from Bill felt like a miracle.

"I want to come home," Bill said quietly.

In spite of all the anguish, in spite of all the difficulties we had been through, I still loved my husband with all my heart and I told him so.

That afternoon Bill went with me for Thanksgiving dinner at Bacci and Eda's, just as he had for so many years. I called Eda ahead of time and told her Bill was coming. Mercifully Eda didn't ask any questions but just put another plate on the table. Most of the dinner conversation was about Billy and Patti's wedding. That was fortunate because I don't think Bill and I could have answered any questions about the two of us even if someone had asked. It was all too new, too uncertain.

That night Bill came home with me to our house on Woodside Drive and we started married life once again. He kept his furniture in his apartment until his rent ran out at the end of the month, but the day after Thanksgiving he moved his clothes back into his custom-built closets, right next to mine. The day after Thanksgiving was also when Billy and Patti borrowed my Mustang to fetch Shannon. They had rented a small apartment in San Anselmo, and that's where they spent their first two nights as a married couple. The day after Thanksgiving they signed all the proper paperwork to get their daughter back. Then they brought her home.

As we all settled into our new lives, I recalled Mamma's final blessing to me, saying how lucky I was to have Bill and Billy in my life. After a long time where I couldn't see the wisdom in her words, they began to ring true again. Even though my husband and son sometimes seemed to create the bitter coffee in my cup, they provided the taste of sugar as well.

CHAPTER 18

Resuming our marriage wasn't just a matter of Bill and I embracing and everything being fine and dandy. We sort of had to get used to each other again. Living separately for more than four months had shattered all the daily patterns that married couples follow without thinking. We needed to re-create our joint life, kind of like a quilt that's been taken apart and then reassembled piece by piece into a different but similar design.

One of the first things Bill wanted me to do was to sell my Mustang. He had all kinds of reasons why.

"Elda, you just didn't get a good deal on that car. We can get you something much better," he told me.

I believed him at the time. Now I wonder if he had other reasons for wanting me to get rid of that flashy car. I think my buying the Mustang really surprised Bill. Instead of falling to pieces without him, I went out and got exactly what I wanted. The car was an unconscious symbol of my independence—and the first thing to go when we got back together. By January the Mustang was sold and I had a different vehicle. I don't even remember what it was, but I'm sure it was a lot more sedate than my lovely light blue 1965 Mustang.

The next thing we got rid of was that cold showpiece of a house on Woodside Drive. For all its luxury, it hadn't brought us much happiness. In a way, that house violated our basic values. Although Bill craved success and I desperately needed security, we both eventually realized that love and family were far more important to us than fancy things or showy places.

A real estate agent told me about a house that was in foreclosure in the nearby town of San Rafael. The place was for sale real cheap because the owner had died. All we had to do was pay the back taxes and delinquent payments—so we grabbed it. We told ourselves that with Billy married and out on his own, a smaller home made more sense. I think we both just wanted out of the Woodside Drive house with all of its bad memories.

Our new home wasn't a dump by any means. It may not have been as fancy as the old place, but it was still real classy. It had three bedrooms, an inground swimming pool, and a nice view. We hadn't stepped down in the world. It was more like we had lost our need to show off, so we picked a place to live that was more real, more homey, and more comfortable. We could still entertain business customers there—and we did, although not as lavishly as before—but it also felt like our home in a way the Woodside place never did.

For years Bill told a story about a salesman he knew who always wore a big, fancy diamond ring. The man would flash it in everyone's face at the slightest opportunity. This man was really obnoxious about that ring. One day the salesman dropped by and wasn't wearing his big diamond.

"Where's your ring?" Bill asked him.

"I'm a success now," the man replied. "I don't need it anymore."

I think our Woodside Drive home was Bill's diamond ring. Once he realized he had all the things he really wanted, he was able to let go of that house. Our business was a success, and I think Bill finally knew in his heart that it wasn't going to suddenly go away. Even if he stopped pushing every minute for the next sale, the next goal, the next challenge, Bill had "made it" financially—he wasn't ever going to be poor again.

So we sold most of our fancy furniture and kept only the pieces we really liked, the ones that would fit comfortably in our new home. Because the master bedroom was a lot smaller, we pushed our twin beds together to make a king-size bed. It was a minor change, and at the time I didn't think much about it. Now I see it was important. Just as our beds were back side by side instead of pushed apart, so were we. Bill and I started spending time together. We listened more and communicated better. It was awkward at first and it didn't happen overnight, but we started building a better relationship, step by step. Gradually I learned to trust him again, and we fell back in love with each other.

It helped that Bill wasn't traveling the way he had before. We had plenty of salespeople to cover the territories, so Bill just supervised. He did go to gift shows occasionally, in places like Hawaii and Florida. The difference was that now I went with him. We were much more of a team, and I could tell that Bill valued both my companionship on these trips and my opinions as we decided which merchandise our company should carry.

Alice still worked for Willitts and Associates, but she stayed out of my way. After a while she made a point of coming into the office to introduce me to her new boyfriend. Bill was there too. I felt pretty confident. I had won Bill back, and Alice was clearly showing us that she had moved on. In fact, after dating hot and heavy for a while, Alice and her boyfriend got married.

It may be hard for some people to understand why I took Bill back into my life, but I truly believe in the power of forgiveness. It took time, but eventually I was able to completely forgive both him and Alice, which left me free to enjoy my life. Staying hurt, bitter, angry, or resentful takes time and energy. It gets in the way of living fully. Truly forgiving and moving on gives room for new things—good things—to happen. Forgiving Bill and Alice wasn't easy, but for me it was worth it.

About a year or so after we got back together, Bill and I were in San Francisco on business. As we walked by a large North Beach hall we heard one of our favorite songs being played by a band at a wedding reception. The front doors were wide open. Bill and I looked at each other, and we just couldn't resist. Without a word he took my arm and escorted me onto the dance floor, where we moved blissfully to the beautiful music. After the song ended we strolled out again with no one any the wiser that we weren't invited guests. It was a small but magical moment that still makes me smile when I think about it.

It seems to me that over the years we melded Bill's midwestern practicality with the warmth of my Italian upbringing, and we were both the better for it. We started the process early in our marriage, and we continued it after we were reunited. The blending didn't always go smoothly—I felt at times that Bill was trying to make me more like him than vice versa—but the end result was that together we became more than we could have been separately.

Unfortunately Billy and Patti were having a pretty rocky time trying to make a go of their marriage. In 1968 they split up and Patti filed for divorce. They had been married less than three years. Billy came to live with us. Patti and little Shannon moved in with Patti's folks. Billy had visiting rights with his daughter on the weekends. Once again the O'Rourkes made sure Patti never saw Billy. They wouldn't allow her to talk with him when he came to pick up or drop off Shannon. He was never allowed inside the house. As she had before, Mrs. O'Rourke figured that if Patti was kept away from Billy, she would get over him and start a new life without him.

At one point Mrs. O'Rourke called me to tell me what a horrible son I had raised. She went on and on about how awful Billy was and what a terrible marriage he and Patti had.

"It takes two to tango," I snapped back at her.

I may not have approved of everything Billy was doing, but he was my son and defending him came naturally. And there were plenty of reasons for me to be proud of Billy. I realized he was still fairly immature, but he had started to settle down a bit. He'd turned into a clean-cut, hardworking young man. He was learning to be a full-fledged plumber and seemed to enjoy his job. When we would drive around together, he'd point out the high-rise buildings he had worked on. His voice was full of pride as he described the various projects. It meant a lot to me to see him starting to have some direction in his life. It meant a lot to my husband too. Bill began accepting Billy more, and the friction between them lessened quite a bit.

The distance between Billy and Patti eased up as well, thanks to a twist of fate. While Patti's parents were on a short vacation, Patti was driving around town, running errands. She glanced at the car next to her at a stop sign and realized the driver was Billy. Rolling down their car windows, they started talking. They drove to her home and spent hours discussing their marriage, their lives, and the fact that they still loved each other. And that they both loved Shannon. I don't know exactly what they said, but in the end Patti stopped the divorce proceedings and moved back in with Billy.

After a bit, Billy and Patty split up again only to reunite after a short separation. It was hard for them to make things work when they were together, but apparently it was even harder for them to stay apart.

Meanwhile Bill's and my travels were becoming even more adventurous. Early in 1969 we went to Tahiti and Moorea in search of a sunscreen tanning lotion to sell in our business. The French Polynesian islands were so lovely. We spent three days on Tahiti with its gorgeous black-sand beaches, then flew over to the neighboring island of Moorea, which was even more exquisite. At this point, I loved my life at home, and being able to travel only made things better.

In August 1969 my oldest sister Beppa and her husband, Giuseppe, celebrated their fiftieth wedding anniversary. Their son and daughter-in-law, Bruno and Virginia, rented a large hall and threw a huge party with all their family and friends. It seemed only a short time since I had watched Beppa get ready for her wedding, donning her simple white dress and threading orange blossoms into her veil. Now it was their golden anniversary and they had a huge room full of people congratulating them and wishing them well.

As a gift, a few days after the party Bruno and Virginia took Beppa and Giuseppe for a vacation at Lake Tahoe, a beautiful resort high in the Sierras right on the California-Nevada border. They had booked rooms in a first-class hotel and planned to see the shows, enjoy the fancy foods, and maybe gamble a bit at the casinos.

Several nights later the phone rang long after Bill and I had gone to bed. I answered it, still half asleep. I could barely understand Bruno's voice. He was crying so hard that it was difficult to figure out what he was trying to say. He had to repeat himself several times before the meaning of his words penetrated my sleep-fogged brain.

"My mother dropped dead of a heart attack, right in our hotel room," he told me, sobbing.

Bruno asked us to come to Tahoe and help him. We got up, dressed, threw a few things into our overnight bags, and hopped in our car. It took several hours to drive from Marin County to Lake Tahoe. When we finally did arrive, it all felt unreal. The ground level of the hotel held a brightly lit casino, full of people drinking and gambling. I kept thinking that my oldest sister was dead upstairs. Beppa, with her stern facade and generous soul, was gone. Her heart had stopped beating. It was hard to take it in, to look around at all the people playing blackjack, ordering more drinks, putting coins in the slot machines, and doing everything they could to have a good time, knowing that Beppa was upstairs, dead. At the same time it occurred to me that since we all have to die, what could be better than in the middle of celebrating your fiftieth wedding anniversary? Perhaps it wasn't such a bad way for my oldest sister to leave this world, but it was rough on those of us left behind.

Bill and I helped Bruno, Giuseppe, and Virginia make all the arrangements to have Beppa's body brought back to the Bay Area for a big family funeral. It was held at Sts. Peter and Paul Church, the same as for Mamma. The place was packed. Beppa and Giuseppe had always lived in North Beach and had lots of friends in the area. Afterward Beppa was buried in a Catholic cemetery in Colma. The pallbearers laid white flowers on her casket just as they had for Mamma.

As far as I know Rico didn't attend the services, but the rest of the family did. We were sad, but we had known something like this would happen sooner or later. Beppa was the oldest of the eight children and had lived to be eighty-one. We felt she had a full life. And by that time we were all pretty aware that we were not immortal.

Several months later, early in 1970, Joe told me that Rico was in the hospital, dying of prostate cancer.

"He's your brother. You should go see him, to say good-bye," Joe told me—several times.

At first I refused to go. I had so many mixed emotions. There was still overwhelming fear inside me any time I thought of Rico. But my husband said visiting Rico was the right thing to do.

"He's your brother, Elda. We need to go," Bill said, echoing Joe's words.

So I went. It was a short visit. What can you say to a man like that who is dying, and he knows it and you know it? And what do you say to someone with whom you had such a tortured past? I stammered a bit and then left. I didn't feel any sense of satisfaction at having done my duty to my brother. I didn't feel I had done my duty. I was still afraid of Rico. Nothing had changed just because I went to see him while he was dying in the hospital. I didn't feel much of anything except to wish that I could have somehow handled things better, years before.

I know I said that I believe in the power of forgiveness. I think that even though I was always afraid of Rico, in my heart I had forgiven him. Deep down I knew that the way Rico had acted wasn't his fault. Perhaps the person I couldn't forgive was myself.

Rico died shortly after my visit. Joe took care of all the funeral details, and my nephew Fred tells me I attended the service. I don't recall any of it. It's just a blank spot in my mind. But afterward my fear of Rico began to fade away. I think I had always known it would take his death or mine to erase the past. I wish I could say I had made peace with him at the end, but at least I was able to let go of the terror that had gripped me for so many years. It's kind of sad that relief was the strongest emotion I felt at his death, but that's how it was.

Rico was buried in the Italian cemetery, in the same crypt as our parents. Joe had bought a four-person site so that eventually he and his wife, Annette, could be buried next to Babbo and Mamma. There wasn't really room for Rico, but Joe arranged for Rico's coffin to be sort of squeezed into the middle, in the space they used to lower the bodies to put them into either side of the underground vault. Babbo's and Mamma's names had already been carved onto the crypt's marker stone. There was only enough room for Joe and Annette's names, when their times came. So Rico lay there unidentified.

Many years later, after Joe and Annette were already dead and buried in the spots reserved for them, I had a narrow piece of stone carved with Rico's name. Installed on top of the crypt, the nameplate was much smaller than a standard grave marker, but it was solid marble and looked good. It was expensive to have it done, but it gave me peace of mind.

It had bothered me that Rico was buried there with no way to show he had even existed. And he did exist, once. When I was a little girl and then as a young woman with my first job, he had been my beloved older brother. He had wined and dined me, made me laugh, and made me feel like a lady. I needed to honor that. Maybe paying for that nameplate was my way of finally forgiving myself for not finding a better answer to the puzzle that was Rico. And maybe having his name added to the family crypt was a way to heal my relationship with him after he was dead and gone. Forgiveness and healing are always the best way go—sometimes it just takes me a long time to get there.

CHAPTER 19

When my grandson Greg was born in September 1970, it was a scene straight out of a movie. My son Billy rushed out of the delivery room and—with a big grin plastered across his face—shouted, "It's a boy!"

By this time Billy and Patti's marriage had gradually become more and more solid. It was clear that they were committed to making things work between them. With a little financial help from Bill and me, early in 1970 they managed to scrape together enough money for a down payment. They bought their first home, in San Anselmo. And Patti's parents had finally accepted Billy as their son-in-law, so we were on much more friendly terms. With five-year-old Shannon at home with Patti's sister, all four of us grandparents were holding a nervous vigil in the hospital waiting room when Billy burst in with his happy announcement. It was a classic family moment.

Greg's birth was followed a little over a year later by the arrival of our second grandson, Jason, in December 1971. This time we didn't gather in the delivery room. Patti's parents stayed home and looked after baby Greg, and I was at our place taking care of little Shannon, now age six. Billy called me with the good news that mother and baby were fine.

"You've got another brother," I happily told Shannon.

She burst into tears.

"Why would I want another brother?" Shannon asked me. "The one I have now stepped all over my phonograph record and broke it."

I tried to comfort her, but it was hard not to laugh. Having been the only female in a house with a husband and a son, I certainly understood her point of view. But I rejoiced quietly to myself at this newest addition to our family. All of my grandbabies were so beautiful, so special. They made me feel blessed in a way that all our business and financial achievements could never really match. Security and success were still important to me and to Bill, but family was even more precious and cherished.

Bill and I were working as a team again, and things were going well. By 1970, William G. Willitts and Associates had a large sales force plus three warehouse employees as well as one part-time and four full-time office workers. We'd outgrown our original building, so we moved to a big warehouse in Greenbrae, only a short distance from our home. And on the advice of our insurance agent and our accountant, 1970 was the year we incorporated our business. The company was now William G. Willitts and Associates, Inc. We'd come a long way in less than ten years.

On one business trip, Bill and I headed off to Tokyo, searching for musical gift items. I loved Japan, but its cuisine was just a bit too exotic as a steady diet for this Italian-American peasant. I wanted something familiar to eat, something I could recognize as real food. So

Bill and I visited the Japan World Exposition and made a beeline for the Italian pavilion. I wolfed down pasta until I thought my stomach would burst, but boy was I happy.

That may have influenced our decision a while later to head for Europe on a business trip. This was my first journey to the continent since 1916, when my family left, traveling in steerage on a steamship. We returned in a bit better style, making first-class business forays to England, Switzerland, Germany, and Italy. We were after new imported gift lines, especially novelty music boxes. At the tail end of our trip, we ended up in the beautiful spa resort town of Montecatini, Italy—not far from my birthplace in Lucca. In Montecatini we visited my father's niece, Cesarina Cioni, who had lived with my family for several years before we left for America. She was in her mid-twenties when we left. She was invited to come to America with us but decided to stay in Italy, where she had a job and other relatives nearby.

Although I was too young when we left Italy to remember Cesarina clearly, my sister Algisa had been writing to her for many years. When we finally met, Cesarina and I just looked at each other and then hugged tightly. She was seventy and I was sixty. We hadn't seen each other for fifty-five years, but I felt as if I had known her all my life. Somehow our souls recognized each other. I felt such a strong kinship with her.

Cesarina was a wonderful tour guide, giving me a real feel for the beauty of everyday life in my native country. We made one trip to my birth town of Lucca, but we didn't know where my old family home was and no one seemed to remember anything about the Del Binos. It felt rather odd, like trying to revisit a past I didn't remember clearly. Everything was familiar and unfamiliar all at the same time. The few hours we spent in Lucca just sped by.

Several more business trips followed for Bill and me, ranging from trade shows in the states and Hawaii to a longer buying trip to Australia and New Zealand. I got rather jet-lagged at times, but my husband thrived on the challenge and adventure.

Things were going well for Billy too. In 1972 he signed up for an extensive master-plumber training course that would put him at the top of his profession. One night he stopped by to see us after his classes. He did that from time to time, calling ahead to say he'd drop by for a late dinner. On this particular occasion Bill and I had already eaten, but I fixed a steak for Billy. Then we sat down at the table with him to talk while he ate. Just before he left, Billy turned to me and asked, "Mom, if Dad died would you be able to run the business without him?"

"No, I couldn't," I told Billy without any hesitation. I had a high opinion of Bill's sales skills and knew I couldn't match them. Then Billy turned to his Dad.

"Could you run the business without Mom?"

"I think so," was Bill's quick answer.

That was all Billy said. He left soon after that.

"What was that all about?" I asked Bill.

"I sure don't know," Bill replied, shaking his head. We had both given up trying to interest Billy in our company, and we could see that he was doing well as a plumber. Both Bill and I had finally accepted that Billy had chosen his own course in life. So we just shrugged our shoulders and forgot about Billy's questions.

A week later our son dropped by our house again. This time he came straight to the point.

"Dad, I'd love to enter the business with you," Billy told him, looking Bill directly in the eye.

I don't know how my husband felt, but I was astonished and delighted all at the same time. Having given up all thought of Billy joining the company, here we were getting exactly what we had yearned for. Of course Bill's reply was more logical than my quick spark of intense joy.

"A man has to like whatever it is he's doing because he's going to be doing it the rest of his life," Bill said. "If you've already got a job that you enjoy now, don't change it."

I know that was a hard thing for my husband to say considering how much Bill had always wanted Billy to keep our business going after we were gone.

Billy told us that he was doing well as a plumber and enjoying it but that he'd finally realized he was using his brawn but not his brain—and that he did have a brain.

"I've started wondering just how long my back will hold out, lifting bathtubs, showers, and toilets all day," Billy said.

Our son was also wondering whether he could accomplish more in this world than just installing plumbing fixtures. He thought William G. Willitts and Associates, Inc., might be a way to find out. But my husband was cautious and still wasn't sold on the sudden switch.

"I'd love to have you in the business, but first I want you to finish your schooling and become a master plumber," Bill said. "Then if you don't like working in our company, you'll have something to fall back on."

So after qualifying as a master plumber, in 1973 Billy Willitts started work in the warehouse of William G. Willitts and Associates, Inc. His dad was determined that our son would know the company from the ground up before he took charge. After Billy proved himself in the warehouse, he was given a sales territory. He turned out to be just as good at charming the customers as his father had been.

With two strong egos in the company—make that three since I wasn't exactly a shrinking violet—everything wasn't always sweetness and light, but things went well. The company continued to prosper. After all those unsettling years—Billy's rebellion, Alice, the separation, Patti getting pregnant—we seemed to have settled into the good times. Certainly there were problems to be dealt with, but they didn't feel insurmountable. We all were healthy and reasonably happy. I had a lot to be thankful for.

Because of my breast cancer history, I had a checkup with my doctor every six months, but things always looked good. When they had removed my right breast, my doctor told me it was likely I'd eventually develop cancer in my left breast as well. I heard what he said, but I didn't believe it. I was sure I was cancer-free for good and it would never return.

By January 1975 it had been more than fifteen years since my mastectomy. That's when my luck ran out. During a routine checkup, my doctor discovered a lump in my remaining breast. He immediately referred me to a surgeon, and I once again found myself scheduled for an operation in Marin General Hospital, not knowing if my breast would be there when I woke up. But medical techniques and attitudes had improved quite a bit since 1959. I was given a lot more details about possible options and what might happen during the surgery. The doctors acted less like gods and more like part of my team in the battle against this disease. And I wasn't an emotional wreck the way I had been in 1959. Time hadn't dimmed the impact of that amazing moment in my garden, when I had felt God telling me I was going to live. Deep down I still felt that certainty, that serenity.

The whole situation—waiting for the surgery date, wondering what the biopsy would show, worrying that I was facing a second bout with cancer—was much harder on Bill. Once again things were totally out of his control and there was at least a possibility he could lose me. Bill didn't talk about what he was feeling, but as we prepared for the operation he had trouble concentrating—which wasn't at all like him—and I could tell when worry got the better of him.

The lump was malignant, and I had a second mastectomy. It may sound odd, but with both breasts gone I felt more balanced, more whole. I felt normal again; both sides of my chest matched. My new incision—which was much smaller than the one from 1959—healed cleanly and quickly and there was no need for chemotherapy or radiation.

Of course it was terrible having cancer again, and I would have avoided it if I could. But the second time around was a whole lot easier compared to what I had gone through sixteen years earlier. In terms of it being socially acceptable for people to talk about the disease, it was as different as night and day. In 1959 the whole subject was taboo. By 1975 I felt comfortable telling my family and friends all about what was happening to me. And I got a lot of support and encouragement. Once again I ended up cancer-free after the operation. It did take several months for me to rebuild my physical strength, but by spring I was back to my old self and raring to go.

And off Bill and I went, for a whole series of journeys—annual trade shows in Hawaii, a buying excursion to Hong Kong, and several other places. We bought an RV and started taking purely recreational trips. Since Bill loved camping and I hated it, the RV was a great compromise. Give me a comfy bed and a bathroom of our own and I'm fine. We could go anywhere—and we did. We chugged up and down the California coast on beautiful, twisty Highway 1. We headed down to Arizona and the Grand Canyon, and anywhere else that struck our fancy. Since we loved the desert in the wintertime, we got in the habit of taking the RV to Southern California at the beginning of each year to spend a few days in a small town outside of Palm Springs.

Although it was a little hard for Bill to relinquish the reins, Billy was taking increasing control of the business. Bill and I were gradually preparing emotionally and financially for our retirement. In 1976 I turned sixty-five and applied for Social Security. To do that I had to send away to Italy for an official copy of my birth certificate. When it arrived, I was shocked to see that my birth date was April 29, 1909; not April 28, 1911. I was totally confused.

"Bill, look at this," I told my husband. "I'm two years older than I thought I was."

He glanced at the birth certificate.

"So what?" he replied. It seemed pretty trivial to him.

I thought back to years earlier, when my sister Eda had made that unexpected trip to my office to tell me I was two years younger than we had thought. From that point on I assumed I had been born April 28, 1911. I used that date on every form I had ever filled out and on every official application I'd ever filed for anything. As far as I knew, it was my birth date and I was sixty-five. But my official birth certificate said I was born on April 29, 1909. That meant I was sixty-seven years old. How could Eda have made such a mistake? I called her right away.

"Eda, guess what? I got a copy of my birth certificate and it says I'm sixty-seven years old not sixty-five," I told her excitedly.

Everyone in the family knew that Eda was exactly six years and three months older than me. If I was two years older, so was Eda.

"Shhhh," she hissed sharply. "Don't tell anyone. Promise me you'll never tell anyone. Promise me. No one must ever know. Promise me."

There was such incredible intensity in Eda's voice and she was so upset and so insistent that I promised her repeatedly I'd never tell anyone. I spent the entire phone conversation reassuring Eda that no one would ever find out that we were both two years older than we had said we were. I was so busy telling her I'd keep the secret that I never thought to ask her why she changed our ages to make us two years younger. After I got off the phone I told Bill that Eda had lied about my birth date so she could be two years younger.

"That's Eda," he laughed, not at all upset by the news. "That's our Eda."

It's true that Eda never did like telling anyone her age.

"It's none of your business," she'd say if anyone asked. "That's something I don't tell anyone."

I still don't know why Eda wanted us to be two years younger. She and I never talked about it again, and her secret eventually went to the grave with her. I kept my promise to keep silent until years later, when other members of my family saw a copy of my birth certificate and found out my real age and birth date. By then Eda was dead, and I didn't see any harm in telling everyone the truth.

Why the lie? Why was that secret so important to Eda? Maybe when she first met Bacci, her future husband, Eda shaved a few years off her age out of vanity. Since everyone in the family knew she was exactly six years and three months older than me, she had to change my age as well to keep her deception from being discovered. I suppose that in 1927 a twenty-six-year-old woman might be considered an unwanted old maid, while a twenty-four-year-old girl was still a desirable prospect as a bride.

The truth is, I have absolutely no idea what prompted Eda's little deception or why it was so vitally important to her that it stay hidden. It certainly added an odd note to my life. At the age of sixty-five— make that sixty-seven—I found out that instead of being two years and four months younger than my husband, I was only four months younger. Ever since Eda had told me her little white lie, I had believed I was five years old when our ship sailed into New York Harbor and we saw the Statue of Liberty. I was actually seven years old. When I first met and started dating twenty-two-year-old Louis, I was twenty-five, not twenty-three like I thought. And when I decided I was destined to be a heartbroken old maid at age twenty-eight, almost twenty-nine, I was really thirty and about to turn thirty-one. When I married Bill, I was thirty-one, almost thirty-two, not twenty-nine going on thirty. When Billy was born, I was thirty-seven, not thirty-five. No wonder I didn't get pregnant when Bill and I tried to have a second child. My body was thirty-nine, almost forty years old, not age thirty-seven as I thought. So if I try to remember when things happened and exactly how old I was at the time, I have to stop and figure out whether I'm thinking in terms of my biological age or my Eda-age. Because for most of my life I believed my Eda-age was my real one.

Aren't secrets funny things? I was willing to tell people my brother Rico had been committed to a mental hospital but not to reveal that he hit me, blackening my eyes. It took a lot of effort for me to finally start telling the truth. As important as that secret was to me, I believe Eda's little white lie about our ages was just as crucial to her—perhaps more so. I eventually got to the point that I could talk about my secret, but Eda never did. And yet to most people Eda's deception would seem pretty trivial. Then again, other people might have concealed Rico's schizophrenia instead of that one moment of violence.

Whether or not something is a secret depends a lot on the viewpoint and feelings of those involved. I think that we all, every single one of us, have things that we tell to only a few close friends or perhaps only God. I doubt if most people would care about these hidden facts. And who knows? Maybe even God is bored by them. But still we keep our little secrets, at least until we're ready to relinquish them and lighten our load a bit.

No matter what we choose to do, life goes on. And not everything turns out well. In 1974 my fourth-oldest sister, Paolina, had been diagnosed with colon cancer. The doctors performed a colostomy, removing part of her intestines. Paolina did fine for quite a while, but eventually the cancer spread to her bones. She died December 23, 1977, just two days before Christmas. She passed away in the home she had shared for more than thirty years with her son Fred and his wife, Norma. It was a blessing when God took Paolina because to see her suffer was worse than the pain of losing her.

Her family held a big funeral with all the traditional Italian Catholic rituals—a rosary, Mass after church, and a graveside burial service for the family. I couldn't help but notice that although there were lots of children, grandchildren, nieces, nephews, great-nieces, and great-nephews, there were fewer living members of my generation. Time was moving on, and whether I used my real age or the slightly younger one Eda had assigned me, we were all getting older.

CHAPTER 20

I started my first job when I was fifteen years old; Bill began even younger than that. By summer 1977 we were both sixty-seven. Together we had put in more than a hundred years of labor. Most of it involved intense effort and long hours, particularly after we started our own company and worked days, evenings, and weekends. It was time to think about retiring and doing something new with our lives.

We wanted to give the company to Billy, but the accountants and lawyers said if we did that we'd be taxed up to our ears. By this time William G. Willitts and Associates, Inc., was an established business with sixteen employees and multimillion-dollar annual revenues. It was worth quite a bit of money, and no matter how we felt about it we couldn't just hand it over to our son. The government frowned on that sort of gift. So we set it up as an official, legitimate sale but with no real money changing hands. It was all done on paper. Billy bought the company from us, and we loaned him the money to do it. The payments stretched out over several years.

When we found out we couldn't just hand everything to Billy and walk away, my husband wasn't at all upset by the delay. He wanted his son to take over the business, but at the same time Bill didn't really want to let go of his baby, so to speak. He had spent his whole life building his success by making sales and satisfying customers. It was only natural for him to be ambivalent about walking away from it all.

Billy was a different story. He was eager to move on the next stage of his life—ownership of William G. Willitts and Associates, Inc. We would think everything was settled and that the business was about to become his. Then the paper-pushers would come up with one more objection. Any time there was another postponement, it made our son just a little bit crazy. It isn't that Bill and Billy weren't working well together. They were getting along great. It's just that the repeated delays in the change of ownership made Bill happy and Billy frustrated.

And me? As far as I was concerned, the sooner it was done the better. I was ready for Bill and I to move on with our lives without the business. Plus I wanted an end to this last bit of friction between my husband and my son.

Finally all the t's were crossed and all the i's were dotted and everything was ready to go. On June 1, 1978, my husband and I sold our business to our thirty-one-year-old son. The three of us sat in our attorney's office, signing the stacks of papers that made William G. Willitts and Associates, Inc., belong to Billy instead of to Bill and me. Once it was done I think my husband was genuinely happy. He accepted it and was glad to have Billy take over. Bill and I were on the company's payroll for the next six months as "advisers," but we were beginning to look forward to a new life—one that didn't involve going to the office every day, calling on customers, or keeping track of a warehouse full of sales orders and shipments.

We had already bought and moved into our retirement home. About the same time we began the long process of turning the business over to Billy, we started looking around for a new place to live during our "golden years." We searched Marin County and all up and down the East Bay—throughout the greater Bay Area. We must have spent every weekend for at least a year looking at homes for sale. They ranged from cozy condominiums to spacious ranch homes surrounded by open acres and everything in between. At each one Bill found something he liked.

"We could put such-and-such here," he'd say, "and I could fix that up over there."

I'd just shake my head. I didn't know exactly what I wanted, but I was sure I would recognize the perfect place.

"My heart will tell me when we find the right home," I told Bill.

This drove my rational, logical husband absolutely nuts. Each Sunday morning he would pick an area, read the "homes for sale" advertisements in the newspapers, and then we would head out full of hope. But none of the available places made me feel "this is it." My heart was silent.

"Your heart is never going to tell you anything," Bill would say grumpily at the end of each day of searching. "We're going to live where we are now until we die."

The next weekend we'd look through the newspapers and do it all over with the exact same results. It's a wonder we didn't end up divorced after all. Then a friend called to tell me she was talking to me from the patio of her new condominium in the Sonoma Valley. That struck a chord in me. I'd been to Sonoma occasionally when I was growing up, and Bill and I had stopped there several times while on our way to the mineral baths in Calistoga, in the more famous Napa Valley.

Located about sixty miles north of San Francisco, in the heart of Northern California's Wine Country, the Sonoma Valley is a gorgeous stretch of fertile flatland cradled between two mountain ranges. Its southern end spreads out into the San Pablo Bay wetlands. The main valley floor holds a combination of housing developments, rich farmland, open fields, and acres of grapevines. There are no interstate freeways or multilane superhighways—the only routes into and out of the valley are two-lane rural roads, adding to the area's relatively leisurely pace of life. In addition to Sonoma, which is the valley's only officially incorporated city, there are several residential communities, all proud of their sleepy, small-town feel.

At the heart of the city of Sonoma is a lovely plaza with a duck pond, a rock fountain, two playground areas, several picnic tables, and lots of leafy trees arching overhead. And in the center of Sonoma Plaza stands the majestic City Hall, built in the early 1900s. The four sides of the building are identical. The architect designed it that way so every Plaza merchant would have exactly the same view and none could complain about being slighted. That's pure Sonoma, all the way.

The Sonoma Valley was about an hour's drive, more or less—depending on traffic and who was driving—from San Rafael and Marin County. I figured that was close enough that we could still visit Billy, Patti, and our grandchildren as well as serve as "company advisers" for several months. It was also far enough away that my husband wouldn't drive our son crazy by popping up at the office all the time. I decided Sonoma Valley was the best spot for our retirement home, and Bill agreed with me. We started exploring the possibilities. At one point Bill wanted to buy a house in a senior development in the southern end of the valley, but I wanted something smaller and easier to take care of.

One Sunday in April 1978 we visited a Sonoma Valley real estate agent about an ad for a house on one acre. I asked if he had any condominiums listed for sale. There were two. He took us to see those first. Bill loved to garden and really wanted a house with a good-sized yard, but he agreed to go see those condos, I think just to shut me up. I didn't like the first place at all, so we went on to the next one. Bill told me later that when he parked the car in front of the second condo complex, my whole face lit up with delight. I'm not surprised. My heart was singing, loud and clear. Even before we got inside the door I knew we were home.

The place was located on the northern edge of town, just a few blocks from City Hall and the tree-filled Sonoma Plaza, which I adored. The complex hugged a hillside—the edge of a mountain range known as the Mayacamas. From the street I could see that the buildings had creamy, pinkish-white stucco walls topped with red tile roofs. The condos were arranged in a rectangle around a central courtyard, with a driveway and a line of carports outside the right edge of the rectangle. We entered the courtyard through a black, wrought-iron gate complete with graceful curlicues, then followed a cement walkway and a series of small stairways climbing gently toward the back of the complex. Off to our right was a swimming pool glimmering bright blue behind a wrought-iron fence. As we walked past the pool, I saw that the rear of the property was terraced with a low stone wall that looked as if it could have been there for years. The buildings were one-story near the street and two-story in the rear; the front porches of the downstairs units were finished with ten-inch-by-ten-inch terra-cotta tiles, adding to the overall Mediterranean feel of the place.

The condominium for sale was the upstairs unit at the back left corner of the complex. There was a lovely front balcony, two spacious bedrooms, two bathrooms, a small dining area, and a nice kitchen. The dining room and kitchen windows provided restful views of the hillside behind the building. To me it was the perfect layout, the perfect location, the perfect atmosphere. It may have been due to the Mediterranean-style design, with its echoes of my native Italy, but my long-silent heart was singing "home sweet home."

Bill wasn't so sure. We had suddenly reversed roles. I kept seeing all kinds of possibilities, and he was wondering what might be wrong with the place. Bill wanted access to a sauna; there was one in the clubhouse next to the swimming pool. Bill wanted to be able to garden; the agent assured us that with permission from the homeowners' association we could plant things on the hillside behind our unit.

Our unit. That's how I thought of it from the minute I walked in the door. My husband soon ran out of objections, and within a half hour we were signing the papers to seal the deal. We never did see the house on one acre that had been our original destination. When we arrived back home in San Anselmo, Bill suddenly spoke up. In the last year he had bought a small electric organ and was teaching himself how to play it.

"Is there going to be room for the organ?" he asked me. "I won't move there if there's not enough room for the organ."

I think this was his last-ditch attempt to assert some reason and sanity into my highly emotional attachment to what I already thought of as our new home. So we went back the next day with a measuring tape. I found the perfect spot for the organ in the living room near the fireplace. Bill never had a chance. My heart knew the condo was meant to be our home, and that was that. After we moved in and got settled down, Bill loved the place just as much as I did.

We went from a three-bedroom house with a pool and a garage to a two-bedroom condo with a carport. Not everything fit, but the important things did. The master bedroom was fairly large, so there was plenty of room for our two twin beds, still pushed together to make one king-size bed. We hadn't lost the hard-won closeness we'd developed after all the difficulties we'd gone through. There was also space in the condo for most of our other furniture, if not all. And since we were already thinking that someday we'd like to have a little weekend house somewhere—maybe in the desert, maybe in the mountains—we rented a storage space for the extra items and got settled into our new home.

By the time Billy officially bought the company in June 1978 we were already commuting to work from Sonoma. We kept doing that for six more months, and then we were done. It wasn't easy to walk away from the business we had started from scratch, but it helped that we were turning it over to our son. He seemed more than ready to take the lead. It also helped that both Bill and I wanted more time for ourselves. Now our annual trips to Southern California in our RV could last as long as we liked because we no longer had to report back to the office by a certain day.

Originally we had driven south each year and stayed in a motel in Palm Springs. Once we bought the RV we started going to the nearby town of Desert Hot Springs, where there was a trailer park with RV hookups. The place also had a swimming pool and natural mineral water. We loved it because we could just hang out if we wanted, or we could travel around the area to see what we might find.

Maybe it was because he grew up in snowy Michigan, but Bill really adored the desert in the winter months. I liked it, but Bill loved it. Several times we talked about buying a second home in Desert Hot

Springs, but it was hard to find the right place. In winter 1978 we spotted a mobile home we liked and wanted to buy, but the owner didn't want to sell. All the other mobile homes in this park were placed parallel to the street, but this one was on a diagonal, which gave it an amazing view of the San Jacinto Mountains. You could even see the aerial tram that went to the top of the mountain range.

We drove by that same mobile home in winter 1979—after our official retirement—and spotted a "for sale" sign in the window. We jumped at the opportunity. This was a complex where you owned the land as well as the mobile home, which made it a great investment. Most of the owners lived in the park year-round, but we figured it could be our vacation home in winter and spring, when the surrounding desert was relatively cool and extremely beautiful.

It was an extra-wide mobile home—two and a half times the standard width and similar to a small house—and was really top quality. Although some people may look down their noses at "trailers," in many ways this place was even classier than our Sonoma condominium. The mobile home was barely a year old, and everything was still new and shiny. I loved the floor plan, which had a spacious master bedroom at one end. It was separated from the other bedrooms by the living room, kitchen, family room, and even a small den. And there were windows everywhere, giving gorgeous views of the wide-open desert and the nearby mountains.

Of course, we could have bought a fancy home in Palm Springs or some place like that—we had enough money. But our experience in that sterile showplace on Woodside Drive had cured us of the need to buy things just because they were high-priced status symbols. All we wanted was a comfortable vacation house in a beautiful spot. This Desert Hot Springs mobile home fit the bill perfectly. Within a few hours of seeing the "for sale" notice, we were signing all the paperwork to buy the place. We planned to spend each summer and fall in Sonoma, to be near our family, and then live in our desert hideaway in the winter and early spring. We were both so happy. It looked like everything we wanted was simply falling into place.

CHAPTER 21

With the mobile home deal in escrow, Bill and I headed north. We figured we'd take care of a few things in Sonoma and then drive back down to Desert Hot Springs after the sale was complete.

As we drove toward Sonoma, Bill told me about something that had been bothering him for a while—there was blood in his stool. He told me he wasn't really worried, and I wasn't too concerned. Bill had a history of hemorrhoids, and I was sure they had simply flared up again. But Bill added that it was getting worse and there was much more blood than was usual with hemorrhoids. I was still pretty calm, but I decided we needed to get Bill checked out as soon as possible.

Because of my cancer history, I went in for an exam every couple of months, just in case. I had one of my appointments scheduled a couple of days after we arrived back in Sonoma. I never did get my routine checkup. I told the doctor about my husband's symptoms, and they immediately brought Bill into the examining room and did a whole series of tests. As soon as the results came back, the doctor gave us the news: There was a growth in Bill's colon that would have to be removed to find out whether or not it was cancerous.

It was a shock, but we stayed pretty calm. I asked Bill how long he'd been having these problems, and he said not long at all.

"So let's hope that if it's cancer, it's early and they'll catch it in time. If it is cancer, you'll beat it," I told him.

The way I looked at it, if determination had anything to do with the outcome, Bill would make it just fine. We had been down this cancer path twice before, with good results. So once again we headed off to Marin General Hospital for surgery. This time it was Bill on the operating table and me out in the waiting room. The news wasn't good; the growth was malignant. The cancer had started in Bill's colon and spread to his liver. The doctors recommended three months of chemotherapy, using harsh medications to attack the cancer cells.

I had never needed chemotherapy, so this was new territory for both of us. We were scared but confident. Because of my two successful battles against breast cancer, we both felt this was something that could be conquered, God willing. And I suspect Bill felt that if I could survive cancer, so could he. But he did ask whether I thought we should go ahead and buy the mobile home. Escrow was about to close, but there was still time for us to pull out of the deal. He wanted to know if buying a second place was too much to cope with on top of his cancer. I didn't hesitate at all.

"Let's keep it," I said. "I know you'll really enjoy it, Bill. We'll enjoy it together, and it's something you've been wanting."

The mobile home became a symbol of hope for our future together. By this time it was early May. Bill was scheduled to have chemotherapy treatments from June to August. Before we were tied down for three months, we decided to visit to Southern California again to make the new place our own.

We already had a routine for the ten-hour drive from Sonoma to Desert Hot Springs. Most of it was on the straight multiple lanes of Interstate 5, which runs north and south down the middle of California. For miles and miles there would be nothing but the dark asphalt slashing through wide, flat fields of what seemed like endless rows of crops—corn, hay, and things I couldn't even identify. We always left Sonoma around 5 or 6 A.M., with Bill driving. We'd stop to eat at about 10 A.M.—always at the same restaurant at an otherwise anonymous off-ramp—and after breakfast I'd drive for a bit while Bill slept. We'd take turns at the wheel all day long and arrive in Desert Hot Springs before dinnertime.

We took our extra furniture out of storage and had it shipped down south so that our belongings arrived when we did. We had a great time arranging our things in our new winter home. Then we went shopping. For the den we splurged on two matching dark green leather recliner chairs—the deluxe models. We also bought a little table to place in between them to hold snacks so that we could sit there side by side, eating, talking, and watching TV.

It was May and the desert temperatures were already climbing sky high. In spite of the heat we happily spent several days landscaping our new home. Out in the scorching sun, Bill and I put in desert plants and surrounded them with rocks from a nearby dry creek bed. Our new neighbors told us we were crazy, but we didn't think so. It was a labor of love and of confident optimism. The place wasn't fancy or ostentatious, but it was comfortable, welcoming, and ours. We had everything set for future visits once Bill's cancer was gone. And at the end of the month we headed back north for Bill's chemotherapy sessions.

The details of those three months of treatments are pretty fuzzy in my memory. As far as I recall, we went to Marin General Hospital once or twice a week for the chemo and otherwise stayed home in Sonoma. I do know that the first time was the hardest. Bill had to have toxic medication administered slowly through a needle poked directly into a vein. We had been told it was crucial to find a good vein because if any of the chemo leaked into Bill's body or onto his skin, it would burn him. It was hard to think that anything could be so dangerous and yet at the same time able to cure Bill of the invading cancer. When you watch someone you love hooked up to chemo—well, it looks like something that should be avoided at all costs. Your mind wants to run away, to somehow make both of you be elsewhere and not in that awful situation.

As the nurse gave Bill his first dose of chemotherapy she said everyone reacted differently to the drugs.

"If you don't get sick in the next couple of hours, you won't get sick at all," she told Bill.

Instead of going somewhere to eat lunch we walked along a nearby creek. We were waiting to see how Bill would feel. When the time was up Bill was still doing okay.

"I didn't get sick," he told me with a huge grin.

So the rest of Bill's chemo treatments weren't as hard to watch as the first one. It became more like getting a shot than having something awful done. I think it would have been different if the chemo had made Bill ill the way it does many people. But in that sense Bill and I were lucky. And Bill didn't lose his hair the way a lot of patients do when they get chemotherapy.

As difficult as that time was, we remained confident and settled easily into a routine. It helped that the hospital was in San Rafael, which was a comfortable, familiar town for us. We knew the hospital and its staff, we knew the area, and we had friends and family living nearby. So going to San Rafael for Bill's treatments felt a bit like going home.

I accompanied my husband to all his chemo appointments, and we spent a lot of time together. We were convinced that Bill could beat this, and we refused to think about other possibilities. As we sat through Bill's chemo sessions we talked about ourselves and our life together. Somehow this experience was gradually melting away the little frictions between us. Our past hurts seemed to be fading away, and only the present was important. Every negative inner voice was silenced. It sounds a bit unreal, but there was no discord, no arguments big or small. We stopped all the back-and-forth, all the push-me-pull-you of daily life. It just dropped away as we looked at what we loved in each other instead of what irritated us.

Perhaps because it was no longer possible to pretend that either of us was going to live forever, we were finally able to appreciate what we had together. We had accomplished all of our dreams, and we were happy to be living them. We had our son, daughter-in-law, and grand-children; we had the satisfaction of knowing that Billy was successfully building up the business we had started; we had our two homes; we were extremely well off financially, with a comfortable retirement income that let us do the things we wanted to do; and we had each other. Most importantly, we enjoyed each other's company.

Bill was certainly at peace with himself in a way he had never been before. I'm sure he did a lot of thinking about what he wanted out of life and what was important. I think it helped that he was concentrating on getting better and being healthy rather than on a complicated business deal, making another sale, his latest project, or whatever had consumed him in the past. Perhaps it's sad that it took Bill's cancer to help us strip away our defenses and just love each other, but I'm glad it happened.

We decided we liked how things were going between us, and we wanted to make the positive changes last. We knew what our past had been, and we didn't want to repeat it.

"Maybe there's a word or a phrase we can use if we start to fall back into our old habits, our old ways of looking at things," I told Bill.

He was reading the book *The Greatest Secret in the World* by Og Mandino and suggested we use a sentence adapted from one of the "scrolls" in the book: "I will greet each day with love in my heart." That phrase became our commitment to ourselves and each other. Billy was also a fan of Mandino's book and recognized the importance of that phrase for Bill and me. So one day our son presented each of us with a gold medallion inscribed with the words "I will greet each day with love in my heart." Billy had them specially made by a jeweler and hung on gold chains. Bill and I were able to wear the small disks around our necks so the spiritual message was never far from our hearts.

It was wonderful when Billy presented them to us. I was almost overcome by my love for these two men in my life—my husband and my thoughtful son. And Bill loved Billy's gift—both the significance of the phrase and the fact that Billy went to all that trouble to give us this incredible present. Bill was never as demonstrative as I was, but it was clear that he was really touched.

Our positive attitude gradually spilled over into other areas of our lives. After years of staying away, Bill started going to church with me again. We still didn't go during services, but we both loved slipping into the sanctuary between Masses. We would light a candle and each pray in our own way, filling ourselves with the silence and sacredness. Afterward we'd go out to a restaurant for a good breakfast and what was usually a great day together. Three months of chemo is a hard thing to go through, but it also helped us grow and develop as individuals and as a couple.

Once the treatments were completed at the end of August, the doctors did a series of blood tests and X-rays. Bill's cancer had gone into remission.

To say we were jubilant is an understatement. With our hearts full of gratitude to God, we resumed our normal lives. But we kept wearing our medallions, and each morning we would say to ourselves, "I will greet each day with love in my heart."

Not all the news in our lives was good. On November 2, 1979, my sister Jenny—the second oldest and the family's comedian—died at age eighty-nine. Only a short time before she had been diagnosed with uterine cancer. It was pretty far advanced and she didn't last long. Joe's daughter, Joanne, nursed Jenny through the worst of it. By the time she died, I believe Jenny was ready to go, at peace with the idea of death. Her husband had died several years before, and they never had any children.

Bill and I were in Desert Hot Springs when we heard Jenny had slipped away. We drove through the night to get back to the family in San Francisco. Once again we all gathered for the rosary, funeral Mass, and graveside service. I found myself looking at my brother and sisters, wondering which of us would be next. Beppa, Jenny, Paolina, and Rico were dead; Algisa, Joe, Eda, and I were the only ones left from our family of eight children. Algisa was eighty-five; Joe was seventy-eight, almost seventy-nine; Eda was seventy-seven (at least according to her birth certificate; the world still thought she was seventy-five); and I was seventy (or, by Eda's reckoning, sixty-eight—take your pick). It was sobering that we four were the only ones left, the only ones who had experienced our family's journey from Italy to San Francisco, the only ones who remembered the flour-sack underwear and the table groaning under Mamma's delicious meals.

That winter, Bill and I returned to Desert Hot Springs and resumed our decorating and landscaping efforts. My husband loved tackling yet another home improvement project and the feeling of accomplishment when it was done. Bill still pretty much directed what we were going to do, but things remained peaceful between us. We had managed to retain our awareness of the beauty in small things and the precious gift of our love for each other. Bill was talking to me more than he ever had before—about how our family was doing, his views of God and spirituality, his feelings on a whole range of topics. It made life wonderful. And there were lots of little romantic moments, like when Bill put a flower in a vase on the table and said he picked it because he was thinking of me.

The only downside was that Bill had to visit his doctor in Marin County every month. That meant we were only able to stay in Southern California for three weeks at a time, instead of half the year as we had planned. Each month, when we dutifully came back to Marin for Bill's checkup, his doctor would listen patiently to our cheerful news of Bill's continued good health.

"Enjoy it, Bill," the doctor would tell him, "because your cancer will eventually come back."

How I dreaded those words. I despised that doctor for bursting our balloon of hope and optimism.

"Why does he have to keep telling you that? I don't think it's true," I'd rant at Bill when we left the doctor's office. "Why can't he just leave it alone? I hate that guy."

But Bill seemed unfazed by the doctor's warning. If my husband was afraid, it didn't show. He seemed convinced that he had beaten the cancer and it would never return.

In general his health was good, but he did catch a bad case of the flu in early April 1980, during one of our trips to Southern California. Bill wasn't terribly sick, but we figured we'd stay in the desert until it was time for him to see his doctor again. Except we had promised to return to Northern California sooner than that. Our friend Jeannette, who had been the first office employee we ever hired and who was still working for Willitts and Associates, was planning to take us out for a special meal on April 19. It would be dinner for six: Jeannette and her husband, Bill and me, plus Billy and Patti. But Bill was still feeling poorly from the flu, so I called Billy to tell him I didn't think we should make the ten-hour trip up north just for the dinner.

"You both have to come, Mom. Jeannette will be so disappointed if you don't," Billy told me.

So we headed north to Sonoma. The trip exhausted Bill; after we unpacked the car he just fell into bed. But he was determined not to disappoint his family or his friends, so he pulled himself together in time for the dinner. I began to suspect something was up when Jeannette told me we were eating at the Elks Club in San Rafael. That seemed a pretty unusual setting for a meal for the six of us. When she added that Billy and Patti would meet us at the club instead of coming to her house first, I decided they were planning more than a simple meal.

Smart lady that I was, I figured out exactly what was going on. They were giving me a surprise birthday party. My birthday wasn't until April 29, but I thought April 19 was close enough. I even convinced my husband that it had to be a birthday party for me. So when we walked in the door and a bunch of people started cheering, I was sure my hunch had been right. Billy was standing there grinning, wearing a tuxedo and looking distinguished. The dining room was filled with long tables covered with starched white cloths and decked with gleaming, flickering candelabra. I started walking around, shaking hands and thanking everyone for coming to my party.

Except the banquet wasn't for my birthday. Bill and I never had a proper retirement dinner, so our son had arranged one as a surprise. The room was filled with family, friends, and longtime company employees. Billy made a speech welcoming everyone. Then he introduced other people, who talked about Bill and me and how we started the company by ourselves. After the speeches were done, our son presented us with a poem he had written, sharing his thoughts on his parents' lives:

To Elda and Bill

Two people dreaming of success,
maturing in a business that at times held the ultimate frustration,
An immigrant lady and her strong-willed man,
Exercising caution in a world filled with trickery
yet not being blinded to life's virtues.

Together they gambled for small winnings
and then gambled again, always increasing their shares.
Sometimes forced to the limit of hearts' endurance,
yet searching on for true success.

This man, pioneering new territory,
braving loneliness and fatigue in his seemingly endless travels,
trying hard to remember where his dream began.

This lady, always giving all she had to give
and then forcing her heart and nerve to give some more.

Pioneers in business, finding their way on a never-before charted
 course.
Together they won.

To their son they surrendered the business they had both
 nurtured.
This meant giving up their labors and business aspirations,
but through it all a new direction was found:
A direction so simple that all mankind
can't see it through the noisy confusion.

No matter what mysteries life holds for these two,
they have found eternal success.
From their souls they have committed to each other one simple
 promise:
I will greet each day with love in my heart.

The whole evening was a heartfelt gesture from people who knew us and loved us. Just thinking about it makes my throat tighten and my eyes fill with tears. It meant so much to both Bill and me, but especially to Bill. I think that had to have been one of happiest nights in his life.

Bill and I continued to travel, both to our getaway in Southern California and elsewhere. In late summer 1980 we flew to Vancouver and caught a bus that took us on a tour of Lake Louise. We visited Banff, on the western side of the lake. Then we took the long scenic way back to Vancouver, going by boat down the Inner Passage. That's an area of such striking beauty that it has to be seen to be believed. In the middle of the trip Bill lost his appetite and didn't eat for several days. Then he perked up and started eating again, so I put it out of my mind. Bill wasn't one to need a lot of attention. He didn't like being sick and in fact tended to pretend he was fine when he wasn't because he didn't like me to fuss over him. He didn't like sympathy.

When he regained his appetite, I assumed that whatever had made Bill ill had gone away. I went back to enjoying the spectacular scenery. But after we flew home to Sonoma, Bill lost his appetite again. He was losing weight rapidly. My always-energetic husband seemed to have no energy at all.

So it was back to the gloomy doctor in Marin, to discover that his predictions had been right after all. Bill's cancer had returned. His days of remission, our days of grace, were over.

CHAPTER 22

*T*he doctors were not optimistic. They said my husband's cancer had returned, and his liver was enlarged. Experimental treatments were being developed, but there was no known cure for the disease that was spreading throughout Bill's body.

Since the staff at Marin General Hospital didn't have any hope to offer us, we asked that Bill be referred to the medical center at the University of California at San Francisco—a teaching hospital and the center of quite a bit of cancer research. Unfortunately, the UCSF doctors were also pessimistic about Bill's chances. After a long consultation, they suggested a couple of radical treatment options. I think one would have required Bill to stay flat on his back in the hospital for a week, getting a complete blood transfusion every day. Bill was determined to try anything that offered a chance to beat the cancer, but complete daily transfusions was more than even he was willing to go through—especially since the doctors admitted they didn't think it would do much good.

We made several trips to UCSF, and my husband did try some of their less radical treatments. Nothing seemed to help. Bill's energy continued to drop, but he was still upbeat. He had gone into remission once—he was sure he could do it again, and I agreed with him. I had managed to win out against breast cancer not once but twice; I knew it could be done.

But there was more bad news in February 1981. Tests showed that the cancer had migrated and was blocking Bill's intestines. The doctors wanted to do a colostomy, the same procedure my sister Paolina had to endure as part of her long struggle with colon cancer. I couldn't picture my fastidious, always immaculate husband losing part or all of his intestines, then having to pass his stool out of his body through a tube in his abdomen and into a plastic bag attached to his side. Bill had an extremely strong sense of innate dignity. I couldn't imagine him going through that level of physical humiliation. Just the thought of it was upsetting. So I asked the doctor if a colostomy was absolutely necessary.

"If he doesn't have it, Bill will be in such pain that he'll want to kill himself," the doctor replied.

That settled it. Even though Bill and I hated the whole idea, we agreed he needed the colostomy. The doctors did say there was a slight hope they might be able to fix the blockage some other way, but they wouldn't know until they cut Bill open and saw exactly what the problem was. Once again, Bill went into the operating room at Marin General Hospital while I sat with family and friends in the waiting room. As far as I was concerned I was getting to know that place entirely too well.

Bill came through the surgery just fine, but again the news wasn't good. There had been no other way to fix the blockage. The surgeons had removed part of Bill's colon and installed a colostomy tube and bag.

Looking back, I suspect that Bill hated the indignity of that colostomy with a purple passion, but he never said so. I think he figured that as long as he was alive, he still had a chance, so he'd make the best of things. Bill spent about a week in the hospital while they taught us both how to live with a colostomy—how to dump Bill's stool out of the bag and into the toilet; and how to flush the colostomy sack and tube with fluid from another bag, which had to be hung high overhead. Everything had to be washed daily to avoid infection.

When Bill was allowed to come home, one of the first things he did was to measure the proper height and pound a nail into the bathroom wall so he'd have a place to hang the fluid bag while he was doing his daily colostomy cleaning. Except Bill never used that nail. When it came time for dumping his stool and cleaning the colostomy bag, he always called me into the bathroom to assist him.

It was a messy process, and at first it surprised me that Bill asked for my help. I had assumed he would want to do this in private. But Bill must have felt awfully vulnerable emptying and cleaning a bag and tube that went directly into his digestive system. I think he didn't want to face the task alone. I sort of gritted my teeth the first time Bill called me into the bathroom to hold up the fluid bag for him. After that it didn't faze me. All I saw was this human being, whom I loved deeply, in need of help. In that sort of situation you just do what you have to do. So my assisting Bill with his colostomy cleaning became part of our shared daily routine.

Beyond that, Bill was able to lead a pretty normal life with the colostomy. He had to wear the bag all the time, but there was no odor or anything that would let other people know it was there.

Our fortieth wedding anniversary was February 21, 1981. For the life of me I can't remember how we celebrated or even if we celebrated at all. It was fairly soon after the surgery, and we were both still adjusting to the changes in Bill's body. Although the colostomy may have fixed the blockage problem, Bill's energy was at an all-time low. He needed to rest a lot. Our friends would call and want to stop by, but we'd always put them off until another time. As a result we were often alone. That was fine with us. In a way, it was a peaceful time.

After a couple of months of recuperation, Bill insisted on heading south to our winter home in Desert Hot Springs. He loved that place. I think he felt comfortable there. And with fewer friends in the area it was easier to live a quiet life, just the two of us.

We still hadn't given up hope. Even in Desert Hot Springs we asked our neighbors and acquaintances about oncologists, trying to find one who might know something that could help Bill. We connected with a doctor who suggested hyperthermia therapy. The goal was to knock out the cancer with heat treatments. This meant injecting Bill with medications to raise his body temperature to 105 degrees. My husband asked the doctor about the chances for success.

"If you were in a room with a hundred people, ninety-five of them wouldn't make it and five would. Those are your chances," the doctor said.

"I could be one of the five. Let's do it," Bill replied.

So Bill literally sweated it out. It was hard to watch. He'd be drenched in perspiration, and when it was over he'd be completely exhausted. But Bill wasn't one of the lucky 5 percent. After several treatments the doctor said they weren't doing any good. Despite his disappointment, Bill kept his upbeat attitude.

"I'm glad I gave it a try," he told me.

This visit to Desert Hot Springs was far different from any of the others we had made. Always before Bill had been puttering here and there, coming up with things we should do to fix up our mobile home.

But this time he didn't do a single project. He didn't even have the energy to go swimming in the community pool, one of his favorite pastimes. For the first time in his adult life, Bill took a nap every afternoon. I think he was trying to rest in the hope that it would make him feel better—but his problem wasn't anything that sleep could fix.

One night while we were watching TV in our matching leather recliners, Bill asked me to come sit on his lap. This was not a common request. In all our married life I had rarely sat on Bill's lap. But he was so calm, so collected, that I just took it in stride and did as he asked. He pulled me close against him, circling his arms around me. Then he began to talk softly about how I should live my life when he was gone.

I had always taken care of our bookkeeping and finances, so he knew I understood our investments and how much we had. Now he talked to me about managing things to ensure I had plenty of retirement income. He talked about Billy, Patti, and our grandchildren. He told me to enjoy life and ended by saying everything would be all right for me because I would always be surrounded by the love of our family. His manner was so confident and reassuring that it didn't upset me at all. I heard what he said and I felt his love and support for me, but I still didn't allow myself to think that he really might die.

By this time Bill's liver was starting to give out. Each day he became a bit more jaundiced, a little more yellow. He was becoming less alert, less focused. Although he was growing weaker, Bill didn't want to go home to Sonoma. I think maybe he wanted to die in his beloved desert, surrounded by its wide open spaces and simple beauty. But I was getting worried about my ability to care for him on my own. I talked to Billy on the phone, and together we convinced Bill that we needed to go back home to Sonoma, where we had family and friends close by.

"Unless I can drive, I'm not going," Bill told me.

"Okay, you can start off doing the driving," I replied.

Maybe it was a matter of pride. Maybe he needed to feel in control. Whatever the reason, we began our trip early in the morning with Bill behind the wheel. It was a good thing we were on a wide, empty freeway because he kept weaving from lane to lane. Bill was lucid and he seemed to be thinking clearly, but he couldn't focus and he couldn't navigate. We'd only gone about ten miles when I spoke up.

"It's my turn," I said as cheerfully as I could. "You've driven far enough to get tired, and I should take over now."

Without any argument Bill slid over into the passenger seat while I walked around the car and got in on the driver's side. I drove the rest of the way home on that ten-hour trip—something I had never done before. Bill didn't suggest even once that he take the wheel again. I think he realized he was no longer capable of driving. It was a long, quiet trip, with Bill asleep most of the way.

When we arrived in Sonoma, he dragged his body up the stairs to our condo and fell into bed, leaving me to unpack the car and haul all our luggage up the steep front steps. That had never happened before in our entire life together. Bill had always carried the suitcases, the bags of groceries, whatever. It was the first time he had left me to cope on my own. That's when I knew deep down that he was seriously ill.

Bill recuperated in bed for a couple of weeks. In mid-June Billy asked us to attend a company picnic. By this time the business was known as Willitts Imports and was located in Petaluma, north of our old location in San Rafael and about a thirty-minute drive from the Sonoma Valley. Billy had really expanded the company. He was now importing gift items from overseas and was beginning to hire artists to create one-of-a-kind designs.

My husband really wasn't well enough to attend any sort of large event, much less a picnic, but he pulled himself together and went anyway. He loved what Billy was accomplishing with the company. Together Bill and I had conservatively built a solid base. Now our energetic young son was taking risks we never would have even considered. Billy was building an expanded and successful operation on the firm foundation we had created. It made us extremely proud of our son. So we made an appearance at the Willitts Imports picnic in a Petaluma park. Bill could hardly walk, so he sat most of the time. We didn't stay long because he quickly became exhausted, but I was glad we did it; that brief visit meant so much to Bill and Billy.

My husband was still able to get out of bed now and then, but his illness was slowly taking over his body and our life together. We had few visitors other than Billy, Patti, and the kids. Bill rested as much as possible, and we rarely went out. On the Fourth of July, Billy called us with a spontaneous invitation. The company was about to move into a brand-new building in Petaluma, and Billy wanted us to come see it.

"Dad, we're here with the kids and the sparklers and the fireworks. Why don't you come out and see the place?" Billy said over the phone.

As exhausted as he was, Bill couldn't resist the dual pull of family and the latest incarnation of the business he had founded. I drove us to Petaluma, and then Billy provided a tour of the custom-built facility. Bill just loved it. He could tell the company was off the ground and flying. Sitting with Billy and Patti, Bill and I watched our three grandchildren set off fireworks in front of the new Willitts company building. Then I drove Bill home. He was so exhausted that he barely made it upstairs to our condo.

The next morning Bill was too sick to get out of bed at all. I think we both knew then that he was nearing the end, but we never talked about it. I called Billy and Patti to say that it was becoming too much for me to care for Bill all by myself. I wanted to hire people to help. Billy and Patti wouldn't hear of it. Instead they moved into our second bedroom. The idea was that we would all take turns helping Bill. Our son went to an electronics store and got the parts to rig up a buzzer so anytime Bill needed help he could alert Billy and Patti in the next bedroom.

Except Bill never once used that buzzer. Instead he'd just roll over and ask me for more water, a back rub, or his medicine—whatever he wanted, all night long. Billy and Patti were sleeping soundly in the guest room and I was up all night. After a short while Billy and Patti went back to spending the night in their own home, and we hired two nurses to work in rotation—from 4 P.M. to midnight and from midnight to 10 A.M. In the daytime, representatives of hospice—which provides care and support for terminally ill patients—would stop by to check on us both.

This meant that I slept in the spare bedroom instead of beside my husband, who remained in our king-size bed with a nurse by his side all night long. I knew that Bill was extremely sick and I wanted to help, but I also knew that there was little I could do. He needed professional care, and I needed to get at least some rest each night. But not being able to sleep next to my husband was frustrating, especially because our bedroom was pretty much unchanged. It didn't look like a sick room. Bill was on mild tranquilizers, but he wasn't in any noticeable pain—thank goodness. There was no medical equipment because he didn't need an oxygen tank, IV drip, or anything like that. There wasn't even a bedside commode; the colostomy bag meant the nurses could easily clean out his bodily wastes without any fuss and use a simple bed pan when Bill needed to urinate.

Without any of the outward signs of extreme illness, our master bedroom was cool, serene, and welcoming. Bill was tucked into what had always been his side of our bed. From there he could look out the back window and see the spreading branches of an ancient oak tree, a corner of the carefully tended yard of our downstairs neighbors, the summer sky, and a short stretch of the open hillside behind our condo complex. He was covered by a soft, blue, quilted comforter I had picked for our bedroom just a few years earlier. It had kept the two of us warm on many cold winter nights. His slippers were under the bed as always, and his clothing hung in the closet. But each night instead of having me snuggled up next to him, a nurse sat on what had been my side of the bed. She watched TV with the sound on low and kept an eye on Bill.

My tall, handsome husband was rapidly losing weight—almost shrinking into the pillows that cushioned his head. And the whiteness of the pillows and sheets only emphasized his increasingly yellow skin, caused by the jaundice from his failing liver. He was steadily going downhill and he knew it. It made him angry, and he would often get stubborn about something a nurse wanted him to do. In the beginning they were still getting him up every day, walking him down the hall-way, and having him sit in a chair in the living room. He kept insisting that he could do everything himself—so they let him try.

He couldn't. He couldn't get himself out of bed; he couldn't get himself dressed; he couldn't walk by himself down the hallway. I think that's when he finally gave up. Defeated, he crawled back into bed and stayed there. By this time it was mid-July. Bill's strength was gone and so was his hope for a miraculous recovery. Gradually he stopped communicating with anyone. He just lay there, looking more and more fragile each day. It got to the point that when the nurses or hospice personnel arrived for a scheduled shift or visit, they were surprised to find Bill still alive. I braced myself, knowing he was getting close to death but at the same time not wanting to face the reality of what was bound to happen soon.

Bill had always been strong-willed and determined; now he was completely dependent on others for everything. He had to be cared for like an infant. Every now and then I'd find myself wishing my husband would let go rather than hanging on to such a diminished existence. And yet he clung stubbornly to life.

"You need to let him know that it's okay for him to die, that you'll be all right when he's gone," one of the hospice people told me.

It was one of the hardest things I've ever done. That night I asked the nurse to leave the room for a few minutes. I sat down on the bed and leaned over so that my mouth was next to my husband's ear. Bill was still breathing, but he gave no sign that he knew who I was or even that I was there.

"Honey, it's time," I told him softly. "You can let go now. I'll be fine. The family will take care of me. I'll be fine. You can let go."

He didn't give any response, but I felt I had done what I could. I left the room with tears in my eyes, and the nurse returned to her duties. The next morning Bill was still struggling for every breath, clinging to life.

"Has his son talked to him?" the same hospice person asked me.

Since it was summer and school was out, Patti came over every day and usually brought the three kids. Shannon was about to turn fifteen, Greg was nine, and Jason was eight. The three of them would cool off in the swimming pool while Patti kept me company with Bill. Billy would stop by after work, and I'd eat dinner with him, Patti, and the kids.

When Billy showed up that evening, I told him what the hospice representative had suggested—that Billy give his father permission to die. Our son went into the bedroom alone and shut the door. I never did ask him what he said to his father, and Billy never told me. I figured that was strictly between the two of them.

The next morning—July 24, 1981—I got up early. I had just finished breakfast when the nurse came to get me.

"He's gone," she said softly.

I called Billy. He said he and Patti would be right over. While I was waiting for them, I asked the nurse what I should do. She told me to trim Bill's mustache. That may sound like an odd suggestion, but I was grateful for this little task. I did it with every ounce of love that I had in me. It felt good that I had a part in making Bill look immaculate, the way he always did before his final illness. Like a true gentlemen or any natural-born salesman, Bill was always attentive to his appearance. I concentrated on carefully trimming the sparse little mustache he had been growing since 1978.

Billy contacted a funeral home in San Anselmo, and they removed the body. That night I went back to sleeping on my side of our king-size bed, right next to where my husband had died. It may sound ghoulish, but in fact it made me feel closer to Bill, as if a bit of him still lingered in that bedroom where we had found such peace and contentment.

When Bill was placed in his coffin, he was still wearing his medallion, which said, "I will greet each day with love in my heart." He wore it all through his illness and died with it around his neck. The mortuary dressed him in a shirt, suit, shoes, and socks—I never did understand why they wanted us to supply shoes and socks—and then they asked Billy what they should do about his Dad's necklace.

"Leave it on him," Billy told them.

The funeral service was held at the Presidio Air Force Base in San Francisco, with full military honors—a 21-gun salute and all. About seventy-five people attended, all notified by word of mouth. There was no announcement published in the newspapers until afterward. It was a simple ceremony. Bill had always told us, "Please don't cry when I die. Have a drink and give a toast and have a dinner." So that's exactly what we did.

It took a lot of effort to get through all the red tape, but a few days after the funeral service my husband was buried in the National Cemetery in Colma, just south of San Francisco. This area that once held farms and open fields was transformed after World War II into a final resting place for military veterans. It was a peaceful site, and I knew it would have been just what Bill wanted.

The first few days after my husband's death weren't so bad because I had my family and friends around me, helping with every detail. Then I was on my own, and the condo felt so big, empty, and lonely. As I had during other difficult times in my life, I felt numb inside and was operating on autopilot.

About a week later I was cleaning our bedroom when I spotted a rather gaudy, hand-tooled leather wallet on Bill's dresser. I started to throw it away because it wasn't at all the type of thing Bill would have used. Something made me look inside. It contained a note in Bill's handwriting. He must have left the wallet on the dresser when he was still active and lucid, or maybe he had one of the nurses place it there before he died. I'll never know.

"My Dearest Wife Elda," the note said. "Just thought that I would write this little note to you in case there might be a little slipup on Wednesday."

When I first saw the letter, I thought Bill might have written it in the last weeks of his life. But it wasn't dated, and his opening line made me think he must have drafted it in February, before his colostomy operation.

"You know how positive my thoughts always are, and they are no different at this writing," the note continued. "But just in case—I would never want you to have to suffer through life like other unfortunate widows we have known."

I remembered the struggles of his mother and of Mamma after their husbands died and left them with young families. I thought about my sister Eda, who had been lonely, miserable, and needy since her husband's death a few years earlier. And I recalled other women we had known, who had faced financial hardships or simply never stopped mourning their husbands. I wiped the tears from my eyes and kept reading.

"You know how much I love you—much! much! more than life itself. So naturally it follows that I would want you to be happy."

I had to wipe away more tears. I reread those sentences before continuing on.

"Should the above happen, please continue to lead a normal life, enjoy shows, plays, dinners out, parties, etc., just as you would were I still with you. Please remember that this is my most sincere wish, to continue to enjoy life to the fullest, and should this involve meeting 'someone else,' please do so without the slightest feeling of guilt. I love you and cherish you so much… Be at peace, be happy, enjoy each and every moment, and always remember I love you dearly, Bill."

My hands were shaking. It took a moment to get my breath back. Then I read that note again and again. It was clear to me that whenever he wrote it, Bill meant for me to find it after his death. He wanted me to have his blessing and approval to go on without him; to enjoy myself and my life even when he wasn't by my side. The note was a gift of his liberating love so that I wouldn't feel tied to his memory. As wonderful as that note from Bill was, it was also heartrending. By reminding me of his deep and abiding love, it made me feel the pain of my loss that much more clearly.

In our years together Bill taught me to value both myself and my immigrant family. He and I had built a family of our own and a business of our own, both of which were thriving. We had worked through deception and anger, then rebuilt a warm, nurturing relationship. Bill's behavior may not have always been the best at all times—his affair with Alice hurt me deeply—but I wasn't always a picnic to live with either. Somehow we had managed to overcome our own fears and weakness to forgive each other and ourselves. I loved Bill deeply and he loved me.

Facing the possibility of his own death, my husband had reached out to me with reassurance and understanding, writing down his hope that I would continue to see the joys, beauties, and small miracles in life.

I held Bill's last letter tightly in my hands. I was paralyzed with fear. After so much that we had and did together, how could I go on without him?

CHAPTER 23

I always say that the spouse who dies first is the lucky one. The survivor's life is never quite the same. There's an endless void, the feeling that something vital is missing. Things can get better; it's possible to once again taste the sugar in the bottom of the cup instead of just the bitter coffee—but it takes a long, long time and a lot of effort.

Bill and I had been married forty years. Now I was on my own. I continued living in our Sonoma home, which was filled with reminders of our life together. There were pictures of each of us, separately and together, and small statues and other mementos we had bought on our many travels. A framed copy of the poem Billy had written for our retirement party hung in a place of honor in the hallway, surrounded by photos of Billy, Patti, and the children. Every piece of furniture was something Bill and I had picked out together. And Bill's organ still stood next to the fireplace, where we had placed it when we first moved in. My husband had gotten really good on it and had played it often—

right up until his final illness. I had loved hearing his melodies as I worked in the kitchen or read a book in the bedroom. Now the organ was silent. The whole place was quiet. I was the only one there.

It hurt to be in those rooms that held so many memories of Bill, but at the same time I couldn't bear the thought of moving. Somehow I kept going, doing what I had to do. It was like pushing a button and starting a machine. I would get up, get dressed, go into the kitchen, fix my breakfast, and then sit at the dining room table, looking idly out the window at the hillside behind our unit.

Shortly after we had moved into our condominium, Bill got permission from the homeowner's association to plant cactus and other drought-resistant plants on the hillside behind our home. One of our neighbors had erected a wooden signpost with a board that proclaimed the area "Bill's Garden." It was in clear view as I ate breakfast, lunch, or dinner. Bill was gone, but his sign and his garden remained. I spent an awful lot of time not doing anything—just sitting there, staring out the window at the "Bill's Garden" sign.

It helped a bit that I still had my close friendship with my sister Eda. We were both widows, and Eda knew some of what I was going through. She was still living in San Anselmo, and since she had never learned to drive, I'd go down there to see her. It took more than an hour to get from my house to hers—longer if traffic was really bad— but I started making the trip often, maybe two or three times a week. Our outlook on life had always been different, but we loved each other. Now Eda needed a companion and I needed to fill my days with something, anything. Her husband, Bacci, had died a few years earlier. Eda had become very needy; she depended on others to make her feel less alone. So we would go out to a show or have lunch or go shopping or just go for a drive together. Anything to keep busy.

But even Eda couldn't fill all the empty time I had on my hands. Worried about me, Billy coaxed me into working three days a week in the company's collections and accounts receivable department. He had changed the business name yet again, to Willitts Designs, to reflect the fact that he now had a large in-house art department designing unique gift items that were manufactured to his specifications in Taiwan. It should have made me proud and excited to see all that Billy and the company's employees were accomplishing, but I wasn't feeling anything at all. Hiring me to work part time was my son's attempt to pull me back into life and activity, but it did nothing to ease my pain or heal my heart. I continued to move around in a daze.

Then in late August my sister Algisa had a massive stroke. We all knew she had high blood pressure, but it was a shock when it happened so suddenly. She was living downstairs from her daughter, Olga. One of her granddaughters found Algisa collapsed in the backyard. The granddaughter immediately called 911, and an ambulance rushed my sister to the hospital.

Once they told me that Algisa couldn't talk, that she didn't seem to know where she was, that she basically wasn't herself anymore…well, I couldn't go visit my own sister in the hospital. I just couldn't. It was too much, too soon after Bill's death. I decided I wanted to remember Algisa as she had been, not the damaged body the stroke had left behind.

After a short hospital stay Algisa was transferred to a nearby nursing home. Mercifully she only lasted a few more weeks. She died on September 18, 1981. I pulled myself together enough to attend her funeral. It was handled by the same San Anselmo mortuary that had arranged for Bill's services and burial. That's all I remember about Algisa's funeral—that I went and that it was handled by the same company that took care of Bill after he died. Other than that, my memory is a complete blank. With Algisa's death coming less than two months after Bill's, both my thoughts and emotions seemed frozen and somehow distant from me.

I had been raised to be a good daughter in a big Italian family, which meant that I was taught to always take care of others first. I had done that all my life, from translating for Mamma when I was just a little girl to always being there for my brothers, my sisters, my husband, my son.

But my son was grown and didn't need me to take care of him. Of my family, only Joe and Eda were still alive, and Joe had a life of his own. Eda needed my love and attention and wanted me to visit her in San Anselmo as often as possible, but that by itself wasn't enough to fill my world. The part-time job kept me busy, but it didn't ease the pain of the gaping void inside me.

Bill was gone—it was still hard to believe it even after burying him and stumbling through two months of living alone. There was nobody at home but me. There was no one for me to take care of anymore. I didn't know what to do if I wasn't trying to meet someone else's needs. Who was I if I wasn't helping somebody else?

I sank into a deep depression. I had no energy and no interest in anything. It was all I could do to pull myself out of bed each morning and go through the daily motions. Everything in my life was gray. There was no color, no joy anywhere, and I was exhausted all the time. My doctor gave me a complete checkup, but he couldn't find anything physically wrong with me. After a while he put me on antidepressant pills. They made me light headed and disoriented without doing anything to ease my inner pain. I needed to get on with my life, but instead I was stumbling around, high on medication and depressed.

I stopped taking the pills and went back to my doctor. I asked him to recommend a psychiatrist or a therapist. Instead he told me that anytime I needed to talk, I could call his office. He would call me back sometime around eight or nine at night, and I could talk to him all I wanted. It's funny—I never took him up on his offer, but it helped a great deal to know that there was somebody out there who would listen to me if I asked. My inner darkness gradually began to ease up a bit. And I remembered what Bill had said to me more than forty years earlier—"Elda, you've got to learn to love yourself."

I hadn't understood him at the time; I hadn't been able to take in his words and apply them to my life. But now I was starting to instinctively grasp what Bill meant. Slowly I began to take delight in the little joys in my life and to do things to please myself. Maybe I didn't need to justify my life by helping others; maybe simply being me was enough reason to want to keep on living.

For decades I had been cooking American-style meals for my husband and son. It started with my mother-in-law's recipe for scalloped potatoes, and I went on from there, learning all sorts of midwestern classics. I never thought twice about it—in the beginning it was part of my quest to fit in and to please Bill. Eventually it became habit. But now that I was on my own I started remembering the delicious Italian meals Mamma and my sisters had made when I was young. I wanted to taste them again—but since I hated housework with a passion, I had never let Mamma teach me how to cook. And because Mamma was illiterate, none of her recipes had been written down.

Fortunately my four oldest sisters had willingly learned how to cook like Mamma. My late sister Algisa had taught her daughter Olga all of Mamma's recipes. So I contacted my niece for details about how to make some of my favorite childhood foods. I also read a couple of Italian cookbooks, experimenting with the instructions and ingredients to make the dishes match my memories. Gradually I found myself fixing Tuscany-style meals just because they made me happy.

I even went out on a few dates. A man Bill and I had known for years—I'll call him Frank—had been widowed not long before my husband died. Several month's after Bill's death, Frank called and asked me out for a cup of coffee. I was flattered; he was a highly professional, accomplished man. We had coffee and a long, pleasant conversation. Everything kind of fell into place—an easy sort of companionship.

A few weeks later Frank asked me to have dinner with him in San Francisco. Frank lived in Marin County, so he drove north to Sonoma, picked me up, then drove us south to the City for a lovely, elegant evening. That meant he had the extra hour's drive north from Marin to Sonoma at the start of our date, plus the return trip from Sonoma to Marin after he brought me home. It was thoughtful of Frank to make that additional effort.

He was a true gentleman and treated me beautifully, like I was an important person in his life. We went out a couple of times over the next few months, and I enjoyed myself each time. It was nice to have a man my age to go places and do things with. I didn't feel any awkwardness or guilt about going out with someone other than my husband because this was really just a friendship.

However, Frank was doing a lot of extra driving to pick me up in Sonoma and take me home again after dinner or a show in the City. On our third or fourth date for an evening in San Francisco, we arranged that I would meet him at his home in San Rafael instead of having him making the extra trips to and from Sonoma.

I was bowled over when I saw Frank's place. It was like a palace, with gorgeous artwork and carved busts on pedestals. It was lovely, it was elegant, it was beautiful, it was tastefully done—and it just left me cold. Living there would have been like living in a museum or a show-place. I had done that once myself, on Woodside Avenue in San Rafael, and knew through experience that fancy things don't necessarily bring good times.

Seeing his home made me think more clearly about my dates with Frank. I had enjoyed myself, but mostly because it was nice to have a classy escort and to be treated so well. One look at his home and I knew there was no hope for any sort of long-term relationship between us. Our lives and our values were too different. And the more I thought about it, the more I realized that deep inside Frank wasn't a happy person.

And do you know what else? I realized that I didn't need a man in my life to be happy. In fact, I was happier without Frank than with him—so I stopped seeing him. I guess I'm just a one-man woman, and I'd already had my forty years with that one man. Dating someone had been a fun and exciting change, but learning that I didn't need him to complete my life made me feel even better. Things were definitely looking up.

I made a few trips down to the mobile home in Desert Hot Springs, to stay for a couple weeks at a time either with Eda or a few friends. But it was a long drive, and it was hard to maintain the place from a distance. After a while, with regret, I put the mobile home on the market and sold it and all its furnishings.

Determined not to slide back into the gray world of depression, I decided I needed a purpose—a goal no matter how minor or simple. I decided to put together a small genealogy. With only Joe, Eda, and I remaining from our generation, I figured it was time to record all the facts so that my grandchildren and great-grandchildren would know who they came from and all that we had done to make it in this country. I began gathering the scattered notes I had jotted down over the years as well as various family documents. I knew my parents had met in a little town called Monsummano, in the Tuscany region of Italy, and that my sisters and brothers had been born there. I was the only one born after our family had moved to the larger town of Lucca.

As I pored over the details, I realized I had no idea exactly when my parents had gotten married. That didn't seem at all odd to me. Since Mamma couldn't read, it wouldn't have been important to her to keep copies of her marriage certificate or our birth certificates, or even to have someone record the exact dates.

I called my cousin Cesarina in Italy, on my father's side of the family. We had stayed in touch after my wonderful visit with her more than ten years earlier. I thought Cesarina could help me locate some of the paperwork about my parents and other family members. I asked her to go to the local church in Monsummano and find the date of my parents' marriage. Since Beppa was the oldest child, I used Beppa's birthday—June 26, 1888—as a starting point and told Cesarina to look in the year or so before that so I would know exactly when Babbo and Mamma were married.

"The church doesn't have anything listed in that period," Cesarina told me the next time we talked.

"Well, do you think it's a whole lot before that? Would you mind checking the earlier records?" I asked her. She kind of "ummed" a bit, sort of at a loss for words, and then blurted it out.

"Elda, your parents weren't married when Beppa was born. In fact, they weren't married until after Jenny was born," Cesarina told me. She'd known all along but wasn't sure what to say or how I would react.

Some of what I had been told was true: Mamma had been the daughter of a well-off family, and Babbo had been their gardener.

What I didn't know was that they fell in love but couldn't get married because her family objected to such a low-class, poverty-stricken suitor. So Mamma and Babbo met secretly. When Mamma's family found out she was pregnant, they shut her up in the family home and told her she could never see Babbo again. When Beppa was born, Mamma was an unwed mother in an extremely small town in rural Italy in the late nineteenth century. It must have been so hard on Mamma to face the shame in the community and the disapproval of her family.

Apparently it wasn't enough to stop her love for Babbo. Somehow she managed to see him again because on February 27, 1890, my sister Jenny was born. She was their second child and both were illegitimate. Her family threw Mamma out and turned their backs on her. That was why only her brother, the priest, kept in touch with her.

My parents were married October 12, 1890. I had the date I had asked for, but it was going to take me a long time to absorb this new information. I wasn't shocked or ashamed or anything like that. It was simply that everything seemed to have shifted a bit in my mind; things that I had taken for granted now took on new meaning.

I could hear my mother's often-repeated words about how we should never bring shame to our family. *"Guai! Se qualche duno dovessa svergognare la famiglia sarebba la mia morte"*—"If that happened, it would kill me," Mamma used to tell us. No wonder Mamma placed so many restrictions on what we could do or where we could go. No wonder she was reluctant to let Eda and me start dating. Mamma made us stay home most nights and weekends because she was worried about the possibility that one of her children might disgrace the family. Mamma worried about it because she had done it herself.

Could this family secret be one of the reasons why none of my older sisters got married while we were still living in Italy? Beppa turned twenty-eight shortly after we arrived in San Francisco. Why did neither she nor any of the others find a husband before we came to the United States? I'd never thought about it before, but maybe this was the answer. Maybe there were no suitors for girls from a poverty-stricken family with a shameful past.

And what about Mamma? What must she and Babbo have gone through, first in trying to be together and then struggling to make it entirely on their own after they were married, with no help from her family and only shame in the community? How must she have felt, having been born and raised in luxury and then serving as a wet nurse to other women's infants and even doing backbreaking labor harvesting crops, all to bring in a little more money for their struggling household?

Of course America had beckoned to them. I remembered that Mamma bundled us onto the train out of Lucca without contacting her brother or anyone else in her family. The fact that their first two children were illegitimate had to have been fairly common knowledge. At a time when few people could read, tongues must have wagged as much as if not more than they do now when a community scents scandal. And back then, in that intensely Catholic society, being an unwed mother and being born out of wedlock were both deeply shameful.

I remembered what Mamma said in the 1950s when Eda and her husband, Bacci, decided to vacation in Italy. They wanted Mamma to go with them. Our mother was delighted that Eda was going to see Italy again and gave her lots of directions about where to go—but Mamma refused to come along.

"Non lasciavo se avevo l'intenzione di ritornare"—"I wouldn't have left if I was going to go back," was Mamma's firm reply.

Now I saw her answer in a whole new light. Mamma had escaped from her shame in Italy. With hard work and determination she had built a life here with her children. No one in the United States knew anything about the family's past. It had become a secret. It seems likely my oldest sisters and brothers must have known that Beppa and Jenny were born out of wedlock, but they never so much as whispered that there was anything out of the ordinary in our family's history.

I've said it before: Our private secrets are funny things. Even in those more conservative times, I suspect most people in San Francisco were too busy with their own lives to care whether Babbo and Mamma had two of their eight children before getting married. And it's unlikely that anyone is shocked when they learn what I kept carefully hidden for so many years, that Rico hit me. Certainly no one except Eda was concerned about her little trick to make both of us a couple years younger.

Today couples live together, even have children without getting married, and no one thinks twice about it. Even my wonderful grand-daughter, Shannon, was born out of wedlock. I remember how Patti's mother tried—and failed—to keep Billy and Patti apart. It felt odd to think about Babbo and Mamma sneaking out and meeting secretly, the way my son and daughter-in-law did.

It's true that Billy and Patti faced strong opposition when Patti was pregnant with Shannon, but Patti's family never abandoned her. Billy and Patti were eventually able to claim their daughter and build a good life together. They never had to keep their past a secret, but only because they were living in a different time and place than Mamma and Babbo. Years and geography made the difference.

I tried to picture my parents as young lovers. She was nineteen when their first child was born; he was twenty-three. He would have been tall, handsome, and strong from his daily labor in the gardens. Almost a foot shorter than he was, she would have undoubtedly been dainty and petite. He would have been muscular and dressed in simple peasant clothes. The daughter of well-off merchants, she would have worn pretty dresses and maybe some simple jewelry or perhaps a bright ribbon in her hair. She didn't know how to read or write, so they couldn't exchange letters. How did they get to know each other well enough to fall in love? To conceive two children? Where did they meet in order to be alone? Maybe I was romanticizing based on a few bare facts, but there seemed to be so many questions that would never be answered.

My parents must have loved each other so much. In the few years that I saw them living together, there were always little gestures and looks of affection, so I knew they cared for each other. Now I realized their love must have been much stronger, much deeper than I understood.

I told Billy and Patti what I had learned about my parents and my two oldest sisters, but it didn't seem important to them. I also let Eda and Joe know what I had discovered. Eda was just like me—surprised but not at all shocked. Joe didn't want to talk about it. The subject appeared to be a bit shameful to him. I don't know if he disliked thinking of his parents as illicit lovers or if he had always known this family secret. He was sixteen when we left Italy to come to America. That would have made him old enough to have encountered any neighborhood gossip about our family.

As I mulled all this over, I remembered a phrase I had heard Mamma say many times when I was growing up—"What happens in the family stays in the family." Secrets should remain secrets. So for a long time I kept the surprising information about the date of my parents' marriage to myself and didn't tell anyone outside of the family.

A few months later, in winter 1983, I became concerned about Eda's health. She seemed unfocused and not entirely herself. I took her to her doctor, who referred her to a neurologist. Eda had a condition that impaired the blood flow to her head.

I didn't understand all the details, but she wasn't getting enough blood circulation in two parts of her brain. There wasn't anything the doctors could do to help her. She still seemed to be able to take care of herself, so we figured it was best to keep her living in her San Anselmo home for as long as possible. She would have hated any kind of institution, or what's now known as "assisted living."

I tried to keep in touch as much as I could. Every weekend and once or twice a week I made the drive from Sonoma to San Anselmo to visit her. I called every day to see how she was. And always Eda would demand to know when I was coming to see her, even if I had been there the day before. It was draining, but there didn't seem to be much more that I could do, other than praying for her and going on with my life. I had survived Bill's death, stumbled my way through the loss of Algisa soon after, pulled myself out of the dark fog of depression, and slowly rediscovered some of life's small joys. Now there was nothing I could do about Eda's health problems except trust in God and wait to see what came next.

CHAPTER 24

*I*n late summer of 1983, Patti and Billy gave me the good news that they had another child on the way, expected sometime in spring 1984. Shannon was seventeen, Greg was thirteen, and Jason was twelve. Patti was thirty-five years old and would be thirty-six by the time the baby was due, yet she was more than ready for this new infant. She loved being a mother. I think if it were possible, Patti would have kept on having babies all her life.

By this time they were living in a town called Inverness in the western part of Marin County, near the coast. Billy, Patti, and the kids had a lovely two-story home surrounded by trees. You couldn't even see the neighboring homes. And if you walked a quarter-mile, there was a view of the ocean. Their place was comfortably furnished with all types of beautiful antiques. The dining room was like a greenhouse, with a table in the middle and a dirt floor on each side where plants could grow indoors. They even had a hot tub in the backyard. Their house was gorgeous—not the usual American home, but very stereotypical Marin County.

In March 1984 my grandson Riley was born in that house with the assistance of both a midwife and a doctor. The whole family watched his birth—even me, although I was reluctant. Who wants to see somebody go through all of that pain? My mother and older sisters had their children with the help of a midwife, but I thought a hospital and painkillers were a better way to go. However, this was Bill and Patti's baby, and they could do what they liked. I wasn't thrilled by the idea of being a part of it all, but I tried to keep that to myself.

Patti went into labor in the evening and didn't have the baby until early the next morning. I came over to their house as soon as Bill called me and spent the night in the guest room, waiting. Patti was upstairs, in their antique bed. I got a bit of sleep but woke when Patti went into the last stages of labor. Everyone gathered in her bedroom—the midwife, the doctor, Billy, Shannon, and even Greg, who was standing by with a camera, ready to get pictures of the whole process. I was still downstairs with Jason. Suddenly Billy called to us from the upstairs balcony.

"Come on up, Mom. The baby is ready to come," he told me. "Hurry or you'll miss it."

I didn't really want to, but Jason and I headed upstairs anyway. And you know what? It was absolutely wonderful. I'm so happy I didn't miss seeing beautiful little Riley coming into this world. There's nothing quite like it.

Unfortunately not everything was so positive. Eda's health was going rapidly downhill. She complained that the woman next door was watching her all the time. One day when Eda and I were in her backyard, she told me to look at the neighbor woman standing over by the fence, watching us.

No one was there.

Once again I took Eda to the neurologist. Hallucinations were just a part of her condition, which was growing worse, he said. There was nothing anyone could do about it. I took Eda back home, and we all tried to make her life as comfortable as possible. It was hard on me, because her condition brought a lot of my fears roaring back to life. She was out of control, and it reminded me of my brother Rico. I tried to keep seeing her as much as if not more than before, but it became too stressful for me to drive down to San Anselmo three or four times each week.

My nephews Fred and Beb—Paolina's sons—both lived near Eda and agreed to check on her on a regular basis. I also arranged for a nearby Italian restaurant to deliver dinner to Eda every night. Eda loved their food, so it worked out well. And I still kept in touch by telephone. I talked to Eda several times during the week for a chat, and I always called her on Saturday, without fail.

One Saturday I called repeatedly, but Eda didn't answer. I telephoned Fred, but he wasn't home. His daughters Carolyn and Nancy went over to Eda's home and found her lying on her sofa, only semiconscious.

They immediately called an ambulance to take Eda to the hospital. She hadn't had a stroke exactly, but her collapse was caused by the lack of blood circulation to her brain. She never regained consciousness. The woman who had once been my vital, lovely, stylish sister, the family's social butterfly, was completely unresponsive for several months. After a short stay in the hospital, we moved her to a convalescent home in Tiburon. Eda died on March 13, 1985.

Once again the funeral arrangements were handled by the same San Anselmo mortuary that had taken care of Bill and Algisa. This time when the family gathered for the funeral, Joe and I were the only members of our generation. All the others were gone.

I wrote Eda's newspaper obituary announcement and arranged for her headstone. I made sure they listed only her date of death, not her birth date or her age. As far as everyone else knew, she was eighty. I was the only one who knew she was eighty-two, and I saw no reason to reveal her little secret. It was the least I could do for my sister, who had been so unlike me and yet so dear to me.

As executor of Eda's estate I was in charge of clearing out her home, disposing of her things, and selling the house. It soon got to be more than I could handle. Once again I felt like I was in a fog and just going through the motions of daily living. As draining as Eda's demands had been, she had needed me. There had been at least one person in my life I could take care of. Now I was once again entirely on my own.

As I started to slide back down into the black depression that had grabbed me after Bill and Algisa's deaths, I recalled my husband's gentle insistence that I needed to love myself. I had never completely accomplished that while he was alive, but now more than ever it was important for me to realize that my self-worth didn't depend on taking care of other people. I could enjoy life without first making sure everyone around me was okay. This was a concept that I was still getting accustomed to, but it helped lift at least some of the emotional darkness that surrounded me.

I also remembered Bill's note, the one I found about a week after his death. He obviously wanted me to enjoy my life without him. As difficult as that was at times, I needed to do it, if for no other reason than to honor his memory and all that he had taught me in our forty years together.

It was good that I was beginning to pull myself back together because I had another medical battle on my hands. In June 1985, just three months after Eda's death, suspicious results from a routine pap smear led my doctor to schedule a hysterectomy. It seemed likely I had uterine cancer, but the operation would confirm it one way or the other. A few days before the Fourth of July, I checked into Sonoma Valley Hospital, which was only a few blocks from my condo. As the staff prepared me for the surgery I was calm, but Billy was worried. He asked me what I thought about it all.

"Well, my mother always told me that everything comes in threes," I told him. "This is the third time I will have had cancer, so as far as I'm concerned it should be my last. I'm kind of looking forward to just dealing with it and getting it over with."

"What kind of logic is that?" Billy asked me in surprise. He was dumbfounded by my reasoning, but it made emotional sense to me. As illogical as it may have seemed to him, adopting that viewpoint helped me stay calm and collected.

I needed that calmness and all of my determination. The growth was malignant. It was indeed my third bout with cancer. The doctor was convinced he'd gotten it all, but for safety's sake he wanted me to take oral chemotherapy. Bill's chemo had been administered intravenously, by a needle into his arm, but mine was done with a daily pill. The doctor thought I would probably have to keep taking it all of my life. There didn't seem to be any side effects—I didn't lose my hair or get nauseous—and my doctor said the oral chemo was mostly a preventive measure, to be extra sure.

I was glad that it was all over, and I was confident that having been vanquished three times, my cancer would never return. Life went on and I continued to celebrate its sweetness. Once again I was able to say to myself, "I will greet each day with love in my heart," and mean it.

Early in 1986 I got the good news that Patti was pregnant again. Even at age thirty-eight she was still delighted to be having another baby. This time there was no talk of a midwife or a home birth; Patti went to the hospital when she went into labor. I stayed at their home and took care of two-year-old Riley. Little Petey was born on September 6, 1986—the same day his father turned forty years old.

By this time I was probably the only one still referring to my son as "Billy." He was the father of five children and a highly successful businessman. Especially at the office, I tried to call him Bill. Gradually—when it became less painful to acknowledge that my Bill was gone—my son also became "Bill" in my mind. Certainly he deserved the more grown-up name. By 1986 annual sales at Willitts Designs had soared to an impressive $17 million, which was 93 percent more than when Bill and I had relinquished the reins in 1978. There had been sixteen employees when we turned everything over to our son; now there were one hundred.

In December 1986, Bill moved Willitts Designs into a custom-built 80,000-square foot warehouse and office space in Petaluma. I was still working part time for the company and was really enjoying it. In the spacious new facility Bill had a special office designed for me. It had two large windows that overlooked the street and a brass plate with my name on it on the door. Believe me, it was a real delight to walk in there to work. It was quite a step up from when I was fifteen years old and thrilled to be in my first secretarial office, where I had barely enough room for my desk, chair, typewriter, and filing cabinet.

The new Willitts building also included an employees' exercise room. It was set up for karate and aerobics classes as part of the company's "Be Healthy" policy Bill had created. Twice a week he trained in Kenpo karate alongside the other Willitts Designs employees. Patti taught aerobics classes. For each day they exercised, the employees got an extra five dollars in their paychecks, up to a weekly maximum of fifteen dollars. As president of the company Bill also stressed emotional health and good communications. Each month there was a "Speak Freely" meeting. Employees could offer suggestions or air their complaints. There was also an "Employee of the Month" award that brought with it a bouquet of balloons and a preferential parking space.

A healthy, motivated workforce was a big part of my son's formula for success. He wrote about this in an article for an airline magazine—one of those freebies you find when you're flying in a commercial airplane. Apparently the magazine story caught the eye of someone at NBC's *Today* show because in the summer of 1987 reporter Mike Jensen and a film crew spent all day at our Petaluma plant shooting a segment on Bill's unusual path to success.

They filmed me, they filmed Patti, they filmed the employees—but the star of it all was my son, Bill. All those hours of shooting resulted in a ten-minute segment that aired August 21, 1987. I woke up extra early and watched the show from my home. There were scenes of Bill karate kicking and making business decisions. Reporter Jensen described Willitts Designs as "an enormous success" and "a kissy kind of company."

"We're committed to success as a business. We're just doing it differently," my son said on camera. I was so proud of him—both for what he had accomplished with the company his parents had started on a shoestring and for the recognition he was receiving for his innovative, sensitive management style.

I also appeared in the *Today* program segment—for a split second. *My gosh, I'm on national television,* I thought to myself.

I didn't like my appearance all that much (I thought I looked much older than I felt), but it was amazing to see myself on TV, even briefly. I went into the office, where everyone was pleased and excited. Bill and Patti thought it was great publicity for the company. Then I went to the bank to make a deposit.

"I saw you on the *Today* show," the teller told me excitedly.

Someone had recognized me on TV. I felt like a celebrity. All of this was pretty heady stuff for a little immigrant girl who quit high school and got a job so she could have enough money to enjoy life a bit.

Everything was going so well for me. My depression was gone. There had been no signs of cancer following my 1985 hysterectomy, and after two years of taking the oral chemotherapy, my doctor told me I could discontinue the medication. It seemed like a good time to celebrate being alive. By this time my granddaughter, Shannon, was away at college, but my grandsons Greg and Jason were still at home. In the summer of 1988 I took the two of them on a tour of Italy as a high school graduation present for Greg. We spent a week exploring Rome, Sorrento, the Amalfi Coast, and Pompeii; then the three of us took a train to Florence, where we were joined by Bill and Patti. After several days in that beautiful city, we rented a car and drove approximately thirty miles to the town of Montecatini, where I once again had a wonderful visit with my cousin Cesarina.

We took a quick side trip to my native Lucca, which was about eighteen miles west of Montecatini. My brother Joe had given me directions to the house where I was born and grew up. We didn't have much time, but we followed Joe's instructions and located a house that I thought might be the right one. I only got a quick glance at the outside of the building. Still, I felt a chill up my spine as I remembered myself as a little girl, eating my breakfast while sitting on the first-floor windowsill and gazing out at the world around me. I didn't know until years later that I was actually looking at the wrong house.

After Bill and Patti flew home, the boys and I continued on to Switzerland and then back into Italy through the spectacular Alps. It was an exciting adventure even though I had caught a cold that I just couldn't seem to shake. At one point I completely lost my voice and couldn't utter a sound. I arrived back home in Sonoma, coughing and with almost no energy.

I made an appointment with my doctor and told him I thought I'd caught some kind of bug in Italy. He sent me for X-rays, but they showed no serious problems. I didn't get any better and after several weeks developed a nasal infection. My doctor sent me to an allergy specialist, who in turn referred me to a nose specialist. He operated on my sinuses, but the surgery gave me no relief. I was still coughing up a storm and getting weaker every day.

Finally I had to quit my part-time job at Willitts Designs because I was too sick. By this time I was using oxygen several hours a day. I slept with it on and kept a tank beside my favorite chair in the living room so I could read or watch television while breathing the extra oxygen. I could go without it for several hours a day, but otherwise I needed it to be able to breathe properly.

I worried that I wouldn't be able to go to my granddaughter Shannon's wedding on September 9, 1989, but I pulled myself together and managed to attend. Shannon married Michael Falk, who is Jewish, in a wonderful outdoor ceremony in Santa Rosa, about forty-five minutes northwest of Sonoma. It was the first time I had attended a Jewish wedding, and I thought the rituals were so beautiful. Shannon was so beautiful. It seemed such a short time since she was born and I worried that I might never see my granddaughter if she was given up for adoption. Now she was a lovely bride.

But I couldn't stay at the wedding for long because I tired so very quickly. I had to go home and get back on my oxygen tank. In the weeks after the wedding I was increasingly irritated by my ill health. There seemed to be no treatment or even a diagnosis. The coughing and fatigue just wouldn't let up. In October I started having even more difficulty breathing and had to be rushed to the local emergency room. I was admitted to Sonoma Valley Hospital. The doctors ran all sorts of tests but still didn't have any answers. They did a biopsy that indicated my lungs were clear and healthy, but still I was struggling for air.

I ended up going in and out of that hospital every two weeks, often gasping for each breath. Finally I was admitted to the medical center at the University of California at San Francisco. Three resident doctors and one regular doctor were assigned to my case.

"Although your lung biopsy was clear, at this stage we can't completely discount cancer," the doctor told me.

I basically ignored his warning because I had already fought cancer three times and, at age eighty, I figured I was done with it. The biopsy hadn't shown cancer, so I was sure there was some other explanation for my breathing problems.

They ordered all kinds of tests on my lungs and heart. They even did a lung scan from my neck to my pelvis. This procedure took four hours; I had to be tranquilized so I wouldn't cough and ruin the test results. I figured it was worth it—with all these experts running so many tests, they had to be able to find out what was wrong with me. Then they would fix it and I could go home to Sonoma and get on with my life.

CHAPTER 25

The view from my room at UCSF medical center was spectacular. The hospital sits atop a small hill—the area is called Parnassus Heights—south of Golden Gate Park. I was on about the third or fourth floor, and the outside wall was all windows. I could see the park, the Golden Gate Bridge, and the spire on the church at the University of San Francisco, where two of my nephews had earned their degrees. They were all familiar, beautiful sights. I was gazing at part of the city that had been home to me and my family for so many years.

My room was spacious and not at all like a typical hospital cubicle. There were two beds, but most of the time I was there I was the only patient. So, of course, I was in the bed nearest the window. That's where they brought me after the four-hour lung scan. Still woozy from the tranquilizers used to keep me from coughing during the procedure, I just lay there enjoying the scenery. It was a crisp, cool fall day late in 1989. I was eighty years old. Although San Francisco can be incredibly foggy and overcast, especially in the summer, that day the sky was clear and bright. It seemed as if I could see forever. Full of the medication, I was completely calm, relaxed, and unconcerned about what came next. That wasn't true for my son, Bill, when he stopped by to see me. He knew all the testing had been completed, and he wanted to know the results.

"They said they won't be able to give me any details for twenty-four hours," I told him calmly.

I may have been tranquil enough to be willing to wait, but Bill wasn't. He wanted answers. He was polite with the hospital staff but insistent, repeatedly asking for anyone who could give us some information.

When it became clear that Bill wasn't going to give up and wasn't going to go away, the nurses produced a young woman who was one of the three medical students assigned to my case. I had gotten to know her during my several days in the hospital, and although she was pretty much the rookie on my medical team, I knew she was conscientious and caring. Now Bill was putting her on the spot.

"We won't have a complete report until tomorrow," she told my son in her best professional manner.

"Even if the report isn't complete, we want to know what you saw during the scan. What can you tell so far?" he asked.

"There are small spots of cancer in both lungs," she told us in a quiet voice. She leaned over the bed and gave me a quick hug, then left the room.

I was stunned. So was Bill, but he recovered first.

"Get dressed, Mom. I'm taking you home," he told me.

I didn't even ask him why. Certainly I'd had my fill of hospitals and was ready to leave. Perhaps my thinking was still fuzzy because of the aftereffects of the tranquilizers. And I was shocked by the news about my lung cancer. I wanted to be somewhere, anywhere else. Or maybe it was just that I had been trained by my family to follow instructions from men without questioning and this information had rocked me back into my earlier, more obedient mode. Whatever the reason, without a single question or protest I let Bill help me into my clothes and gather up my things. When we started to walk out of the room, the medical student suddenly reappeared, blocking our way.

"You can't take her home," she told Bill. "Her lungs are so weak that they could collapse at any moment and she would have to be rushed to the emergency room."

"If that happens, then I'll take her to the emergency room. She's coming home with me," Bill replied.

I never officially checked out. We just left.

By this time Bill and Patti had gotten tired of the continually gray, foggy weather along the Marin coastline and sold their house in Inverness. They had moved to Petaluma, in a much sunnier area that was also nearer the Willitts Designs building. They bought an older home on a half-acre lot, complete with an ancient water tower on the property. The existing house only had three bedrooms, so in addition to totally renovating it, Patti and Bill added a mobile home in the backyard. This served as a bedroom for their oldest son, Greg. The next oldest, Jason, slept in a room at the top of the water tower. Their younger two, Riley and Petey, slept inside the main house with Patti and Bill.

My thoughts were blank as Bill drove me north to this comfortable, rural setting. I still wasn't thinking clearly as Bill and Patti settled me into Petey's bed and arranged for Petey to sleep in Riley's room. For that first night I was content to just relax and regroup, surrounded by my loving family.

The next day, of course, I wanted to go home—to my home, not Bill's. I wanted to be back in familiar surroundings. My son wouldn't hear of me staying at my place on my own, so he got on the telephone and started calling people, trying to work something out. We'd gotten the bad news about the cancer on a Friday. By Sunday Bill had located a young woman—a highly recommended friend of a friend—whom he hired to sleep in my spare bedroom every night. It was only then that he was willing to let me move back home. She wasn't there to take care of me, just to be on hand if anything happened.

Although I had left the UCSF hospital abruptly, that didn't mean we had given up hope of finding a medical cure. We contacted the doctors, and they recommended chemotherapy treatments. The only good news—if anything about needing chemo could be called good news—was that the doctors believed the cancer had originated in my breasts, which meant I would get a lighter dose of chemotherapy than if the disease had started in my lungs. After checking various treatment facilities throughout the area, I picked the comfortable familiarity of Marin General Hospital and an oncology specialist who had worked with Bill. Despite the fact that Bill had lost his battle with cancer, I trusted this doctor and felt that if anyone could help me, she could.

So in mid-November 1989 my niece Olga drove me from Sonoma to Marin for my first chemotherapy appointment. It was about a forty-minute drive. Olga kept up a cheerful conversation, but I could tell she was worried about what I was about to go through and was trying hard to keep my spirits up. I was scheduled for several months of chemo, going in for three or four days in a row one week and then taking the next week off to give my body time to recover. Friends and family members had agreed to take turns driving me to my appointments.

On that first visit Olga took a seat in the waiting room while the nurse showed me into a small private treatment room. Olga had offered to keep me company during the procedure, but I asked her not to. I remembered how hard it was for me to watch the first time my husband was given chemotherapy. I didn't see any reason to make Olga share the experience with me. I felt I was better off doing it alone.

I sat upright for the procedure. The main piece of furniture in the treatment room was a comfortable chair with a wide armrest. It was important to keep my arm relaxed and still. Unlike the oral chemo I took after my uterine cancer, this time I was on the "real" stuff—nasty chemicals seeping slowly into my body through an intravenous needle and tube, just as Bill had experienced eleven years before. It was still clear in my mind how important it was to find a good vein, because if any of the chemo leaked into my body or onto my skin, it would burn me. And again I found the first time to be the most difficult. It was incredibly hard to sit back and watch the nurse push that needle into my arm.

Once she found a vein and carefully inserted the IV, she put a device on my head that was supposed to keep my hair from falling out. It was sort of like having an old-fashioned cone-shaped hair dryer on my head. It cost extra to use this thing, but I had decided it was worth it because I dreaded the idea of going bald. For the next twenty to thirty minutes I sat with that strange contraption on my head while the caustic chemotherapy medication flowed drip by drip into my body. As I waited I found myself unable to believe that this was truly happening to me. It seemed unreal. I had been so sure that I would never have to face chemo, and yet here I was with a needle in my arm, a strange device on my head, and horrible chemicals flowing into my system.

When I was done, they gave me a bunch of medications to prevent nausea and vomiting as well as a whole host of prescriptions to avoid other nasty side effects. The nurse kept talking as if it was a foregone conclusion that I would get sick to my stomach. I hate to upchuck, I just hate it, so I was determined to do anything I could to avoid it.

As Olga drove me home we intently discussed the details of how, when, and where to get the prescriptions filled and what might help keep me from vomiting. As we talked I kept telling myself that I was not going to get sick. I focused on staying relaxed and calm so that stress wouldn't add to the problem. We stopped at a local pharmacy on the way home, ending up with a bag full of various—and expensive—medications. When we got back to my condo, I found Patti and all her kids waiting for me.

"Please go home," I told them. "If I get sick to my stomach, I don't want anyone around."

"Just go ahead and get sick," Patti cheerfully replied. "We're not leaving. We're here to help."

Oh great, just what I wanted—an audience. Even Bill left work early and showed up at my place in the late afternoon.

"I had to come, Mom," he told me. "I had to be a part of this. I kept thinking about you, and I couldn't stay at work another minute."

I love my son and was glad to see him, but if I was going to be violently ill I wanted to do it in peace and quiet—not in the middle of my family. Of course nobody listened to me when I told them I'd rather be alone. Fortunately I was one of the lucky ones. I never did get nauseous or throw up from the chemo. That first night I was even able to eat a light supper. In fact, although I spent a small fortune getting the prescriptions filled, I never needed any of them. I skipped most of the standard side effects from chemo.

Unfortunately, I didn't skip them all. My hair was a different story. I had paid extra money for that cone thing and wore it on my head during my first two series of treatments, hoping against hope that it would somehow protect my hair and keep it from falling out. I had no idea why the doctors thought that contraption would help, but I figured they knew what they were doing and it had to do some good or they wouldn't have suggested I use it.

Ha.

After a couple weeks my hair starting coming out in great big clumps. I kept waking up with less and less hair on my head, until finally it was all gone. I didn't care what anybody told me; I felt ugly when I was bald. And I discovered that I really missed washing my hair. I hadn't understood how relaxing it was and how much shampooing every other day was part of my normal, non-cancer routine. So there I was, bald and feeling ugly. I tried on some wigs, but they were scratchy, hot, and uncomfortable. Instead I bought a bunch of soft fabric berets in strong colors—red, white, blue, and black—that matched most of my clothing. I convinced myself that the berets looked jaunty, and after a while I grew to like them.

It helped that down deep inside me I knew I was going to beat cancer for a fourth time. I could still close my eyes and remember that moment when God spoke directly to me in my garden so many years ago. The message hadn't changed or faded in the least. I knew I was going to make it. There was no inner communication telling me that God had changed His mind and my time had come. I was still absolutely certain the cancer was not going to win.

My son was not as optimistic. I didn't find this out until much later, but right after Bill took me out of UCSF medical center he had a doctor friend of his review my medical records. The friend told Bill that I had about six months left to live. Fortunately I never heard that gloomy prediction. I don't think it would have mattered if Bill had told me. I still would have listened to my inner voice, which was softly saying I was not going to die from this cancer.

I completed three series of treatments over a six-week period, going one week and taking the next week off to recover. Just as I was getting ready to start my fourth series of chemo appointments in late December I woke up feeling feverish. I pulled the thermometer out of my medicine cabinet and checked: 103 degrees.

I had been told quite clearly that patients with a fever can't take chemo treatments. I called my doctor and told her that overnight I had gone from normal to 103 degrees. She quizzed me about how I had taken my temperature. My doctor wasn't impressed with my old mercury thermometer, which I had to shake down, put in my mouth for several minutes and then read the results against the tiny lines and numbers.

"Elda, you're reading it wrong. Get a digital thermometer," she told me.

Someone immediately went out and bought me a digital model—my family and friends were always around to help—but the result was exactly the same: 103 degrees. So definitely no chemo treatments that week. The doctor said I could resume the treatments in two weeks, when I was scheduled for my next round of appointments.

That gave me three straight weeks off chemo. For the first four days I was feverish and miserable. I spent most of my time in bed. I barely had enough energy to walk down the hallway to the living room to sit in my favorite chair. If I did get up, I couldn't stay up for long; I was too weak and light headed. I wasn't able to cook, so everybody took turns stopping by to see how I was doing and to bring me food. My refrigerator was soon stuffed full of all kinds of tempting tidbits, but I didn't have much of an appetite.

Finally the fever broke and I immediately felt better. I called my doctor, and she told me to resume the chemo treatments as scheduled. But she also sent me to have my chest x-rayed to see exactly what was happening with the cancer in my lungs.

It was gone. All gone. Everything was dormant. Once again I was in remission. It felt great. I was certain I had won the battle against cancer for the fourth time—but my oncologist wasn't as optimistic.

"The cancer may be dormant now, but you need to continue the chemo treatments," she told me.

Dutifully I went for my next round of chemotherapy. But as I sat there with an IV needle letting those toxic medications seep into my vein, I wondered why I was doing it. If there was no sign of cancer in my lungs, why should I continue punishing my body with chemotherapy?

A friend had given me a copy of Deepak Chopra's book *Quantum Healing*. Reading it was pretty hard going—I think you almost have to be a doctor or nurse to understand everything in his book—but it gave me a lot to think about. One of the easier parts for me to understand was when he told stories about his patients' recoveries. He talked about a woman who broke into a high fever and then went into remission. Since that same miracle had happened in my body, it made me pay close attention to what Chopra was saying in his book.

I took stock of my situation. I was in remission. I was bald. I was tired of the harsh chemo. It seemed like a good time to try alternative, holistic methods of healing. In January 1990, I made all the necessary arrangements to spend ten days—February 1 to February 11—at Deepak Chopra's Ayurveda Clinic in Pacific Palisades, in Southern California. Once again my heart was telling me loudly and clearly what I should do next, and the message I got was to go to Chopra's clinic.

CHAPTER 26

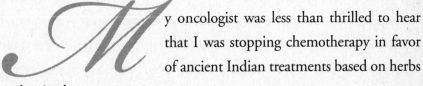y oncologist was less than thrilled to hear that I was stopping chemotherapy in favor of ancient Indian treatments based on herbs and attitude.

"If you stop your chemo now and your cancer comes back, then there will be nothing that can be done to save you," she told me.

"I guess that's the chance I have to take," I told her firmly and went ahead with my plans. This was my life, and this was my choice to make. I was ready to try something different.

And it was definitely different from the Western medicine I was used to. Chopra's clinic mailed me herbal sticks with detailed instructions about how to prepare for my visit there. Starting on January 12, I had to soak two of the herbal sticks overnight in one cup of water. The next morning I added a half-cup of milk, then boiled the whole thing down until there was only a half-cup of liquid, which I drank. That night I soaked three herbal sticks and went through the same routine in the morning, then four sticks, and finally five herbal sticks on the fourth night. I didn't know what was in those herbal sticks, but I figured if I was going to do this at all I might as well do it right. I followed the instructions to the letter as I packed for my trip.

I was also supposed to drink three to four glasses of hot water daily; keep my body warm; avoid strenuous exercise; and eat warm, well-cooked foods like steamed vegetables, soups, or lentils. I had to stop eating heavy foods such as oils, butter, or pizza; cold foods such as ice cream or yogurt; and raw vegetables or fruit. It seemed silly to go the clinic if I wasn't going to do as I was told, so I altered my diet and drinking habits to follow all these new rules.

I felt drawn to alternative medicine, especially as taught by Dr. Chopra. But my thoughts were full of other things as I flew to Chopra's Southern California clinic. My granddaughter, Shannon, and her husband, Michael, were expecting a child in a little over a month. Just days before I left on my trip, Michael had been diagnosed with cancer in one lung and one kidney. The doctors had spotted it early, before it had spread far, and said Michael's best hope was an operation to remove his diseased kidney before the malignancy spread any further.

I put my worry about Michael and Shannon aside as I checked into Chopra's clinic. For ten days I did nothing but focus on my own recovery. I ate a prescribed nonfat diet: no meat, no coffee, no tea, and no alcohol. The only thing I really missed was my daily glass of port with dinner. After all those years I was still following the advice of the doctor from my first battle with cancer and using a glass of port to relax me. I didn't like port at lunchtime or late at night, but it had been a staple on my supper table for more than forty years. However I gave it up gladly to follow the clinic's strict regime in the hope that the change would let my body heal itself.

Every day two staff people gave me a soothing, two-hour body massage. It was done in three phases—first a standard deep-muscle massage, then a health treatment that varied from day to day, and finally gentle rubbing with soothing oils as I listened to soft music. They also taught me how to meditate, which I did daily. Several times a day I watched videos of Chopra talking about health and healing.

The kitchen was open twenty-four hours a day. I would fix my own breakfast and snacks. For the vegetarian lunch and dinner, a staff member would roll a steam table into the dining room and we'd help ourselves. Since I didn't have a car, I couldn't go anywhere except to stroll along the beach. I would walk to see the sunset every night. It was always so beautiful, with amazing colors filling the sky as I walked on the soft sand. For those ten days, that beach and Chopra's clinic were my entire world.

It was quite an experience. In the past the place had been owned by movie stars. You could tell everything had once been rather elegant, but now it had definitely seen better days. Everything was reasonably clean, but a good maintenance man could have made a fortune there. In the center of the property was a pool, with all the rooms around it. They were sparsely furnished, and there was paint peeling off the wall in my bathroom. I had only two lamps in my room. The one on the chest of drawers didn't work at all, and the one sitting on a cardboard box next to my bed had a permanently crooked shade. Other patients' rooms were just as dilapidated, and there was no maid service. We cleaned up after ourselves and fetched our own clean towels.

As strange as the place was, I adored it. In a way I wish I had it all to do over again because it was the most relaxed ten days of my life. It gave me a chance to slow down and pay attention to my body. The staff was warm and dedicated. Everything was geared toward a healthful, healing environment and to understanding Chopra's philosophy. Each night I called my son with a progress report.

"You know, Bill, maybe now I know what it feels like to be in a cult—and I love it," I told him.

Perhaps I was brainwashed; I certainly took in a lot of new information in a short time without any outside input or feedback. But it all made sense to me—and it worked. I left feeling better than I had in years. My upbeat, healing attitude had been reinforced; my body had been carefully nurtured; and I had learned enough to keep caring for myself in positive ways. I was calm and stress-free. In a way I hated to go back into the "real world."

Things were certainly hectic when I got home. Patti picked me up at the San Francisco airport and took me straight to UCSF medical center, where Shannon was sitting with Michael, who was due to have his kidney removed the next morning. Michael had a private room, but it was not as spacious as mine had been and he didn't have any sort of view. I don't think he noticed or cared. Although he tried to hide it, it was clear he was scared right down to his bones.

Shortly after Patti and I arrived, Michael's surgeon stopped by to tell him exactly what to expect for the operation the next morning. With all of us crowded into that nondescript little room—Michael in bed, surrounded by me, Patti, and an extremely pregnant Shannon—Michael peppered the doctor with questions, trying to understand everything that might happen and all the implications. Michael had read somewhere that even though the patient was unconscious it was important to have soothing, familiar music during an operation. He had put together a tape of his favorite songs—including some by Bruce Springsteen and Santana—and asked that it be played during his surgery. The doctor quickly agreed. I guess he figured anything that reassured a nervous patient was worth doing.

After the doctor left, we stayed around for a bit, which gave me a chance to tell Michael all about my time at Chopra's clinic. Maybe the conversation simply helped take Michael's mind off of the looming operation, but he seemed genuinely interested in everything that had happened to me and whether I felt it had helped me. I definitely gave him a positive report. I think he could see how much happier and calmer I was than before my trip.

Michael went into the operating room on schedule and had his kidney removed on February 12, 1990. All went well. The lab tests showed they had caught the disease early. The doctors said Michael wouldn't have to go through radiation or chemotherapy treatments. He just needed to recover from the surgery, and then he could go home. Since his and Shannon's baby was due in a few weeks, that was good news.

For the past few weeks, of course, Shannon had been spending every moment she could with Michael at UCSF hospital. At night she stayed in a nearby hotel room. It was an extremely stressful time, so it's not surprising that she went into early labor while she was visiting Michael at UCSF. The medical staff whisked Shannon off to the maternity ward, which is where they discovered the baby was in breech position—feet first. Because of all the dangerous complications this can cause, little Max was delivered by cesarean section at UCSF on February 17, 1990, while his father lay in another UCSF hospital room recovering from cancer surgery. Both Shannon and Michael were in the hospital for several days—she was on the second floor and he was on the third. As soon as they felt well enough they were allowed to visit each other.

It was a busy, anxious time, but in a way it was a lot of small miracles all at once. My lung cancer was in remission; I didn't need more chemo or other treatments. Michael's cancer was also in remission, and the doctors said his prognosis was good; he didn't need chemo or radiation. Shannon came through the cesarean surgery with flying colors. And in the midst of all the worry about lung cancer and kidney cancer and emergency operations and chemotherapy, I got to meet my great-grandson, Max. So many things were happening at once that I almost couldn't keep up, and then suddenly I was a great-grandmother.

It was wonderful. Little Max was so beautiful and perfectly healthy. Ten toes, ten tiny fingers—a tiny bundle of yawning, burping life, snuggled into my arms. Once again I knew everything was going to be fine. The doctors could worry all they wanted about the long-term prognosis or the potential for a reoccurrence. I had triumphed over cancer for the fourth time, and God had graced me with a wonderful great-grandson. I was deeply thankful for all the blessings in my life.

As soon as he was well enough, Michael flew back east to spend ten days at another of Chopra's clinics. He loved it every bit as much as I had. He even went back for a second visit. Michael thanked me for all the healing he received, and I told him I didn't do anything; he did it all.

Gradually life began returning to normal. My hair started growing out again, and eventually my head was covered with pure white ringlets. My hair always had a lot of body and shape, but it had never been this perfectly curled. And the color was gorgeous—so white it was almost silver. I had been coloring my hair for so many years that I honestly didn't know what my "real" shade was when I started the chemo. But the end result was a luxurious, luminous crown of short, shimmering white curls. Something good had come out of something bad.

My son was still worried that I had a death sentence hanging over me and that, like his father's, my cancer would suddenly come roaring back. Fortunately he didn't tell me or anyone else about this until years later. As it was, I felt the cancer was once again behind me and I was ready to enjoy life again. I didn't go back to work at Willitts Designs; there were too many other things I wanted to do with my time.

Every Wednesday I went to Petaluma to babysit my grandsons, Petey and Riley, and to let Patti have some time to herself. At this point Petey was four years old and Riley was six. I adored them. Patti would drop them off at school in the morning and then have the day to herself. I'd pick up Petey at preschool around noon and take him to his home and feed him lunch. Sometimes I took him out to eat, as a special treat. Then when first grade let out, we'd go get Riley at his school and the three of us would spend the afternoon together. I loved it.

A couple of times a month I'd go down to the peninsula south of San Francisco and visit my brother Joe. Right up until the Loma Prieta earthquake in 1989, Joe and his wife, Annette, had lived in an apartment they rented in San Francisco's Marina district. The earthquake hit that area hard. Joe and Annette weren't hurt, but the building they were living in was badly damaged. After the quake their apartment had no running water, no gas, and no electricity.

That meant they needed to move somewhere, fast. Joe and Annette were in their nineties by then, and their kids, Jon and Joanne, didn't think they should live by themselves anymore. They found a retirement home in San Mateo, on the peninsula. After a short while Annette's health got a lot worse, and she had to be transferred to a convalescent hospital, where she could get better medical care. That left Joe on his own in the retirement home. It was clean and neat and not a bad place to live—but Joe didn't like it much. In particular he hated the meals. He was real Italian about his food, and this place was definitely not run by Italians or for Italians. He would eat what they served because it was the only thing available, but he was always eager to dine somewhere else.

So at least once a month, maybe twice, I'd drive down and take Joe out for a drive and lunch somewhere with food that was more to his liking. Sometimes my nephew Fred and his wife, Norma, would drive me down and we'd visit Joe together. In good weather we'd pack a picnic lunch with all of Joe's favorites, like mortadella and proscuitto lunch meats and Italian-style olives. Joe loved Italian olives. We'd take him to a park where we could enjoy the food and the sunshine. I looked forward to these visits. Joe still had his same calm, easygoing temperament. Plus, he was my brother and the only other member of my immediate family who was still alive. I made sure we kept in touch.

I also spent a lot of time with my friends, visiting and doing things I loved. The way I saw it, death had stared me in the eye one more time, and I was still here. Everyone was healthy and doing well, so I figured I'd enjoy life to the fullest. I didn't do anything elaborate, like traveling extensively or buying new things. I simply spent all the time I could enjoying my friends and family, which is what mattered the most to me.

I kept following a lot of what I had learned at Chopra's clinic, except that I kind of modified it to fit me. Each morning I'd eat cereal and fruit for breakfast. After that I would meditate for a while, then— as I had every morning for decades—I'd light a candle and pray, spending a long time just talking with God. Following Chopra's lifestyle didn't change the Catholic in me.

Just the morning meditation and prayer took about an hour. Then I'd put a small saucepan on the stove and heat a bit of sesame oil. My master bathroom has a walk-in shower with a built-in bench on one wall. I'd carry the pan into the shower, sit down, and massage my entire body with the warm oil as I'd been taught at the clinic. It always felt wonderful. Then I'd take a long, long shower, rinsing all the oil off while relaxing my aging muscles.

It took me several hours to get ready to start each day, and I rarely got out of my house before noon. Even my grandchildren knew that Grandma Elda shouldn't be disturbed during her morning routine. But I figured I had spent so many years taking care of everyone else that I deserved to spend this time taking care of myself.

And I felt I deserved my glass of port at dinner each night. It was a comforting habit that I wasn't willing to give up, even if Chopra clearly said "no alcohol." I continued to eat the nonfat diet they had taught me at the clinic, with no meat, no coffee, and no tea—or at least I did that for about six months. Then I went back to my own Italian-style cooking. I did keep following Chopra's advice to drink warm or hot water rather than ice-cold beverages. And I found a local massage therapist and treated myself to a full body massage every week.

I walked a lot—all over sleepy downtown Sonoma, stretching my legs as I visited the farmers' market and the local grocery stores while enjoying the backdrop of the tree-studded hills that surround the valley. I had triumphed over cancer a fourth time, and my life was sweet. I didn't need to take care of someone else to feel like I had self-worth. I knew deep inside that I was enough just as I was. After all those years, I had finally managed to do what Bill had suggested—I had learned to love myself.

Meanwhile my son had a lot of worries on his mind. The business was doing great, but the gift import industry is difficult and complex. The company had changed a lot under Bill's guidance. Each year

Willitts Designs was creating as many as five hundred or more new products, which were manufactured in factories in Asia. There were many things that could go wrong from the initial idea to the final product. Bill had to oversee every step. With the manufacturing done so far away, quality was a big concern. Bill was always trying to spot little problems before they became big ones and to solve the big ones when they surfaced.

He was also routinely attempting to second-guess the market. The company did about 60 percent of its business just before Christmas, which meant it needed lots of money to have gift items manufactured and waiting for customers during the holidays. It also meant trying to anticipate which items would be popular and which ones wouldn't do as well. My son was constantly calculating how to avoid having too few of his top sellers and too many of the slow-moving items.

And Bill really cared about his employees. By this time, Willitts Designs employed more than 160 people. In Bill's mind that was 160 families depending on the continued success of the company. One day Bill told me he had realized that Willitts Designs was at a crossroads. If he was successful and could keep everything running smoothly, he would have more than five hundred people working for him. If he didn't make the right choices all down the line, there would be no employees because the company wouldn't make it. He didn't like either option.

"You know, Mom, I'm really getting worn out," he told me. "I think if I have a chance, I'm going to sell Willitts Designs."

"Go ahead," I told him. "I know what it's like to be buried in paperwork and overwhelmed by the details, to have the business take over your life."

It was our company, the one my husband and I had started from scratch, but I didn't want to hang onto it at the cost of my son's health and happiness. I knew my son was working way too hard for far too many hours. He was a family-oriented man with overwhelming business responsibilities. He was a local community–oriented man who had to travel extensively. As far as I was concerned, Bill couldn't keep up the pace he had set, and I didn't want him to.

So when the Hallmark Company showed an interest in Willitts Designs, we were definitely willing sellers. Hallmark had a good reputation in terms of how it treated its employees and customers. It also had the corporate structure and resources required to let Willitts Designs expand to the next level.

Of course it wasn't that simple. There were a lot of negotiations involved, a lot of back-and-forth. I wasn't a part of it; Bill handled it all. He wanted guarantees that all the employees would keep their jobs. And obviously we wanted to receive the highest price possible, while Hallmark wanted to pay the lowest. So it took time to come to an agreement. Occasionally we despaired of ever reaching a compromise. Sometimes it appeared that we'd have to look for another buyer, if one could be found.

It got to the point that it was time to fish or cut bait. On a Friday in the fall of 1991, Bill and his attorneys went to the offices of the law firm that was representing Hallmark. The meeting was in San Jose, in the southern end of the San Francisco Bay. Everyone involved knew it was a final negotiating session. Either a contract would be signed or the deal would fall through—and we weren't sure which way it would go.

To distract ourselves, Patti and I arranged for a babysitter and spent the evening in the East Bay at a seminar on self-growth and dysfunctional families. It was led by a man who was famous for his dynamic presentations and wonderful insights, but I'm not sure we learned all that much. We were both pretty distracted and anxious. A couple times Patti called home to see if there was any word from Bill. There were no messages, either good or bad.

The workshop ran late into the evening. Patti didn't get me home to my condo in Sonoma until almost 11 P.M. Still no word from Bill. Patti drove to her home in Petaluma and called me as soon as she arrived. Still no word from Bill. I couldn't believe it. What could they be talking about for so long? Bill finally called me well after midnight.

"The company is sold," he told me, his voice weary but jubilant. "It's all done. We made a deal."

Under the terms of the contract, the exact purchase price was—and still is—confidential. However there was more than enough cash involved to make Bill and Patti financially independent. Since I owned stock options in Willitts Designs, I was also financially independent.

My lifestyle had already been comfortable because of my husband's and my own hard work and careful investments. Now I had more money than I had ever dreamed of. The worry deep inside me that I could end up as poor as I was in my childhood—that concern, truly, was a thing of the past. I don't think the money brought me happiness, but it did bring me comfort. It was an amazing feeling to know that I would never be in need again.

I couldn't even imagine what Mamma would have said if she knew how much money I now had. She and Babbo risked everything to come to this country so their children could prosper. I wanted to be able to tell them how well things had worked out. I don't know, maybe in some way Mamma and Babbo knew about my good fortune.

Other than easing my deep-seated inner ache for security, the sudden influx of money didn't change my life. I kept on living in my Sonoma condo, which is comfortable and nice but nothing pretentious. Much more importantly, the place is full of reminders of my husband and our life together. And I didn't go out and buy a lot of new stuff. I already had everything I wanted and, again, most of it was connected to positive memories of my past.

I love what money does for me, the freedom and the choices it gives, the fact that it lets me help out my family or my friends when they're in need—but I don't love the money itself.

All I could think about was how incredibly blessed and lucky I had been. If I hadn't met and married Bill, none of this would have taken place. If the two of us hadn't poured all our time, energy, and money into the business, things never would have ended so positively. If our son hadn't turned that company into something even bigger and better, the sale wouldn't have happened. And it goes back even farther, to my parents' hard work with the hope that their children's lives would be better and easier than theirs had been. It even gets down to the fact that I was the youngest of my family's eight children and therefore the one to benefit the most from our move to this country.

The patterns of my life were so beautiful. I had been through a lot of turmoil and hardships, but in retrospect it seemed as if the bad times were needed in order to reach the good times. Every phase of my life was important and happened when it needed to. Now I had a loving family, a comfortable home, supportive friends, renewed health, and more money than any one person really needed. I didn't see how things could get any better.

CHAPTER 27

*I*t's amazing how society's perspectives and attitudes can shift over the years. When I was young, other people's reactions at school and at work left me deeply ashamed of the fact that my family and I were strangers to the ways of this country. I spent a lot of time and effort trying to fit in and become a "real American." Yet in the last dozen years or so I have been repeatedly honored for my immigrant background; it has brought me some of the best moments of my life.

It all started in 1990 when I began getting letters from Lee Iococca, who was in charge of raising money to restore Ellis Island in order to preserve its history as a port of entry for so many immigrants. I had read Iococca's autobiography. I knew what he had done when he was in charge of Chrysler and I knew he was Italian-American. And I remembered Ellis Island and how my whole family cried when we finally made it through the customs inspection and saw the Statue of Liberty. So even though I knew they were form letters and were probably sent to thousands of potential donors, each time Iococca "wrote" to me I'd send a donation check. It got to be a family joke.

"Has your friend Lee Iococca sent you a letter lately?" my son would ask me with gentle teasing in his voice. "Gosh, Mom, you must be at the top of their sucker list."

Maybe I was, but restoring Ellis Island meant so much to me. I kept sending a check in reply to each one of Iococca's requests for money and, of course, his letters kept coming on a regular basis.

But then there was one that was different. It was a note from Paul Sigrist, head of the Ellis Island Oral History Project. Instead of talking about the need for more financial support, it asked former immigrants if they were willing to do a taped oral interview about what it was like when they were processed through Ellis Island. The idea appealed to me. I had been working on my autobiography off and on so my grandchildren and great-grandchildren would know who they came from. I loved the idea of making an audio recording of my memories of Ellis Island.

I sent Paul Sigrist a letter describing my family's experiences going through the immigration processing center. After I filled out a detailed questionnaire, Paul told me I had been chosen for an oral interview. He said he would come to California sometime in the near future, but I suggested instead that I could meet with him in his office on Ellis Island.

This was in the fall of 1990, before Willitts Designs had been sold to Hallmark. Bill was still traveling to all the trade shows, lining up retailers and others to sell our company's gift line. He had a show scheduled in New York City. Patti and I decided to go along, and I made an appointment to meet with Paul Sigrist on November 8.

When the time came, Bill, Patti, and I took the tourist boat across the harbor from Manhattan to Ellis Island. Of course the first thing I looked for was the Statue of Liberty. We weren't going to visit her that day, but she represented so much of my parents' hopes and sacrifices. Here I was, coming back to do an interview that I hoped would honor their memory.

The immigrant processing building at Ellis Island is beautiful but overwhelming. It was designed and constructed at a time when public institutions were meant to be majestic and impressive. It certainly had been imposing, even frightening in 1916 when my family was just a handful among the thousands of people being herded through like cattle. Now I was back to make my memories part of the permanent record of the place. At least this time I could appreciate the grandeur of the architecture—the high ceilings, the carefully crafted details in a building that was slowly being restored as a memorial to all the tired and frightened people who had passed through there so many years ago.

We followed Paul's directions and easily found his office. He asked if I wanted my son and daughter-in-law to stay with me during the interview, but I said no. I had never been interviewed before, and I thought I'd be nervous if anyone was listening and maybe judging what I said. So Bill and Patti wandered off to tour Ellis Island on their own while I sat down in a tiny, windowless conference room with Paul and some audio tape-recording equipment.

It was easier than I expected. Paul and I really hit it off from the first moment we met. He was comfortable to talk to and so interested in what I had to say. I gradually forgot all about the tape recorder and started to enjoy telling my story. My family had relived our trip through Ellis Island many times; they had laughed and interrupted each other while repeating the familiar tale. The details were etched in my memory. It was certainly easy for me to recall my terror when the doctor approached me with the little hook, wanting to look into my eyes. That's not a moment you forget no matter how old you become.

The words simply flowed out of me, and before I knew it the interview was done.

I didn't know it then, but that one-hour tape recording would lead to all sorts of new adventures in my life. A few months later, in summer 1991, I got a call from a young man named Will Parrinello. He and some other young Marin County filmmakers were working on a documentary about Italian-Americans. They'd been to Ellis Island and asked Paul Sigrist for suggestions of people to contact. Paul gave them several names, including mine. They listened to the tape of my oral history interview and apparently liked what they heard. Will called and asked if I'd be willing to be videotaped for their documentary. I said I'd be honored. But when the day arrived for them to film me at my home in Sonoma, I was a bit nervous. I had no idea what to expect.

It turned out to be great fun. Will did the interview with John Antonelli as the cameraman and Jim Iacona on sound. All three of the boys—that's how I think of them, even to this day, as "the boys"—all three of them had grandparents who had come to this country from Italy. They decided to make the documentary after talking about their shared backgrounds.

They were so charming. Maybe I should have been upset because the first thing they did was come in and rearrange all the furniture in my living and dining rooms. But I was too busy talking and laughing with them; I wasn't really bothered by the disruption. The process took all day. In addition to moving my furniture, they set up a lot of lights, tripods, screens, electric cords, and other equipment in the morning. The four of us ate lunch together at my dining table, and then Will sat me down in one of my dining room chairs. With the camera rolling, Will asked me questions for most of the afternoon. And just as it had been with Paul Sigrist, the words flowed out of my mouth. I forgot about the lights, I forgot about the camera, and I just talked.

Maybe there was something freeing about having an attentive audience for tales that had been part of my family lore. All three of the boys seemed genuinely interested in and impressed by what I had to say. In a way it made my Ellis Island experiences feel less shameful. The more I talked about what had happened, the prouder I was of what my family had gone through to get here and what we eventually accomplished in this country. It also felt as if I was telling my story not only for me but for Mamma and Beppa and Jenny and everyone else in my family. Only Joe and I were still alive, and his health was gradually failing. It was up to me to record our experiences.

And as I said, that was just the first of a whole series of events that happened because I did that Ellis Island oral history interview with Paul Sigrist.

In October 1992, the National Trust for Historic Preservation made a presentation in San Francisco's elegant Herbst Theater, showing a video and trying to raise money to support the restoration of Ellis Island. The event organizers called me and asked me to attend as their guest. It turned out that some of the oral history interviews were included in the fundraising video. At the end you could hear my voice quite clearly, talking about my family's journey through Ellis Island as well as our relief and gratitude at being allowed into this country.

When the movie was over, the master of ceremonies invited me up on the stage. He explained that I was the woman heard talking at the end. As I stood in the spotlight on that beautiful stage, everyone stood up and applauded. For me. It was incredibly thrilling. Here I was in San Francisco, where I had felt some of my strongest shame that my immigrant family members weren't just like everybody else in this country, and I was being applauded for what years ago had brought me only embarrassment.

There was still more to come—a lot more. Because of family emergencies and other problems, it took a long time for the boys to get the documentary finished, but finally *Little Italy* was completed. It aired on KQED, the public television station in San Francisco. It was a big deal for the boys and for me. It turned out that I was in pretty fancy company. Some of the other people included in the documentary were August Coppola, who was the dean of San Francisco State University, author Gay Talese, and poet Lawrence Ferlinghetti.

On October 30, 1995—the day *Little Italy* was first broadcast on KQED—Will and the boys held a fancy reception in the television station's San Francisco lobby. They served Italian wines and the buffet had all kinds of Italian food, including a giant wheel of parmesan cheese. Hundreds of people were there, and I got to meet everyone else who had been featured in the documentary. Bill and Patti attended with me. We had already seen the movie—the boys gave me a copy on videotape, and I bought several more to give to my family and friends—but that night we got to watch it in KQED's screening room. It was quite a thrill.

I sent a form letter to all my family and friends telling them exactly when *Little Italy* was going to be on local TV. My phone rang for days after it aired.

"Elda, it's such a wonderful show, and you were the best one in it," one friend said. In fact, several people told me that. I figured they were biased. Still, it was great to get all the compliments. And nobody, absolutely nobody, seemed to be looking down on me because I was an immigrant.

It's amazing what time will do.

That still wasn't the end of it all. In 1997 Bill called me asking if I got the History Channel on my cable TV because they were showing a series that included a segment about Ellis Island. My voice, telling my family's story, was part of the soundtrack. Bill bought the three-video series so I could hear myself again.

Meanwhile Paul Sigrist was working to overcome the bureaucratic hurdles he faced in trying to make the Oral History Room a reality on Ellis Island. I was one of eleven people chosen to be featured in a "Children of Ellis Island" exhibit. The first phase was unveiled in April 1997, with mine as one of four life stories on display. Paul asked me to be there for the opening event, but I chose to delay my visit. I wanted my whole family to be with me, and because of school and other commitments we couldn't make the trip from California to New York until June. It was worth the wait because Paul told me later that the opening ceremonies were just a madhouse. This way I got to see the exhibit quietly, surrounded by my son, my daughter-in-law, my grandchildren, and my great-grandchildren.

As always, there were long lines to catch the boat to Ellis Island. Unfortunately I wasn't walking as well as I used to. The chemotherapy for the lung cancer had caused a condition in which my feet were becoming increasingly numb, which made it hard to keep my balance. I could still walk, but it was difficult to stand in line for long periods of time. So instead of making us take the tourists' ferry with everyone else, Paul arranged for me and my family to ride on the employees' launch over to Ellis. He met us at the dock, and he even had a wheelchair for me. Normally I didn't need one, but that chair made it possible for my grandchildren to push me all over the island so we could see absolutely everything. Paul headed back to work but asked us to be sure to meet him in the Oral History Room at 2 P.M. When we got there Paul sat me in a place of honor in the Ellis Island Theater and then started the afternoon's presentation.

"Each day we have an actor portray the life of an immigrant, based on the oral history interviews," Paul explained to the crowd that had gathered.

A young woman stepped onto the stage and began talking. She was dressed in a plain white blouse and a long skirt. It took me several minutes of listening to realize that she was me. It was my story she was acting out. She was being Elda Del Bino and recalling her terror during the medical exam on Ellis Island. She spoke of all the planning and hard work it took for my family to come to the United States, everything that happened on our trip, and how we were reunited with Babbo and Rico in San Francisco.

I have never cried so much in my life as I did that day. I sat there, surrounded by my loving family, with the tears just streaming down my face as I listened to this beautiful young woman tell the tale of Mamma and Joe and Beppa and Jenny and Algisa and Paolina and Eda and Rico and Babbo and me. She even got all their names right. And she did it in the middle of Ellis Island, where Mamma had been so afraid we wouldn't make it through the examinations and I had been overwhelmed with terror when the doctor tried to look at my eyes. There's no other way to describe it. Listening to that young woman tell my life story was one of the best moments in my life.

And still there was more to come. The boys were starting to enter the *Little Italy* documentary in various film festivals, hoping it would be picked up by a distributor or other public television stations. Amazingly it was selected to be shown in October 1997 at the first-ever Sonoma Valley Film Festival in the historic Sebastiani Theatre, which is right on the Sonoma Plaza and just a few blocks from my home. A reporter from our local newspaper came out to interview me, and the paper's photographer took a whole roll of pictures just of me. A few days before the film festival began the newspaper published a full-page story about me on the front of its Valley Life section, complete with a huge, wonderful photograph.

The 323-seat Sebastiani is one of the grand old theaters. Built in the 1930s, it has long, impressive red curtains and glittering chandeliers high overhead. When it came time to show *Little Italy*, the place was sold out. Several of my friends were there, but I didn't recognize most of the people in the audience. They had read the story in the paper and simply wanted to see the documentary.

It was wonderful to watch *Little Italy* on a huge screen in a large, dark theater, surrounded by an attentive audience. The boys had managed to capture so much in a sixty-minute film, and I was proud of what I considered my small part in it. I was much more proud and even a little stunned after the movie ended. The emcee introduced the filmmakers. Then the boys introduced me and had me join them on stage. I got a standing ovation. At age eighty-eight I felt like the belle of the ball.

The thing was, I didn't expect that much attention. I hadn't even invited my family to the film festival. They had all been given copies of the videotape. Bill and Patti had attended the KQED event. It didn't seem important for any of them to come see it again. I had honestly thought there would be a relatively small audience, with most of the attention on the documentary itself and the three young men who had made it. Instead I was treated like a celebrity with lots of people asking me questions about my life and my experiences as an immigrant. My husband, Bill, had always told me I should take pride in my family, their hard work, and their good values. Now an amazing number of people were showing not only interest in our story but also respect for my family.

A few weeks after the film festival I got a phone call from Patricia Henley, the reporter who had interviewed me and wrote the article for our local newspaper. She had been intrigued by my story and wanted to learn more. Patricia knew I had already written a small autobiography for my family, but she convinced me to work with her on a more detailed version of my life experiences. We developed a real friendship as we spent more than six years digging into my recollections, ideas, and outlook on life.

And the outside interest didn't stop there. Mondo Publishing produces textbooks and other classroom materials. In 1999 they contacted Paul Sigrist at Ellis Island because they wanted to feature the story of a young immigrant from northern Italy. Paul gave them four or five oral history tapes, and they chose mine. The first I heard of it was when someone from Mondo called me, asking for permission to turn my taped interview into an illustrated storybook for third- and fourth-graders.

Did they really think I might say no?

"We can do wonders with your story," the author told me excitedly.

And believe me, they did. She used the oral history tape as the basis for the simple text. The artist worked from copies of my old family photos to make the illustrations look like us. *Journey to a New Land—An Oral History* was released in November 2000. It was so incredibly gorgeous. Each page had a drawing of me or members of my family. It wasn't us exactly, but it sure looked a lot like me and Babbo and Mamma and everyone else. The artist had caught our family's physical traits.

In beautiful, simple language the book told all about my parents' difficult decision to send Babbo and Rico off to America alone, the dreadful voyage in steerage, my fear of the doctor, our tears at the sight of the statue of liberty, the cross-country train trip, and how we were reunited with Babbo and Rico in San Francisco—everything, absolutely everything that had happened. I bought a hundred copies of the book and gave them out to my family and friends. When those ran out, I ordered fifty more. And of course everyone wanted me to autograph their copy. Once again I felt like a celebrity and all because of my oral history interview with Paul Sigrist.

The book came in two sizes. There was a student version that was about eleven inches wide and nine inches high. The teacher's version was about twenty inches high and twenty-three inches wide. It was meant to be read aloud in front of a classroom of students. I kept one copy of both types and had them mounted in a special frame. They're hanging in a place of honor in my hallway, alongside family photographs and the lovely poem our son gave Bill and me at our surprise retirement party.

Then in summer 2002 I got a call to be in yet another PBS documentary, *They Came to America*. As before, they chose me because of the oral history interview I'd done with Paul Sigrist. They were friendly and wonderful people, and once again I enjoyed myself. By the end of the year they gave me a copy of the finished videotape. When I watched it, I didn't like it as much as *Little Italy*—but only because I thought I looked so much older than I had when the boys made their film in 1991. In my mind I hadn't aged, but the camera told me differently.

The people who made *They Came to America* said they would let me know when it will be shown on KQED television. I haven't heard from them yet, but I keep watching for the show, just in case. Even if it made me look older than I felt, it would be fun to see it broadcast on TV. Meanwhile, "the boys" had even more success with *Little Italy*. It was picked up by public television and shown nationwide during pledge week. It was big success, both for the PBS stations and for the filmmakers, Will, John, and Jim. It was startling to think that people all across America—at least the people who viewed PBS at the time— had watched me tell my story in *Little Italy*.

It's not that I think I'm all that special. I'm still the same person I always was, a mix of good and bad. I believe it's my story that captures people's attention. It's my family's grit and courage that has people asking me questions and wanting to know more. And it's mind-boggling how much attention I've received because of my immigrant background and my Ellis Island experiences.

When I first started working at age fifteen, I had to deal with labels like "dago" and worse. I still remember the man who said loud and clear that people who didn't speak English should go back to where they came from. Now I've been given honor after honor for that exact same background.

So many people say it's not the same today, that the Latino immigrants are different from those in the past because they aren't learning the language and the customs. I'm here to tell you it's not true. It's the same now as it was eighty-seven years ago when I arrived in San Francisco with Mamma and Joe and all my sisters.

We lived in a predominantly Italian neighborhood. Mamma never did learn English, despite the fact that she loved this country and stayed here for almost half her life. Neither Beppa or Jenny were ever able to speak much English. Both of them were too busy working or keeping house for their husbands. Beppa had a son, but I don't think he pushed his mother to learn English. Jenny never had children. Both Beppa and Jenny got along just fine in the North Beach district, where almost all of the storekeepers and even some local officials spoke fluent Italian. Paolina didn't learn a lot of English either; she worked full time in an Italian-speaking environment while struggling to raise her two boys by herself.

Algisa became fairly fluent, even learning to read and write in English—but Algisa had a quick mind and was the only one of my four oldest sisters who had learned to read and write in Italian as part of the Catholic catechism classes. She also had two children, Guido and Olga, who actively encouraged their mother to learn more of the language and customs of this country.

Rico, Joe, Eda, and I became equally as comfortable in English as we were in Italian—perhaps even more comfortable. But we were the youngest, the most flexible members of our family when we came to this country. We had the most opportunities to mix with people outside our neighborhood and culture. And unlike Mamma, Babbo, and our four oldest sisters, we were allowed to attend school when we were young.

I think our family was pretty typical. Most of the older immigrants stayed in North Beach or similar Italian-American neighborhoods. They lived, worked, and spent time with other people who spoke Italian and shared their cultural traditions. Some of the younger family members ventured out into a wider world and became more Americanized, but many of the older immigrants clung together in little enclaves, where they could live their lives in Italian.

For many years I had a Mexican-American housekeeper who cleaned my home every other week. She didn't speak much English, so her preteen daughter always came with her to work, but also to translate. Each time I looked at them I saw Mamma and me all over again. People who think things are somehow different now are conveniently forgetting their immigrant grandparents, great-grandparents, or great-

great-grandparents who huddled together in native-language neighborhoods, living among people they could understand while struggling to get a toehold on a successful life in this country.

My housekeeper's husband made a fairly good wage. They probably could have lived on it reasonably comfortably. But she went out and cleaned houses every day because that's how they saved the extra money they needed so their children could go to college. Each time she mopped my kitchen or made my bathroom shine, she had a little more cash to invest in her children. Those are good values just as my family had good values. They may have spoken Spanish in their home while we spoke Italian in ours, but the immigrant experience was the same—hard work, separation from all that they had known before, and lots of hope.

But I've kind of gotten ahead of myself here. Visiting Ellis Island and telling my story isn't the only thing I've been doing in the last decade or so. There were lots and lots of other things going on in my life.

CHAPTER 28

*I*n summer 1992, Eda's little secret about our ages came to light simply because Bill took his son Greg on vacation in Italy. I was still working on my autobiography for my family. Realizing my literary and organizing skills were severely limited, I had hired a local writer to assist me with the project. Wanting to be helpful, Bill picked up a copy of my birth certificate for my records. He hadn't said anything to me in advance, or I would have explained that I already had a copy.

Of course Bill read the document, including my real birth date. I had kept my promise and hadn't told anyone about Eda's slight reduction of our ages. So I had to explain it all to Bill. My son thought it was hilarious. He convinced me to include it in the manuscript the writer was preparing. I did. I also put in the details about my parents getting married after Beppa and Jenny were born. Bill persuaded me that no one was still alive who could be hurt by the truth and that these particular secrets no longer needed to be hidden.

But even in that autobiography—which was photocopied and given only to my family and friends—I couldn't bring myself to tell how Rico had hit me in anger. That was still a deep, dark secret for me, and I wasn't yet willing to put it down in black and white. So I gave everyone copies of my autobiography in December 1993, but it didn't include that one bit of information. I guess it's easy to see that other people's secrets—like Eda fudging our ages—might not be as shameful or as important as they believe them to be. It's a bit trickier to realize that other people might think my own carefully guarded secrets are actually just minor facts from the past.

There were other things going on in my life that claimed my attention. Late in 1993 Bill told me that he and Joe Walsmith, the president of Willitts Designs, were thinking about buying the company back from Hallmark. Bill explained that Willitts Designs was losing money and its prospects were not good. Before it was bought by Hallmark, Willitts was a small, entrepreneurial type of company that moved into and out of different markets quickly, keeping up with the trends of the gift industry. The Hallmark people were wonderful, Bill said, but a major shift in direction that would have taken thirty days in the past took Hallmark twenty-four months. It wasn't working.

Walsmith was the one who got Bill interested in the company again. At first Bill was reluctant—he was enjoying his early retirement—but Joe wouldn't take no for an answer. So for a sum of money that was once again considered confidential, they bought the company back from Hallmark. Willitts Designs became an independent business with Joe Walsmith in charge. Part of the deal was that Hallmark kept quite a few of the company's assets so Willitts Designs was really just a shell of its former self. Bill helped finance the deal and served as a consultant. It was Joe who took the reins and eventually turned things around, making the company profitable again. I wasn't part of this process at all, but I was glad to see it happen rather than have Willitts go belly up. I had let go of the company once with no regrets, but it was wonderful to see it back in familiar hands and thriving.

I was in my early eighties by now. My health wasn't perfect, but considering that I'd successfully battled cancer not once but four times, I was doing pretty well. As I mentioned, the chemotherapy had done some damage to my body. It created a condition in my feet called peripheral neuropathy. For many people this causes excruciating pain, and there isn't much the doctors can do about it. I've been fortunate because my feet have never been painful. They've just gradually gotten more and more numb. I started losing the feeling in my toes in 1991, and by 1993 it had spread to the rest of my feet.

When I stood up or walked around, the bottoms of my feet felt round instead of flat because so much of the ball of each foot was numb. As I walked I started mentally telling my feet "you're flat, you're flat, you're flat." And you know what? It worked. I couldn't walk all over downtown Sonoma as I had before, but I was able to keep going on my own two feet. Anytime my balance started to sway because of the neuropathy, I'd mentally repeat to my feet "you're flat, you're flat, you're flat" and my feet would stay under me.

Things were not going so well for my brother Joe. He was still alert and active, but he kept gradually getting weaker. The doctors said he had congestive heart failure. On March 23, 1994, Joe's gentle, loving heart stopped altogether. I think his body just wore out. He'd been born in 1900 and died in 1994—quite a long, full life. But oh it hurt that my brother was gone. I was the only one of the eight children who was still alive. I was surrounded by loving family, but they were all younger than me. They knew the stories, but they hadn't lived through them. I was the only one left who had.

But it's not in my nature to dwell on sad things. Soon I was caught up in the plans for my grandson Greg to marry Debbie Chapman in August 1994. Her family put on a high-class wedding with two hundred to three hundred guests. It was beautiful, really beautiful.

All of my immediate family was there—Bill and Patti with their two youngest, Riley and Petey; their middle child, Jason, just out of college with a job and an apartment in the East Bay; and their oldest, my first grandbaby, Shannon, who attended with her husband, Michael, and their baby, Max. And of course there was Bill and Patti's second child, the groom, Greg. Every time I looked at Greg I saw his grandfather. He looked just like my Bill. Greg even has my husband's high-energy, type A personality. It's uncanny.

Greg and Debbie were married in San Mateo on the San Francisco peninsula. After the wedding they moved to Oregon, where her sister lived.

Bill and Patti were also getting restless, wanting to move out of California to somewhere more laid back and rural to finish raising their two youngest, Riley and Petey. Bill and Patti took a scouting trip, driving through Idaho and Montana, but they didn't find anything that made them willing to pull up stakes. On their way back to California they made a side journey to central Oregon, near the Cascade Mountains. They fell in love with the small town of Sisters, Oregon, located among the pine trees at about 3,100 feet elevation.

Sisters has kept the feel of an old pioneer town, with old-fashioned storefronts and shingled roofs. It looks as if it never left the 1800s. Once a lumber producing town, Sisters is now filled with specialty stores and galleries. The chamber of commerce promotes it to tourists as the "Gateway to the Cascades." The nearby Three Sisters Wilderness Area gives spectacular views of the "sisters," the three mountain peaks that give the area and the town their names. I suppose it sounds a bit like a chamber of commerce brochure, but the air is clear and crisp and everywhere you look you see incredible natural beauty.

As soon as they saw Sisters, that was it—Bill and Patti knew they were home. In summer 1995 they bought one square mile of land a few miles outside of Sisters and custom-built a large, comfortable home for themselves, Petey, and Riley. They made sure the road into their house zigzagged as needed to save as many of the existing trees as possible. Bill and Patti had purchased a lovely bit of wilderness, and they wanted to keep it that way. Construction was completed in 1996, and they all moved up north.

Of course, they wanted me to pack up and go with them. They even built me my own little cottage, right next to the main house. But instead of pressuring me to live with them in Oregon, Bill and Patti asked me what would make me happiest. The answer was staying in Sonoma; it's where I belong. All my friends are here. I know which store is the best place to buy meat and which has the best bread or cheese. The woman at the organic produce stand remembers me and talks to me as I pick out my purchases.

My heart sang "This is home" when my husband and I first spotted our Mediterranean-style condo complex in 1978, and my heart is still singing "This is home." We had lived there only three years before Bill died in our bed—the same bed where I still sleep each night. I eat my meals sitting at my dining room table and looking out the window at the "Bill's Garden" sign in the middle of the cactus he planted. I have no musical talent and can't play a note, but my husband's electric organ still stands next to the living room fireplace. There are too many memories here; I'm not able to leave them behind.

I love Bill and Patti's place in Sisters, but my heart is silent when I'm there. It isn't my home. However, I didn't want to stop Bill, Patti, and the kids from moving to a place that so obviously called to them and made them happy. It was hard to let them go—probably just as hard as it was for them to leave me behind—but I have everything I want and need here in Sonoma, and they have what they want and need up in Oregon. I still have the love of my family even if I can't see my grandsons, my son, or my daughter-in-law every week the way I did before. But there is always the telephone, and I quickly started a tradition of flying up to see them several times a year. They always make me welcome, and I'm equally glad to see them when they come to stay with me.

It's bittersweet when I go up for a visit or head back to Sonoma. When I'm here, I miss my family; when I'm up there, I miss my home. Yet that's how it has to be. I couldn't bind them to me by asking them to stay in the Bay Area, and they couldn't bind me to them by asking me to move up north when I didn't want to go.

I know I'm jumping all over, jumbling up these events, but I think that's what happens when you get older. The memories don't come smoothly in the order they occurred, but in bits and pieces as they leap into my mind. So all that stuff about Ellis Island came popping out first, even though some of it happened after Greg's wedding, Joe's death, or Bill and Patti's move up to Oregon. I think getting so much attention for my immigrant past has healed something inside me. Maybe it's taken all this time to ease the scars of the taunts and insults I heard when I was young. Whatever the reason, the results of that oral history interview were so important to me that they all come tumbling out together. Then I have to go back and recall everything else going on in my life in those same years.

One of the most important events was my ninetieth birthday party. Early in 1998 I decided that I wanted a huge party when I turned ninety on April 29, 1999. I didn't want someone to give me a party; I needed to be in charge. I wanted to invite everyone I knew and cared about. I was sure that if anyone else organized the party for me, someone would get left off the list. I felt that turning ninety was a special time in my life, and I wanted to share it with everyone.

It was the first big birthday party I had ever given for myself, and it was a doozy. I spent a full year planning it with the help of two good friends, Linda Grange and her husband, Frank, who had been an executive at Willitts Designs. I think if Linda had known how big a party I wanted and how much work it was going to be, she never would have told me she'd help with the details.

I picked the location—Viansa Winery, which sits atop a windswept hill overlooking vineyards, open fields, acres of wetlands, and most of the southern end of the Sonoma Valley. I chose it because the place has ties to the Tuscany region of Italy, which includes my native town of Lucca. I selected the menu for a complete sit-down dinner for 125 people, with lots of Italian varietal wines and a fresh strawberry cake. The expenses started mounting up, and my son had no objection to the fact that I insisted on paying for it all myself instead of expecting him to foot the bill.

"Oh Mom, you're saving me so much money," he would joke each time I told him about a new idea I'd had for my party.

The best part was drawing up the invitation list. They were people from all the different parts of my life. There was my friend Etta, whom

I met on my first day at high school, and her husband, Jimmy. There was Etta's older sister, Ena. There was my son and his wife and all their children and grandchildren; all my nieces, nephews, great-nieces, and great-nephews; and my husband's relatives from Michigan.

There was my financial adviser, his wife, and his secretary; my accountant and his wife; my weekly masseuse; the woman who gives me a facial on a regular basis, sharing details of her life and of mine; two of the nurses who cared for my husband in his final days; and my primary care doctor and his secretary, who helped me through Bill's death, my lung cancer, and a host of other health problems.

There were "the boys" who made *Little Italy*—Will, John, and Jim—with their wives and girlfriends, as well as Will's father, whom I had gotten to know at various parties for the documentary; Paul Sigrist from the Ellis Island Oral History Project; the actress who had portrayed my life at Ellis Island, and her boyfriend; Patricia Henley, the local newspaper reporter who was working with me on a more polished version of my memoirs; my longtime friend Jeannette, who was the first office employee hired by William G. Willitts and Associates, and her dear husband; numerous other employees of Willitts Designs who had become cherished friends; and business associates of my husband who had kept in contact with me after all these years.

They were all people who had touched my life in one way or another, and I wanted them to share this special day with me. They came from all over California as well as Oregon, Texas, Michigan, North Carolina, New Jersey, New York City, and even Thailand. The only people who couldn't make the party were my nephew Fred and his family. After a long battle with the complications caused by diabetes, Fred's wife, Norma, died of a heart attack on April 30, 1999. The party was just a few days later, on Sunday, May 2, so of course they couldn't attend. I fully understood the depth of Fred's loss. My heart went out to him.

Just about everyone else on the guest list was able to attend. We had a wonderful Tuscany-style meal. Bill and other family members told silly stories about me. Bill and Patti presented me with a scrapbook she had been secretly compiling for months, with photos and messages from all of the guests. I cut the huge strawberry birthday cake—my favorite. And everyone laughed, ate, talked, and laughed some more. I felt surrounded by love. I spent an awful lot of money that day, but I've never regretted a single penny. They say no one can have a completely happy life, but we can all have happy days. My ninetieth birthday party was one of my happiest of days. To me it was the pinnacle of success. The whole thing was exactly what I wanted— a gift to myself.

My actual birthday was April 29, but I thought it would be better to hold the party on Saturday, May 1, to make it more convenient for the people from out of town. But even though I made the reservations a year in advance, the winery's large dining area was booked for May 1. I was disappointed, but I settled for holding my ninetieth birthday party on Sunday, May 2, 1999. A few weeks before the party, it finally dawned on me that May 2, 1999, was exactly eighty-three years to the day from when my family had been processed through Ellis Island and admitted as immigrants to the United States. What a sweet, sweet coincidence.

And what a wonderful day May 2 was—both in 1916 and in 1999.

CHAPTER 29

I was treated like a queen when I visited my native town of Lucca, Italy, in the summer of 2000. I think it was because I tried my best to talk to everybody in Italian. They all said I had a delightful accent. Even after more than eighty years in America, they could tell I was from Lucca.

I thought I spoke standard Italian, but I guess it makes sense that my words would have a bit of a regional flair. I learned the language from my family, who all lived in Lucca and nearby small towns. Back then, before our 1916 trip to America, poor families like mine didn't travel around much. If they went anywhere, they walked. Cars and television had not yet made it easy to see more of the world and to follow outside influences, which meant people hadn't started sounding so much alike. That's why when I talk in Italian, it's Mamma's Lucchese accent that comes out of my mouth. And undoubtedly there's also an American edge to my words. Yet everyone in Lucca seemed to easily understand me, and they all were happy to help a white-haired Italian-American lady explore her native town.

The idea for my journey started in 1999, while I was planning my ninetieth birthday party. I began thinking about how I wanted to welcome the year 2000. I decided I wanted to be in Lucca with my entire family. The original plan was that I would pay for everyone, down to the last great-grandchild, to fly to Italy for New Year's Eve so we could see in the new century together in my native land. It was an exciting idea, but it wasn't practical. What with Christmas and all, it wasn't a good time for everyone to get away. And the weather probably wouldn't have been all that great. Instead we scheduled the trip from June 15 to July 1, 2000. Rather than my entire family, only Bill, Patti, and their sons Riley and Petey were able to come with me. In its own way it was absolutely perfect. At age ninety-one, I was returning to Lucca for a good, long visit.

I was really excited the morning we left. I'd been back to Italy before but had never spent more than a few hours in Lucca. For this trip I wasn't going to play tourist, trying to see as much of the nation as possible. Instead I wanted to spend the entire time in Lucca so I could really get to know the place. We flew Al'Italia, nonstop, San Francisco to Milan. Bill had made all the arrangements, and there was a rental car waiting for us when we landed in Milan in midafternoon. We made the four-hour drive to Lucca, grabbed a quick dinner, and then I fell into bed. I had flown first class, but that didn't make the trip any less tiring. The flight to Italy took eleven hours, which is a long time for a ninety-one-year-old body to be squeezed into an airplane seat.

It was wonderful to wake up in Lucca. I'm biased, but I love my native town. Surrounded by gently rolling hills and farmland, Lucca—like all of Italy—is filled with a sense of history you can never get in the United States. According to the guidebooks for tourists, it isn't even known for certain when Lucca was founded. It may have been an Etruscan town before it became a Roman colony in 180 B.C. In medieval times it was ruled by a resident duke. Now it's part of modern Italy, but the signs of all this ancient history are everywhere. The downtown is surrounded by a massive medieval wall known as Le Mura—"the wall." The heart of Lucca can only be entered through one of the wall's four sets of huge, ancient gates. Inside Le Mura is a complicated series of narrow, winding cobblestone streets. In daytime they are caressed by dappled sunlight that filters down between the ancient two- and three-story buildings—all of which are topped by bright red tile roofs. At night the moonlight bathes everything in a soft glow that makes it feel as if the duke and his party might suddenly walk around the next corner. Everywhere you look there are second- and third-floor balconies that would be perfect for Romeo to come calling on Juliet.

Since each prominent medieval family had to have its own church, there are cathedrals, churches, and former churches all over. Every couple of blocks there's a beautiful central fountain or a picturesque piazza. Even the shape of a Roman amphitheater is preserved by the Renaissance buildings that were constructed over its ancient site. Because only police cars, taxis, and a few other vehicles are allowed to drive inside the walled city center, the cobblestone streets are mostly filled with foot traffic, just as they would have been centuries ago. Everything is so old and yet at the same time so vibrant and alive.

We stayed at the Hotel San Marco in northeast Lucca, a few blocks outside Le Mura. Once I got a full night's sleep to recover from the plane ride, the first order of business was to find the house where I had been born. Armed with the directions my brother Joe had given me years before, we set out in the rental car, determined to find my birth-place. After a surprisingly quick search, we found my family home. This time, unlike years earlier, I knew I had the right place. The house was fenced off, boarded up, and appeared to be abandoned, so Bill parked the car in a driveway that ran up one side of the property, and we all hopped out to get a better look. My two teenage grandsons, Riley and Petey, were fascinated by the idea that this was where their grandma had been born. I could tell it was something they had to struggle to grasp mentally—to make the leap from the old woman who was standing beside them to the tiny baby and the young girl I had once been.

The place was smaller than I remembered. Made of brick and cement, the house had an outside layer of crumbling concrete that gave a rambling, decaying texture to the walls. The building faced what used to be a quiet residential street but was now a busy commercial avenue. Traffic whizzed by in a steady stream. The driveway was shared with a thriving auto-repair shop; the neighboring buildings all held businesses of some sort. The house sat forlornly, encased by a chain-link fence and a yard choked with brambles and weeds. They were so thick that there was no longer any sort of path to the front door, and it was hard to see the "for sale" sign in the yard. The fine print on the sign indicated that the building was available for use as a warehouse.

I wanted it. I wanted to buy it and make it ours again, to fix it up and have it be part of our family. A glance around clearly showed me that this was not at all a good investment as a vacation home, but I wanted it anyway. All my great business sense had vanished. So had my son's. I guess sentiment runs in our family because Bill's idea was that he and Patti could buy the place and start fixing it up. When their youngest son was out of high school and off to college, Bill and Patti could come over and spend a year living in this house in Lucca, just the two of them.

So I called the real estate agent whose phone number was listed on the "for sale" sign. I left a message saying we were interested in buying the house, and we needed to see the inside. Then we went off to see a bit more of Lucca.

I found portions of the moat—il fosso—that at one time encircled the entire city, just outside Le Mura. It was basically a man-made ditch. If I remembered correctly—and I make no promises about the reliability of my memory—it was also where Mamma and my older sisters washed our clothes by hand and then hung them on the bushes to dry.

Bill, Patti, and the boys got a chance to walk on Le Mura, which is about two and a half miles long and massive enough to have a wide, paved boulevard on its top, as well as trees and grass. Cars are no longer allowed to drive up there, so the road is filled with tourists, joggers, bicyclists, young lovers holding hands, and mothers pushing baby carriages. Just about everyone travels along the top of Le Mura.

Except me. I really wanted to see the view from up there, to walk where I knew Mamma, Babbo, my brothers, and my sisters each must have walked at one time or another, but I couldn't make the long hike to the top of the wall. It was beyond my abilities to climb any of the many staircases built into Le Mura or even to inch my way up the remaining street ramps to the top of the wall. Because of my neuropathy most of the bottoms of my feet were numb. I was still telling my feet, "you're flat, you're flat, you're flat," and I was able to get around fairly well, but my balance was awful and walking long distances made my condition worse. So climbing up its steep sides and strolling the two and a half miles around Le Mura was out of the question. Yet I really wanted to be able to get up there, to circle around my native town and see it from above, from the many different perspectives offered by a two-and-a-half-mile loop.

Bill, Patti, and the boys stayed in Lucca a day or two and then took off to travel throughout Italy. They planned to return to Lucca for the last few days before we were all due to head home. Meanwhile Patricia Henley, the newspaper reporter from Sonoma who had become a friend of mine, flew over to stay with me while my family played tourist. Patricia had arranged for a rental car to be waiting for her at the airport. We used that car to tour the area around Lucca.

But I also wanted to go to the city archives inside Le Mura, where our rental car wasn't allowed. With my numb feet I couldn't walk there. So we had the hotel arrange for a taxi to pick us up and take us to the archives—taxis are allowed inside Le Mura—and that's how we met Franco Cipriano, our taxi driver. He was exactly what I thought of when I thought of Italians: warm, friendly, sincere, and completely up-front and straightforward. The more I talked with him, the more something about him touched a chord deep inside me. For me Franco had a million-dollar smile and a million-dollar personality. We chatted together happily in Italian as he drove Patricia and me straight to the city's archives. He agreed to pick us up a couple of hours later at the nearby Piazza San Michele and gave us detailed directions so we would be sure to meet him in the right spot.

Franco was a few minutes late for our rendezvous and apologized profusely for the delay. He explained that he had been caught in traffic after driving some tourists to the nearby town of Pisa. From that point on, anytime we wanted to go somewhere inside Le Mura where Patricia couldn't drive our rental car we arranged for Franco to pick us up in his taxi.

He showed us all the sights in the heart of Lucca—the imposing

Duomo Di San Martino, a cathedral dating from 1060 and filled with sacred works of art; Palazzo Guinigi, a stone tower built in 1300 that has full-grown trees on its rooftop garden; and the birthplace and home—now a museum—of the famous composer Giacomo Puccini; as well as lovely little cafes and other aspects of central Lucca.

In addition, each day Patricia and I put a lot of miles on our rental car. We traveled along the coast one day, into the marble hills around Carrara another, and stopped in Pisa to see the famous leaning tower. We saw medieval towers in a town called San Gimignano and rode an ancient tram car to eat lunch in Montecatini Alto, built on the top of a steep hill. My cousin Cesarina was no longer alive, but we went to visit her daughter, Lorena, and Lorena's grown son and daughter in beautiful Florence. After taking us on a tour of the city, with wonderful Italian hospitality, Lorena fixed us a delicious meal in her home.

Following the directions in a guidebook, Patricia and I drove to Villa Bernardini, one of the historic family homes in the hills around Lucca. Members of the Bernardini family met us at the door and collected the fee for touring their house. When I began to speak to them in Italian, they welcomed me like a long-lost family member. They were delighted to have an Italian-American come visit. They gave us a personal tour of their castlelike home, which was built in the seventeenth century by a Luccan nobleman, Bernardino Bernardini.

As they showed us their ancient family treasures it occurred to me that if my family hadn't gone to America, Babbo might have been their gardener. It was an odd thought because I doubted their reaction would have been the same if I had come calling as the former gardener's daughter. I don't mean that I thought any less of them or their hospitality. It's just that I was struck by how different things were for me—for all of us—because my parents decided to make the difficult journey to the United States.

Patricia and I continued to explore in and around Lucca. Everywhere we went I spotted things that vividly reminded me of my family—a sign naming a street or a town they had mentioned, old landmarks that had been included in their stories. It was like getting unexpected flashes of a long-forgotten past. It was sad and sweet and wonderful all at the same time.

And I was still trying to figure out a way that I could get to the top of Le Mura so I could see all of downtown Lucca. Patricia had already strolled around the top of Le Mura several times by herself, but she couldn't think of any way to take me with her that didn't involve walking long distances or breaking the no-cars-on-Le-Mura law.

I asked at the hotel desk to see if they knew of any options. Several clerks conferred together, then told me there used to be a man who gave horse-and-buggy rides along the wall—but he had moved away or his horse had died or something. They weren't quite sure what had happened to him. Whatever the reason, the man with the horse and buggy wasn't available, and they didn't have any other suggestions.

Then I mentioned my problem to Franco. He told me not to worry. He'd get permission to go on Le Mura in his taxi. After several days of wrangling with city officials, Franco showed up with a permit to drive me around the top of the ancient wall. I guess he convinced the bureaucrats that a ninety-one-year-old Italian-American woman who had been born in Lucca couldn't be deprived of what could well be her last chance to visit its medieval wall.

Franco picked me up at the hotel in the early evening, when the light was still good but it wasn't too hot out. He drove slowly through the gates and up one of the ramps to the top of Le Mura. It was magical. I had thought there was no way I would see any of this, and here I was able to slowly savor it all. Franco stopped the car repeatedly to let me get out and enjoy a particular view or inspect a certain aspect of Le Mura. He was a fountain of information. As solid as it felt under our feet, the wall was hollow inside. In ancient days they kept soldiers, horses, cannons, and other armaments inside the wall—a medieval arsenal to repel any invaders.

I especially loved the view of the area immediately east of the city—the outlying district where I had been born. From the vantage point of Le Mura I could clearly see the portion of the moat, il fosso, where I imagined Mamma and my sisters scrubbing our laundry. I'm sure my family must have walked around Lucca from the vantage point of Le Mura. Now, at age ninety-one, I was getting to see the same sights for myself. As I said, it was a magical evening.

At the end of the tour of Le Mura, Franco gave me another treat—although I don't think he realized how much it would mean to me. He suggested that Patricia and I have dinner at Trattoria Giulio, located just inside Le Mura's western gates. One of the first things I spotted on the menu was farinata, a soup that Mamma used to make. It's like minestrone except it's made with savoy cabbage and thickened with polenta instead of rice or pasta. I hadn't tasted it for years—not since Mamma died. I got tears in my eyes when I took my first sip. It was exactly the way Mamma used to make it—exactly. One taste and I knew I was home.

And there were so many other familiar dishes on Giulio's menu. I wanted to taste them all. I even tried baccala, which is dried cod fish soaked, boiled, and served with garbanzo beans. It was something

Mamma fixed often, especially when there wasn't much food or money in the house. Again Giulio's version of the dish was exactly the way Mamma had made it. The trouble was, I no longer liked fish, so I didn't enjoy the baccala. But I knew it was authentic, and it was wonderful that I got to try it even though I didn't like it. As far as I was concerned, we were tasting the real Lucca at Trattoria Giulio. From then on, every chance I got I ate at Giulio's.

Franco arranged another surprise. He contacted people at the local newspaper, and they sent a reporter to interview me as well as a photographer to take my picture. The story and photo ran the next day under the headline "Torna dall' America dopo 84 anni. E compra la casa della sua infanzia," which loosely translates as "Returns from America after 84 years and buys the house where she was born."

Strictly speaking that wasn't true because I was still trying to reach the owner of the house so we could see the inside before deciding whether to buy it. But it was still a great feeling to see my story in Lucca's newspaper. The first paragraph read "Eighty-four years were cancelled in a flash when she saw the home in which she was born in Arancio on the via Romana. She became a child again, annulling the years she spent in the hills of California."

By this time we were getting near to the end of our time in Italy. Patricia headed back to Sonoma on the same day that Bill, Patti, and the boys drove back to Lucca. I had finally managed to make an appointment with the owner for all of us to tour my family home, to see if we wanted to buy it. The weeds were so thick in the front yard that we had to enter through a side door. The owner told us no one had lived in the house for ten years. You'd think he would have cleaned it up a bit in that time. There was trash everywhere—empty wine bottles, part of an old bicycle, a broken table, an ancient mattress on the floor, pieces of a bed frame scattered around. There was even a crucifix still hanging on the wall. I jokingly told Bill that it couldn't have been Mamma's because she wouldn't have left it behind.

Over the years someone had added a toilet upstairs—it certainly wasn't there when I was a child—and faucets in the bathroom and kitchen. But there were things I recognized. The kitchen had the wide windowsills where I used to sit and look out while I ate my breakfast and the open fireplace where Mamma cooked all our meals. It was rundown and dirty and a complete mess, but it was the house where I had been born. I was sure of it. The question was, did we want to buy it? The owner had told us the price in advance, before showing us the home. Converting from lira to dollars he was asking around $175,000. I told that to Franco, who happened to live near my family home.

"He's crazy," Franco said when he heard how much the owner wanted for the place.

Logic won out over sentiment, and we decided not to buy the house. It was disappointing but also a relief. The place would probably have been nothing but a headache. Even repaired and restored it would still have been located in the heart of a commercial area on an extremely busy street.

The owner didn't seem surprised by our decision. I suspect the high price he quoted may have been only for crazy American tourists and that he would have asked a lot less from a Lucca resident interested in warehouse space. Perhaps the owner knew all along that we were unlikely to buy it and just gave us a tour inside as a favor to us. He might have nursed a slight hope that we would be sentimental enough—and rich enough—to pay his outrageous asking price.

I'm glad I got to see the inside of that small building. Many times in my life I've felt that I've come full circle, and this was another one of those times. Yet I had to move on and accept that it did not make sense for us to buy the house. To console everyone I took my family to Trattoria Giulio to taste real Luccan cooking just like Mamma used to make. Bill, Patti, and the boys had been traveling around Italy when I discovered Giulio's and hadn't had a chance to eat there yet. And I had been visiting neighboring towns, so I hadn't been to Giulio's for a few days. When we walked in the door, Giulio greeted me personally. It turns out he had read the newspaper article and was just waiting for me to come back to his restaurant. He wouldn't give us menus; he insisted on choosing our meal for us. Oh lord, what a feast. Every morsel reminded me of Mamma and my family. It was heavenly, but we all ate way too much. However it was the perfect end to my stay in Lucca. It was time to fly back to California.

And you know what? I kept finding wonderful little pieces of my past in Lucca. I felt at home there. But when I got back to the United States, my heart told me that Sonoma is my home now. My roots are clearly Italian, but I'm thoroughly American. For decades I kind of forgot my immigrant past. I was too busy working, too busy living my longed-for American lifestyle. And I enjoyed that lifestyle. I enjoyed the success Bill and I created together. I love my family —my son, my daughter-in-law, my grandchildren, and my great-grandchildren. But following Bill's death I gradually became interested in my Italian roots.

When I was in Lucca, I was as comfortable as I am when I'm visiting my family in Oregon. But that means I have the same problem with Lucca that I do with Sisters, Oregon. They're both beautiful places. They both mean a lot to me. They both hold wonderful people whom I love spending time with. But neither Lucca nor Sisters is home. So now I have two bittersweet relationships. When I'm in Sisters with my family, I love being there, but I miss my home in Sonoma. When I'm in Sonoma, I miss my family in Oregon. And after my visit there in 2000, I find I also miss Lucca, Italy, and Italians. It would be marvelous to be able to go back there every year to recharge my childhood memories. But I can't. Old age won't let me.

CHAPTER 30

For me there's a tremendous amount of difference between age ninety-one and age ninety-five. It's a good thing I went to Lucca when I did, because I doubt that I'm capable of it now, only four years later.

My mind can still function, but my body is slowly falling apart. In August 2002 I started having what I thought was really bad heartburn, but it turned out to be congestive heart failure. My doctor put me on several medications, but some of them made me feel worse instead of better. So it's been a slow process of figuring out how much of which prescription to take and how often. For a long time I would start feeling badly every few weeks and have difficulty breathing, as if I was getting a cold. I'd go to the doctor's office or the emergency room at the hospital, and they'd use a needle to extract excess fluid from my right lung. Then I would feel better for a while—until the fluid built up again. That's gotten better—they haven't had to drain my lung for more than six months, since just after Christmas 2003.

But lately I've had a tight feeling around my chest. They took X-rays and did a CAT scan, but they didn't find anything that could be causing the problem. I've learned to live with it.

I'm more bothered by the fact that I'm starting to lose my eyesight. A few months ago my doctor diagnosed macular degeneration in one eye; now it's in the other eye too. It's a real bother because I love to read. I've been trying out different types of magnifying devices, including TV-like video machines that make the type really, really big. It helps, but not enough.

I can't do much. Up until this last year I could get along pretty well by myself. The housekeeper would clean my place every other week, but otherwise I was able to cook, clean, and grocery shop for myself. I felt satisfyingly self-sufficient.

Now I don't have the energy. My son hired a caregiver to live with me. Before this I would have sworn I would hate sharing my home with a stranger, not to mention being so dependent on someone else, but it's worked out fine. The first woman who lived with me was a sunny, always-smiling woman from the Philippines. Although she herself was fond of fish and rice, she gradually learned to cook my food Italian-American style. And she brightened my day. I never once heard her complain about feeling tired or out of sorts.

Then she went home to her family in the Philippines, and I had to find someone else to take care of me. I thought it would be a hard adjustment, but my current caregiver—also an immigrant from the Philippines—is every bit as nice as the first one. So as I said, it's worked out better than I would have thought. She cooks and cleans for me and does my laundry and other tasks. And she used to own a restaurant, so my meals are fantastic—both tasty and beautifully presented. She also loves to play my husband's little electric organ—even after all these years, it's still sitting next to the fireplace—so I can sit back and listen to music just like when Bill was alive. I'm able to bathe myself, and I pretty much take care of my own personal needs. But this isn't a life I would choose.

My mind still thinks of lots of things to do, but my body isn't capable of any of them. If you ask me to do something while I'm sitting down, I'll immediately say, "Yes, that sounds like a great idea." Then I stand up and realize maybe it's not such a good plan after all.

It helps that I've been able to keep living in my own home, in my familiar California condo in its Mediterranean-style complex of buildings with creamy stucco walls and red tile roofs. The architecture, the surrounding hills, and the vineyards of the Sonoma Valley—they all evoke echoes of Lucca and Italy. In a beautiful way it blends both my past and my present.

Although my body is fading, I try to keep active. I still see my friends when I feel well enough, and I go out on errands with my caregiver. We've even gone to a couple of movies together. It's hard for me to follow the plots of TV shows because I can't hear the dialogue unless I crank the volume up so loud that my next-door neighbor starts complaining. I do watch my beloved sports—especially football. I can still see enough to tell what's going on. My family and friends know not to bother me during football broadcasts. And I try to keep up with the news. I also walk up and down my outside balcony daily to get some exercise and sunshine.

But if I'm at all busy one day, I have to take it easy the next—or even the next two days. And sometimes when friends call suggesting we meet somewhere or even just wanting to stop by for a few minutes, I have to say no. My body only has so much energy left in it, and it seems like there's a little less all the time.

I'm not afraid of death. I read somewhere that life is pleasant and death is peaceful; it's the transition that is troublesome. I'm finding out the truth of that daily as my body slowly wears out. So each and every night I tell God, "I'm ready whenever You are."

But then I wake up the next morning and figure God isn't ready for me yet. I know you can't change God's patterns, so I just have to be patient. Who knows? Maybe He still has something wonderful planned for me. I'll have to wait and see.

Even if I die tomorrow I feel like I had quite a nice life. I wouldn't change places with anybody—not with anybody. There have been difficult times—when Bill was away during World War II, dealing with Rico, my husband's affair, when Patti was pregnant with a grandchild I thought I might never see, my deep despair after Bill's death, my own four bouts with cancer—but in the end I can honestly say they have all made me stronger and a more tolerant person. How would I know happiness if I never knew sorrow? I think difficult times are a bit like fertilizer. It's messy and hard to deal with, but if handled properly it nourishes good things and helps them grow. Even the bad times in my life have been good because they've brought me to where I am today.

When I was younger, I thought loving myself meant being selfish. Now I know that's not true at all. It's just the opposite. It took me a long time to understand that concept, but it's made my life much more rich and fulfilling. Because I realize it's important to love myself, I continue to do the things that nurture my heart and spirit. I still wear my gold medallion, the one that says "I will greet each day with love in my heart." I repeat that phrase to myself each morning, and I really believe it makes things go better. It certainly lifts my spirits.

I still meditate and pray for at least an hour daily. Instead of rubbing myself with warm oil, as I did in the past, my caregiver gives me an hour-long massage—which is another reason I consider her an incredible blessing in my life. And I read positive thoughts to myself daily. I've filled a small spiral notebook. It's full of sayings like "Lord, make me a blessing to someone today" and "Add a daily dose of laughter in your life for your health and well-being."

I love my little book and the ideas I've scribbled in it. Some of them are things I've read. Some are things I've heard. I don't remember where most of them came from—I just know that reading them makes me feel good.

"Happiness hides in life's small details. If you're not looking, it becomes invisible."

I've only started writing these things down in the last few years. I think before that I was too busy with all the details of daily life. But taking the few minutes needed to jot down a positive thought or to read one already in my notebook has been time well spent.

"If you're not criticized, you may not be doing much."

Even when my body ached, it's amazing how good I felt after reading these each day. As my eyesight grew worse, I found I could still make out a word or two here or there. Fortunately, I had most of the notebook memorized, so a word or two was enough for me to figure out which phrase I was trying to read.

"Everyone is a teacher, for regardless of age and education, everyone has a wisdom to share."

Then my range of vision got increasingly narrow and fuzzy. I had trouble reading even one word at a time. So on their last visit to see me, Bill and Patti got out my tape recorder and took turns reading aloud every phrase in my notebook. Now I just listen to that tape each day and let those upbeat sayings flow over me. It may seem simplistic, but it helps me keep my positive outlook on life. Sometimes the simple things are what work.

Even on my worst days, physically, I thank God for everything. And one of the things I'm thankful for is that I can still sit in my favorite chair in my living room, right next to my fireplace, and immerse myself in the familiar lines from my little notebook. I may not be able to do a lot of the things I used to do, but I'm grateful I'm still capable of concentrating on the good parts of my life and savoring the small daily miracles. I'm getting close to the bottom of my cup, and I can definitely say that there's a lot of sweet sugar here.

I'm aware that it's a pretty scary world out there right now, making it seem difficult to maintain a positive outlook. I remember the morning of September 11, 2001. My granddaughter Shannon phoned, distraught, and told me to turn on my TV because a plane had smashed into the World Trade Center. As I switched on the television I watched in stunned disbelief as the second plane hit the tower. I had to go back into my bedroom and pull myself together. But even 9/11 hasn't changed my philosophy. I've seen miracles happen throughout my life. It's just ingrained in me that there will be more to come. I have to believe that somehow things will be resolved without guns or bombs. I don't know how, but I believe it will happen. The only thing I can do is to keep love in my heart, because it works—at least it has in my life.

I know I've been extremely fortunate. God has blessed me many times. Financially I'm not hurting. It would be a lot harder to cope with my ill health if I didn't have the money to hire someone to live with me so I can remain in my beloved home. But if I depended on finances to bring me happiness, I'd be waiting a long, long time because it really doesn't do that. Money is a necessary evil; it only matters if you don't have it. Once you have enough to not worry, it's the other things that are important—family, friends, love, even self-love and self-nurturing. That's what having money lets me do—concentrate on what really matters.

So every day I listen to the tape of my favorite sayings.

"Nothing's going to happen today that God and I can't handle together."

And every night I tell God I'm ready if He is. One of these days He's finally going to listen to me. And that will be good, because death is a part of life. If you're born, you're going to die. Every life is a story, I guess. Sometimes mine has surprised even me.

FAMILY RECIPES

Mamma never measured anything when she cooked. It was always a pinch of this or a bit of that. I'd ask her how much rice to add to a dish to make it the way she did. *"Un paio di manate"*—"Oh, a couple of handfuls," Mamma would reply. I was never sure exactly how much that was.

Since Mamma couldn't read or write in any language, none of her recipes were ever written down. All she needed to know was stored in her head, and everything always came out perfectly.

But I didn't learn to cook from Mamma. I helped her in the kitchen when I was young, but I detested any kind of housework so strongly that I didn't pay any attention to how she did things. Once I was married and had a kitchen of my own I was much more interested in how to make "American" dishes, such as scalloped potatoes, than in learning Mamma's Italian-style kitchen secrets. It wasn't until after my husband died that I started wanting to cook the food I'd grown up with. Sadly, Mamma was no longer there to teach me.

I'm indebted to my sister Algisa and her daughter, Olga, for most of these recipes. Algisa learned to read Italian before the family left Italy. As her children grew up, she became more fluent in English and eventually taught herself enough to read the daily newspapers. She could follow a recipe in English and loved trying new ones. That meant Algisa wrote down her own recipes just the way she learned them from Mamma. She passed them along to her daughter, Olga, who is also an outstanding cook. When I finally started wanting to cook Italian style, just the way Mamma did, it was Olga who was able to show me how. For that, I'm grateful.

Friends today tell me I'm a good cook, but my family knew better. Mamma, Beppa, Algisa, Jenny, and Paolina were all wizards in the kitchen. It was their kingdom, their place to nurture and support their loved ones, and they always excelled.

Pressed Chicken

This dish was one of Mamma's specialties. She always kept a big brick in her kitchen just so she could cook this dish. I use a great big rock, which I found in my garden. I store it in my cupboard with my pots and pans. If you press chicken flat as it cooks, it absorbs more moisture. Somehow even the texture of the chicken becomes different—I'm not sure why. It really gives it a unique taste.

Ingredients

1 broiler chicken (about 2 1/2 pounds), cut in half
olive oil
crushed garlic
rosemary
salt and pepper
1/2 cup white wine

Flatten the chicken on a hard surface. Place chicken in frying pan greased with olive oil over a medium flame (it has to cook through slowly), and brown on both sides. Season with salt and pepper.

Place a flat, heavy dinner plate on top of the chicken—it doesn't have to be airtight. Then place a six- to eight-pound brick or rock on top of the plate.

Cook about 20 minutes, until brown, then remove brick and plate, and turn chicken over. Add garlic, rosemary, salt, and pepper. Sprinkle with wine. Replace plate and brick, and let the wine evaporate. Remove the plate and brick, and pour the juices over the chicken. Discard the garlic and rosemary. Serve immediately.

Mamma's Meat Sauce

My mother made meat sauce all the time. It was one of her staples. This recipe may not be exactly the way Mamma made her sauce, but the end result matches my memories of her cooking.

Ingredients

1 large yellow onion, chopped
olive oil
1 pound lean ground beef
1 can (28 ounces) tomato sauce
1/2 can water
1 small can (6 ounces) tomato paste
1/2 pound dry porcini mushrooms, soaked in hot water
  and chopped
minced garlic
dry basil
bouillon cube

Fry onion in olive oil until limp. Add beef, and brown it. Add tomato sauce, water, mushrooms, garlic, basil, and bouillon. Bring to a boil and simmer for a least an hour and a half.

Biscotti

I loved Mamma's biscotti, which was a good thing because it was the only kind of cookie she ever made. I still remember how wonderful they tasted dunked in my glass of milk after I got home from school. This recipe makes four loaves.

Ingredients

2 cups sugar
1/2 pound butter
4 tablespoons anise seed
4 tablespoons anisette (or other spice-flavored liqueur)
3 cups whiskey
2 cups coarsely chopped almonds
6 eggs
5 1/2 cups unsifted, all-purpose flour
1 tablespoon baking powder

Mix sugar with butter, anise seed, anise liqueur, whiskey, and nuts. Beat in the eggs. Mix flour with baking powder, and stir into the sugar mixture. Blend thoroughly; then chill the dough for two to five hours.

On greased baking sheets (without sides) shape dough with your hands to form flat loaves about 1/2 inch thick and 2 inches wide and as long as the baking sheet. Place no more than two loaves parallel and well-spaced on the pan.

Bake at 375 degrees Fahrenheit for 20 minutes.

Remove from oven. Let loaves cool, leaving them on the baking pans until you can touch the loaf.

Cut loaves in diagonal slices about 1/4- to 1/2-inch thick. Lay slices cut side down close together on the baking sheet. Return pans to 375-degree oven for 15 minutes, or until they are lightly toasted.

Cool on wire racks and store in an airtight container.

Fried Zucchini Flowers

These are considered a delicacy nowadays, but my family simply figured that since the plant produced them we would eat them. Nothing should be wasted. This dish is a lot of work and isn't something you can prepare ahead of time. The flowers have to be eaten hot, straight out of the frying pan.

Ingredients

1 dozen zucchini flowers
1 cup flour
2 eggs
1/2 cup cold water
1/2 cup vegetable oil (enough to generously fill the bottom
   of the frying pan)
salt and pepper to taste
lemon wedges

Wash the flowers gently, and remove the center knob. Drain the flowers, handling them with care (they bruise easily). Refrigerate the flowers until you're ready to use them.

Mix the flour, eggs, and water to make a pancake-like batter. Use more water if necessary. Holding each flower by the stem end, dip them one at a time into the batter.

Fry the batter-dipped flowers in oil until crisp on both sides. Cook until brown (it only takes a few minutes), and then place them on a paper towel to drain off the oil. Sprinkle with salt and pepper, and serve with lemon wedges on the side.

Stuffed Zucchini

We ate a lot of stuffed zucchini when I was growing up. It was Mamma's way of using up any leftovers. I love this dish because it's so tasty.

Ingredients

8 zucchini, a nice size for stuffing
about a pound of leftover meat or a combination of ground meat
1 medium yellow onion, chopped
Swiss chard, cooked, squeezed dry, and chopped
1/2 cup parmesan cheese
3 eggs
1 teaspoon thyme
salt and pepper to taste
olive oil
minced garlic
bread soaked in broth or bouillon water, squeezed, and
   then chopped
parsley
1/2 cup tomato sauce

Cook zucchini in boiling, salted water for about five minutes. Remove from water and let stand until cool.

Sauté onion and garlic until soft. Add parsley and meat. (If using ground meat, brown first.) Add bread crumbs and seasoning. Combine in a mixing bowl; then add eggs (don't beat them) and parmesan cheese. Mix well.

Trim the ends of the zucchini. Cut lengthwise; then scoop out and discard the seeds. Sprinkle the zucchini shells with salt.

Brush edges of zucchini with olive oil; then mound the filling into the shells. Spoon a bit of tomato sauce on each stuffed zucchini. Place in oiled baking dish. Cook uncovered at 350 degrees Fahrenheit for 25 to 30 minutes.

Polenta

If someone had told Mamma that polenta would be served in fancy restaurants for high prices, she never would have believed it. This simple cornmeal dish can be served lots of different ways. The texture can be modified by changing the amount of water to make the mixture thicker or thinner. My husband, Bill, loved it when I would let the polenta cool, refrigerate it, then fry it in the morning and serve it with butter and honey or maple syrup. I like it that way, but this is my favorite, served hot with butter and cheese on top.

Ingredients

4 cups water
2 1/4 cups coarse polenta (cornmeal)
olive oil

Add cornmeal to 2 cups water and stir; then add the remaining water. Doing it this way keeps the cornmeal from getting lumpy.

Add olive oil and salt. Bring to a boil, then lower the heat and simmer. Cook for one hour, stirring frequently.

Cherries in Brandy

When Babbo made his cherries in brandy, I wasn't old enough to learn how he did it. Again, I'm grateful to my niece Olga for providing this recipe linking me with an important part of my past. These are so simple to make and so delicious. Prepare them when Rainer cherries are in season, usually in late spring, and they should be ready to eat around Thanksgiving.

Ingredients

1 quart of brandy (makes 2 1/2 quarts of brandied cherries)
5 to 6 pounds of Rainer cherries (if you don't use them all, they're still good eating)

Wash the cherries; then cut off half the stem, leaving only a short length. Pat cherries dry. Place cherries in a sterilized jar with cinnamon stick, and fill the jar with brandy.

Chicken and Veal Ravioli

Unfortunately, no one saved the recipe for Mamma's ravioli filling or wrote down how she used it to stuff a Thanksgiving turkey. *Fortunately,* my nephew Fred gave me this recipe, which is just as good. He remembers that raviolis were usually made with leftover roast or chicken. Fred said it was almost unheard of to cook meat for the sole purpose of making raviolis. However, things changed and he recalls his mother, Paolina, buying a four-pound cross rib roast to make approximately three hundred raviolis. Since then Fred has developed this recipe, which he says is just as tasty and a lot simpler to make. You'll need a pasta machine and a ravioli cutter.

Ingredients

2 pounds chicken thighs
1 1/2 pounds veal stew meat
1 package (10 or 12 ounces) frozen, chopped spinach
1 large onion, finely chopped
1 clove garlic
8 ounces ricotta cheese
1 1/2 cups grated parmesan cheese
3 ounces or 4 thin slices of mortadella
1/2 teaspoon nutmeg
2 egg yolks
1/2 teaspoon salt

Combine chicken thighs and veal in an ovenproof skillet; season and add garlic and onions. Cook until tender and meat pulls off the bones of the chicken thighs.

Cut veal in small pieces. Place chicken, veal, and mortadella in food processor. Chop to a medium grind (not too fine). Transfer meat to a large bowl.

Cook spinach as directed on the package. Let cool and squeeze any water out of it. Add spinach to ground meat along with the ricotta, egg yolks, nutmeg, salt, pepper, and parmesan cheese. Mix with your hands. Sample to see if you have enough seasoning for your taste.

Pasta ingredients

2 1/2 cups all purpose flour
4 large eggs
2 tablespoons olive oil
pinch of salt
warm water as needed

Except for the water, mix all ingredients in a large bowl. Blend together with a fork until it starts to gather. Turn the mixture out onto a well-floured counter, and knead, adding water a few drops at a time until the consistency is good; add more if needed. Knead for at least 10 minutes, or until the dough feels smooth and elastic. Let rest for 10 minutes.

Using your pasta machine, cut pieces of the pasta and roll into 15- or 16-inch-long sheets. Always rub a little flour on the sheets of pasta as you are passing it through the machine. Fred suggests a #2 setting for the final pass.

Place the sheets of pasta on a well-floured tablecloth. Let the pasta sit on the tablecloth for a couple of hours, until dry. Using your favorite ravioli cutter, place small mounds of the filling on the sheet of pasta, cover with another sheet, and cut out your ravioli.

Bring salted water to a boil in a large pot. Add ravioli. When they start floating to the top (about 10 to 15 minutes), prick them with a fork to check for tenderness. Serve covered with Mamma's meat sauce.

THE DEL BINO FAMILY

Maria Sabina Fedi (born Jan. 14, 1869; died Dec. 10, 1961)
Domenico (Babbo) Del Bino (born Dec. 19, 1864;
died Feb. 28, 1922)
Married Oct. 12, 1890.
They had eight children:

Giuseppina (Beppa) Del Bino (born June 26, 1888;
died Aug. 17, 1969)
Married Giuseppe Vinci on Aug. 10, 1919.
They had one child, Bruno.

Giovanna (Jenny) Del Bino (born Feb. 27, 1890;
died Nov. 2, 1979)
Married Giulio Nelli on April 11, 1925:
They had no children.

Algisa Del Bino (born Feb. 23, 1894; died Sept. 18, 1981)
Married Lorenzo Parenti on June 12, 1921.
They had two children, Guido and Olga.

Rosa Paolina Del Bino (born June 2, 1895; died Dec. 23, 1980)
Married Luigi Abballo on Jan. 5, 1919.
They had two children, Alfred (Fred) and Albert (Beb).

Amerigo (Rico) Del Bino (born Feb. 4, 1897; died 1970)
Never married.

Giuseppino (Joe) Del Bino (born Mar. 27, 1900;
died Mar. 23, 1994)
Married Annette Biagini on July 27, 1937.
They had twins, Jon and Joanne.

Gilda Eda Del Bino (born Dec. 19, 1902; died Mar. 13, 1985)
Married George (Bacci) Parodi on May 5, 1928.
They had no children.

Teresa Elda Del Bino (born Apr. 29, 1909)
Married William Gray (Bill) Willitts on Feb. 12, 1941.
They had one son, William Guido (Bill).

To order additional copies of
The Sugar's at the Bottom of the Cup
contact:

Zucchero Press
P.O. Box 529, Sonoma, CA 95476
www.vom.com/zucchero
zucchero@vom.com

• • • • •

Experience Elda Willitts telling her immigrant story as part of *Little Italy*, a sixty-minute documentary that takes an intimate look at the struggles and triumphs of three generations of Italian-Americans. Directed by Will Parrinello and produced by John Antonelli and the Mill Valley Film Group, *Little Italy* also features Gay Talese, Robert Mondavi, and Lawrence Ferlinghetti.

Walter Goodman of the *New York Times* called *Little Italy* "a warm look at the Italian American experience." The *San Francisco Chronicle* described the film as "riveting…wonderful and uplifting."

To order a copy of *Little Italy*,
send $19.95 for a DVD or $10.95 for VHS tape to:
Mill Valley Film Group
1058 Redwood Highway, Suite A
Mill Valley, CA 94941
mvfg@aol.com
(415) 381-9309

Recipe Corrections

Page 367 Pressed Chicken
Use 2 or 3 cloves crushed garlic
Use rosemary, salt and pepper
to taste

Page 369 Biscotti
Use 3 tablespoons whiskey
not 3 cups

Page 371 Stuffed Zucchini
Use 3 slices of bread

Page 372 Polenta
Use 1-1/4 cups polenta
not 2-1/4